STATE SECRETS

POLICE SURVEILLANCE
IN AMERICA

STATE SECRETS

PAUL COWAN,
NICK EGLESON, AND
NAT HENTOFF

WITH BARBARA HERBERT

AND ROBERT WALL

NEW YORK   CHICAGO   SAN FRANCISCO

HOLT, RINEHART AND WINSTON

Copyright © 1974 by
Paul Cowan, Nick Egleson, and Nat Hentoff
All rights reserved, including the right to reproduce
this book or portions thereof in any form.
Published simultaneously in Canada by Holt, Rinehart
and Winston of Canada, Limited.

Library of Congress Cataloging in Publication Data

Cowan, Paul.
  State secrets.

  Includes bibliographical references.
  1. Privacy, Right of—United States. 2. Intelli-
gence service—United States. I. Egleson, Nick.
II. Hentoff, Nat. III. Title.
JC599.U5C67   323.44   72-182774
ISBN 0-03-001031-4

First Edition
Designer: Ernst Reichl
Printed in the United States of America

Portions of "Beating the Machine" by Nat Hentoff appeared
in different format in *Playboy*.

"Inquisition in the Courtroom," © 1973 by Paul Cowan, was
first published under the title of "The New Grand Jury"
in *The New York Times,* Volume 122, Number 42099, on April
29, 1973.

"Jack Weatherford" was first published in *RAT*, Number 17,
on January 6, 1971.

"Boyd Douglas" was first published in two parts under the
titles of "Intruder in a Gentle Community" and "Minister
with Portfolio" in *The Village Voice* of April 15, 1971,
and March 16, 1972. Reprinted by permission of The
Village Voice. Copyrighted by The Village Voice, Inc.,
1971, 1972.

"Twelve Anguished Jurors" was first published under the
title of "What Went Right in Middle America," Parts I and
II, in *The Village Voice* of February 1 and February 8,
1973. Reprinted by permission of The Village Voice.
Copyrighted by The Village Voice, Inc., 1973.

For
the Citizens' Commission
to Investigate the FBI
and
William O. Douglas

Contents

Introduction

With Watergate and the cascade of revelations it has prompted, many Americans have become familiar with some of the more visible signs of surveillance and repression. The signs have been alarming enough to persuade radicals who, in the late 1960s, had discounted the Bill of Rights as a "bourgeois relic" that the Constitution does afford vital protections. And millions of Americans who had begun to take the Constitution for granted have now been alerted to the danger that government—and not just the Nixon Administration—could subvert their freedoms.

Nevertheless, for the most part this country is still far from understanding the actual workings of the machinery of fear. And despite the shock of the revelations, the machinery continues to grind on through complex devices like data banks, grand juries, and increasingly sophisticated taps and bugs. Charges of "repression" and pervasive invasion of privacy can no longer be discounted as simplistic rhetoric. Still required, however, is the disentangling of the garish myths of repression from the more subtle measures government is actually taking, and that is our intent in *State Secrets*.

In "The Machinery of Fear," Nick Egleson attempts to ascertain the actual strength of such domestic intelligence-gathering organizations as the FBI and to counterpose that reality against their James Bond–like images. He seeks to estimate the extent to which electronic devices like bugs and telephone taps are in fact used, and to explore in detail the psychosocial reasons that the groups of resisters who tended to overrate the government's technology were vulnerable to the flawed, human informers-provocateurs who eventually betrayed them.

Often, when the government has failed to infiltrate left-wing organizations, the Internal Securities Division of the Justice Department has convened investigative grand juries to obtain the information it wants. In "Inquisition in the Courtroom," Paul Cowan shows how the venerable institution of the grand jury, once a shield for potential defendants, has become an instrument of prosecutors.

The documents from the files of the FBI's branch office in Media, Pennsylvania, have a mordantly comic tone to them. Though the best-known extract from those files concerns the FBI's intent to increase New Left paranoia with the prospect of an "agent behind every mail box," their essential flavor is captured more accurately by the informer PH-27-S, who, in 1967, told his superiors that Martin Luther King was scheduled to speak before the Women's International League for Peace and Freedom, a fact that had been advertised publicly for months. Yet, in a sense, the foolish informer is a more ominous threat to American freedom than his more competent public image suggests. For the FBI takes quite seriously the conclusions such informers draw from barely understood information. How many agents are infiltrating legally constituted groups, filing insinuating, innuendo-filled reports on people who are doing nothing more subversive than speaking their minds? How many of them are hustlers like Boyd Douglas, willing to weave a few scraps of left-wing fantasy into allegations that will whet the FBI's appetite and earn the informer thousands of dollars?

Can anything be done to dismantle the machinery of fear? Nat Hentoff, who sees electronic surveillance as a more immediate, pressing threat than does Nick Egleson, argues that there are legislative ways to regenerate the

Bill of Rights and that the courts too can be made to work for libertarians through lawsuits that will result in decisions that restrict the government's information-gathering activities. And in the book's concluding essay, "Twelve Anguished Jurors," Paul Cowan extrapolates from interviews with jurors in the Harrisburg case to suggest that both the Nixon Administration and its urban liberal opponents are wrong in assuming that Middle America constitutes a ready constituency for political repression. In that "conspiracy" trial, jurors from a rural, Republican region of the country exhibited a stronger concern with justice than with the government's emotional appeals to their patriotism. Such common sense may prove to be the best possible safeguard against the current attempts to reduce America's freedom.

Finally, *State Secrets* is essentially an attempt to suggest an approach to the issue of political repression. We have tried to show that clear and present dangers to America's traditional freedom do exist, but that they can be coped with rationally, without apocalyptic rhetoric that inflames fear and encourages paralysis. By understanding the dimensions of the present and potential threats to our rights, we can develop effective tools to deal with those threats and prevent them from overwhelming us in the future.

We would like to thank the National Action Research into the Military-Industrial Complex for their help in interpreting the Media FBI documents.

I
THE
MACHINERY
OF FEAR

The Surveillance Apparatus

NICK EGLESON

Introduction

One has to have a good eye to take the measure of the surveillance apparatus. Ten years ago eyes had to be sharp to see the traces of it. Political meetings then proceeded on the alternate assumption that police did no watching or watching did no good. Few people looked for and fewer people saw evidence of surveillance.

Four years ago the signs were easier to see, but it took diligence to put them together. There was a short newspaper column on the wiretap on Martin Luther King, Jr. There was Senator Ervin's investigation into army intelligence. And though military espionage was a hundred times larger than the operations of the White House plumbers, the investigation into it went almost unnoticed.

Today, with the deluge of evidence about surveillance, the task is to distinguish a G. Gordon Liddy campaign fantasy from a (former) police chief Rizzo around-the-clock watch, or to set aside the phone booth antics of former New York City detective Tony Ulasewicz, leave him wondering if the wrong person will find his stack of $100 bills taped beneath the callbox, and see beyond to the serious business of the New York City red squad where Ulasewicz worked until the plumbers hired him away.

Today it takes eyes that will not be distracted by an investigation or two. The first Ervin investigation—his 1971 hearings on army surveillance—did a remarkable job of exposing a type of surveillance unsuspected until that time. It also created, among those who knew of it, the illusion that a major cog in the machinery of surveillance had had its teeth removed. Teeth may be gone, but the cog was, relatively, tiny. The second Ervin investigations—the Watergate hearings—are equally remarkable and much more illusory. They have made surveillance a household word and the staple of newspaper punditry, but they have not cast more than an occasional glance toward the core of the surveillance apparatus.

What follows is a study of that machinery of fear, of its overall size, of its major data-collecting parts, and of the uses it makes with what it collects. It is a close look at the apparatus and the agents who have been watching, are watching, and will continue to watch the forces of political "insurgency" inside the United States. And it is a comment on the reactions—proper and paranoid, countervailing and counterproductive—that the targets of this surveillance have to being watched.

The Overall Dimensions

The heart, but not the whole, of the domestic political intelligence apparatus consists of three interrelated networks: local police, the FBI, and Military Intelligence.

Local police departments have police intelligence units, commonly called red squads. They are loosely affiliated in a national organization, the Law Enforcement Intelligence Unit (LEIU) and, collectively, do the greater share of the spadework of domestic political surveillance. Most of the units are attached to city police departments, the rest to the state police and to local district attorneys' offices.

The Federal Bureau of Investigation devotes a substantial percentage of the time of its 8,700 Special Agents to political surveillance. Some offices contain special squads that do only political work (called security work), but all agents are somewhat involved.

The army operates the U.S. Army Intelligence Command (USAINTC). During its heyday (1968–69), many of its 1,200 agents spent part of their time watching antiwar and black activists. The operation is now somewhat curtailed, yet its files are still available to civilian authorities. Overseas, Military Intelligence appears still to pursue surveillance of civilians, as indicated by disclosures in the summer of 1973 of MI operations in Germany.

A crude estimate puts the collective strength of these agencies at a force of 8,500 operatives employed on a full-time basis. That figure is very rough and is intended only to give an idea of the operation's scope. The actual work is distributed among a larger group of people, some of whom work in this area only part time. The figure does not include the number of unpaid informer sources cultivated by the agencies; nor does it include service personnel such as secretaries or file clerks in FBI or police offices.

Many other agencies are often listed as part of the surveillance apparatus. None, however, ranks in size with these central three. The most comprehensive essay on this subject to date, Frank Donner's piece in the *New York Review of Books*, lists twelve others.[1] Seven of them do have investigative personnel in their employ. These are the IRS, the navy, the Air Force, the Coast Guard, Cus-

toms, the Civil Service Commission, and Postal Services.
One unit of the IRS, the Alcohol and Tobacco Tax Division,
has been known to check library records for the users of
books on explosives.[2] It has participated in investigations
of radical organizing efforts in at least one place, Fall
River, Massachusetts.[3] The IRS is said to have a seven-
person unit assigned to check left- and right-wing political
organizations and their leaders for tax violations.[4] That the
IRS receives requests to investigate somewhat more
establishment groups is clear from the Watergate memo
from Charles Colson to John Dean asking for a check on
Teamster maverick Harold Gibbons.

Navy and Air Force agencies did collect and publish
intelligence summaries, but it appears that most of their
material came from the army and the FBI, whose operations dwarfed theirs.[5]

The investigative staff of the Civil Service Commission
appears to consist of seventeen clerks who clip articles
from dissenting publications and file the names of people
mentioned favorably therein. They have compiled a list
of one and a half million names.[6]

I cannot find evidence of Customs Department involvement.

The Post Office has been known to "cover" mail—to
record the return address on mail addressed to a suspect.[7]
John S. Lang reported for the Associated Press that the
Post Office told a Senate committee several years ago
that it had such covers on more than 24,000 Americans.[8]
According to Seymour Hersh of *The New York Times*,
however, these covers, which were conducted by the Post
Office under the direction of the FBI, were terminated
in 1966.[9]

Put together, these seven agencies form only a small
part of the surveillance apparatus.

The other five agencies cited by Donner do not even
have their own investigative staffs. These are Immigration;
Justice's Community Relations; Health, Education, and

Welfare; the Office of Economic Opportunity; and the Passport Division. They may pass along information to the police or FBI, either at their own initiative or upon request. For example, the Passport Office is known to keep a "lookout" list including the names of some 14,000– 15,000 suspected "subversives."[10] Reports on passport applications and movements by designated people are sent to the agency requesting the information.

These agencies are all easy sources of information, but they are not parts of the collection, evaluation, or dissemination machinery of the surveillance apparatus. Many nongovernment organizations are in almost the same position. Credit bureaus, banks, and telephone companies are constant sources of employment and financial information for police and FBI units, as the Media FBI documents prove.

The Secret Service, the Bureau of Narcotics and Dangerous Drugs (BNDD), and the CIA are each more important than these twelve, but because of one factor or another (see pp. 28–34), none is as important as the FBI, the police, or military intelligence.

If the domestic surveillance operations of these fifteen government agencies, as well as those of banks and other private organizations, were suddenly halted (as of course they should be), the overall surveillance picture would be only slightly altered. On the other hand, if the role of the police or the FBI, or possibly the army, were reduced, the impact would be enormous, for they are the major practitioners of political police work. Each of these agencies deserves careful scrutiny.

The Military Collectors

Until recently, the military, led by the army, ran a huge file-gathering operation. It was as superficial as it was vast. It served almost nobody, least of all the army. The army subdivision most engaged in civilian surveillance was and is the U.S. Army Intelligence Command (USAINTC)—approximately 1,200 men working out of regional and field offices across the country. Security checks on army and defense-contractor personnel have been its traditional function, although it has always watched some civilians. In 1963, the army watched Boston's Arlington Street Church for signs of antiwar activity. Civilian surveillance became a major preoccupation after the ghetto riots of 1967. Before the Newark riots of July, 1967, were over, USAINTC had been ordered to establish an early warning system for domestic insurgency. By 1969, the army had developed files on most political organizations, black and white, and on countless individuals. Army files by now contain the names of 25 million citizens. Most of the names in the files came from the field checks the government routinely runs on potential employees.[1] According to Senate testimony, only "a small fraction" came from USAINTC's political surveillance activities. A small fraction of 25 million is still a substantial number.

The army claims that only 5 percent of the time of all 1,200 USAINTC personnel went to civilian surveillance. Agents who came forward at the Ervin hearings said it was much more. One said 10 percent, another said even that was too small.[2] But, even supposing that half of USAINTC's time was thus employed, the 600 man-years involved would still be rather small compared to the efforts of police and FBI units.

Most of the information that went into army files did not come from army investigations. At least 80 percent came from the FBI, and other material came from local police sources.[3]

When the army ran its own investigations, its techniques depended on whether the group in question was attempting to organize army personnel. Against military-oriented groups, the army used agents who infiltrated as deeply as did any agent working for a civilian agency inside a civilian group. A memo circulated by the U.S. Servicemen's Fund, for instance, stated that Military Intelligence agents became friendly with the staff of the UFO, a GI coffeehouse in Columbia, South Carolina; later, these agents, according to the memo, testified against UFO staffers in a civilian trial. Reis Kash, a Criminal Investigation Division (CID) investigator for the army's First MP Division (Washington, D.C.) posed as a veteran to befriend the people who ran the Oleo Strut coffeehouse near Fort Hood, Texas.[4] The Fort Jackson 9, a group of GIs indicted for organizing on their army post, became the Fort Jackson 8 when one of their number turned out to be an army intelligence agent.[5]

Army surveillance of GI organizing groups has received relatively little publicity. But military surveillance of civilian groups, including antiwar groups, prompted a public outcry that led to Senate hearings.

Senator Ervin's hearings established two important facts about military surveillance of civilians. On the one hand, the army cast a broad net; its files contained the names of hundreds of organizations. On the other hand, the information it collected was superficial; its techniques were not very penetrating.

Most army intelligence operatives worked as anonymous observers who never risked personal contact with their targets or ventured into meetings where their active participation might have been required. Army agents marched with the Chicago demonstrators at the Democratic convention in 1968.[6] Some wore concealed radios and transmitted their reports to army trucks disguised as delivery vans.[7] Other army agents attended classes at New York University in 1968 to monitor the black studies program.[8] Still others attended public planning meetings

at MIT to plan for the October Moratorium in 1969 and
went to town meetings in Andover, Massachusetts, to
listen to debates over a proposed ABM missile site in the
town.[9] But they never assumed major roles in those
activities.

Army agents who needed to play a more active role
frequently disguised themselves as members of the press.
One agent used forged credentials from a real paper, the
Richmond Times Dispatch. Two agents won fame within
army intelligence circles for pictures of demonstrations
they took while posing as representatives of a fictitious
outfit, Midwest Camera News. Their *pièce de résistance*
was the only "press" interview with Abbie Hoffman in
the week before the Democratic convention demonstration.[10]

All the information gathered by those agents produced
very little action. It was forwarded to the USAINTC headquarters at Fort Holabird, Maryland, where it was com-
puter-indexed and microfilmed. The computer there had
the ability, among other things, to produce a list of all
demonstrations in which any specified individual had
participated.[11] The information was then redistributed in
three principal ways.

—Many reports were retransmitted over the special
teletype network that linked Fort Holabird with USAINTC
offices in every major city in the country. One sample
surfaced at the Ervin hearings.[12] It was the "intelligence
summary" for the week of March 18, 1968. It alerted each
outpost to a Women's Strike for Peace–sponsored antidraft meeting of 200 people in Philadelphia, a speech to
100 people by a leader of the Black Christian Nationalist
Movement in Detroit, and a demonstration by 300 Veterans and Reservists for Peace in Chicago. During one
mobilization in Washington, the USAINTC teletype carried the numbers of most cars passing beneath an outpost

over the Baltimore–Washington Expressway. The FBI used the list to identify 400 "movement" vehicles.[13]

—Other army units, including the Directorate of Civil Disturbance Planning and Operations (DCDPO), the Continental Army Command (CONARC), and each of its six regional headquarters, received these and possibly other reports from USAINTC. DCDPO tried to use the reports to prepare for riots, reportedly without much success.[14] CONARC combined these reports with reports from its own agents who numbered fewer than 300 nationally (in contrast to USAINTC's 1,000-plus) to produce its own intelligence summaries.[15] One source characterized these reports as too general to be useful and distinguished only by occasional bursts of florid style. He reconstructed: "The sun rose over the Pacific Heights in a glory of red and gold. This was the morning to enjoy the scenic beauty of the country—but not for a grim band of fifty dedicated radicals . . . ."[16]

—The third and principal user was the Counter Intelligence Analysis Branch (CIAB), attached to the Office of the Assistant Chief of Staff of Intelligence (OACSI). Ralph Stein was stationed there for fourteen months, from July, 1967, to October, 1968, and says about his experience:

I was directed to start and maintain a left-wing desk. My responsibilities would include being thoroughly familiar and conversant with all aspects of the New Left and traditional left-wing activities as well as with antiwar activities so as to be able to prepare summaries, reports, and briefings when requested. . . . From the day I assumed responsibility for the left-wing desk until my departure, I received thousands of FBI reports and a great number of Military Intelligence reports on groups and persons engaged in dissident activity. The amount of information received seemed to increase monthly. I retained much of the information, placing the material into the CIAB microfilm data bank or into a hard copy file. . . . Some of the information was used to write reports or briefings. Most of the information received did not concern violence nor did it concern any situation which involved the United States Army. The monitoring of civilian political activities did not in any way enhance or improve the army's ability to perform its legitimate civil disturbance activity. . . . In late October, 1967, the deputy chief of the CIAB outlined his concept for a new CIAB publication which would serve as an encyclopedic reference book of dissenters and their organizations. This was the beginning of the . . . Compendium. It was published in early 1968, I believe, with about 375 copies being printed and bound in yellow, three-hole, looseleaf binders. The classification of this document was secret. The Compendium was published in two volumes. Organizations and personalities were divided into left-wing, right-wing, and racial categories. At a later date, a cities section (containing logistical information for troop deployment) was added, and this constituted the only part of the Compendium which was relevant. Each organization and personality was represented by, on the average, one page of text, which summarized the person's or organization's beliefs and activities. Distribution of the Compendium was restricted to Military Intelligence units and federal internal security agencies. . . .

On a daily basis the information collected was put to two main uses: the preparations of briefings and the written responses to requests for information, commonly called actions. Briefings were delivered to the Assistant Chief of Staff for Intelligence (ACSI) and to personnel in the Army Operations Center (AOC) during riots and commitment of federal troops. AOC briefings generally constituted a legitimate function and were often relevant to the crisis at hand. [Stein testifies elsewhere that these briefings were to "keep the Pentagon generals abreast of riot developments, and troop movements, and had nothing to do with 'new-left desk' routine or MI surveillance."] The briefings for the ACSI, however, were often a different story. These . . . dealt almost exclusively with civilian groups and personalities.

Sometime after the Pentagon demonstration, the ACSI, Major General William P. Yarborough, requested a weekly briefing on a group engaged in dissident activity, either left wing or racial. [CIAB also had a right-wing desk.] As a matter of convenience, we alternated weeks with the racial desk. . . . The connection between the army's role in civil disturbances and the material presented in these briefings was highly tenuous or wholly absent. . . . I personally briefed on the YSA, SDS, Fifth Avenue Peace Parade Committee, and the NMC, to name a few.[17]

Other agencies within the military also collected information about civilians. The Army Security Agency (ASA) operated the monitoring equipment for agent transmissions during the Chicago demonstrations in 1968.[18] A source close to ASA reported that a team was dispatched to Texas in 1969 to decode mysterious words in ham radio broadcasts there. The army was under the impression, which proved unfounded, that they were part of a left-wing paramilitary plot. ASA may be the source of eavesdropping reports that came into CIA. Stein reported that he heard tapes of Ralph Abernathy's phone conversations. They had already been "sanitized" so he could not tell their origin. He saw similarly sanitized transcripts of discussions between Dave Dellinger and other persons during one of Dellinger's trips to Europe.[19] ASA seems to have had no role outside communications monitoring.

USAINTC counterparts in the navy and Air Force, the Office of Naval Investigations (ONI), and the Office of Special Investigations (OSI), reported on left and black dissent, but again their sources seem to have been army, FBI, and police agents, rather than their own field personnel.[20] Their operations, like those of the Coast Guard and the National Guard, were minor compared to USAINTC.

The overall picture is of a moderately large bureaucratic apparatus built to conduct formal interviews for background checks and trying to do the impossible job of predicting major social disorders. It sponged off the FBI for most of its information and used plainclothes operatives for the rest. The information filled numerous computerized files, caused irrelevant briefings, and did little else—*within the army.*

But civilian surveillance units may have profited from the army's operation.

—Army intelligence training, which consisted of a course at the U.S. Army Intelligence School at Fort Holabird, helped the careers, and probably the competence, of some civilian agents. Bob Pierson, for example, as Jerry Rubin's bodyguard at the 1968 Democratic convention, had been to USAINTC and worked for Military Intelligence in Chicago as USAINTC liaison with the city and state police intelligence units.[21] Tom Charles Huston, drafter of the 1970 domestic security plan requested by the Nixon Administration but perhaps never implemented, served with army intelligence just before joining the White House staff.

—Army personnel sometimes reciprocated the aid of federal and local surveillance. Near Fort Bragg, North Carolina, a CONARC unit supplied the FBI with reports on a church group.[22] Laurence Lane, a former MI agent at Fort Carson, Colorado, told the Senate hearing that his unit had formal exchanges of information with the FBI, the Colorado Springs Police, the El Paso County Sheriff's Office, and sometimes more distant police departments.[23] He knew that army information had been used to track one black militant on the FBI's most wanted list.[24] John O'Brien, a former agent with the 113th MI in Chicago, testified: "We sent official reports to the FBI. Practically every federal agency who maintained subversive-type files received information from us, and we received information from them and virtually every nonfederal investigative agency in the region."[25] O'Brien said the justification for such assignments was the FBI's insufficient manpower. "Besides," he was told, "it doesn't matter who collects it. It all ends up in the same place."[26]

—One civilian intelligence unit did profit from this roundabout nonsense. It was the Inter-Divisional Information Unit of the Justice Department (IDIU). In late

1967, Ramsey Clark, then Attorney General, established IDIU "to make full use of available intelligence" in dealing with urban riots.[27] The first of the long hot summers had just cooled off. The unit did not, and does not now, have its own investigators. For its first two years most of its information came from the army intelligence network, through the Counter-Intelligence Analysis Branch (CIAB), where Ralph Stein worked. Its staff of less than a score of analysts turned this data into intelligence estimates for the Attorney General and his assistants. Sometime before army surveillance was curtailed, IDIU received the entire USAINTC computer index of persons and organizations, and retains it to this day, even though the army version has been ordered destroyed.[28]

The unit now gets between 80 and 90 percent of its information from the FBI. Since most of the information it formerly received from the army came originally from the FBI, the only change effected by the much-publicized abridgment of the army's role is that the information no longer passes through a military middleman before arriving at the Justice Department.[29]

Justice Department computers are as versatile as the ones formerly in operation at the army's Fort Holabird center. They provide weekly printouts for the different regions of the department in their respective jurisdictions. They create reports for particular cities. They can provide background information on particular planners or participants in a designated demonstration.[30] By its own count IDIU has computerized files on 14,000 people and an equal number of civil disturbance incidents.[31]

The Ervin committee hearings and other publicity have curtailed the army's operation. How much is not certain. To judge from news accounts, army intelligence still spies on civilian groups in West Germany. Stein reported to the committee that acquaintances of his employed at

USAINTC were still engaged in some surveillance and were evading orders to destroy their files. Certainly in Chicago, and perhaps elsewhere, army files were turned over to the local red squad when they should have been destroyed. Nothing has come to light to suggest that what continues is different from the unwarranted but superficial surveillance that marked army work in its heyday. The IDIU is the only known permanent, active repository of the army's work.

Civilian Collectors:
Police, FBI, and Others

The first step in assessing the surveillance apparatus is to establish its size. Estimates of the number of people involved in surveillance work range from 200,000 to 80,000 to 20,000. Assumptions about the apparatus's capabilities vary as widely. So much about the operation is in fact secret that it is widely presumed that the size itself is unknowable, but that is not the case. It can be estimated by considering separately the two major parts of the civilian apparatus, the police and the FBI.

It was a rule of thumb in the late 1960s that intelligence functions should use 1 percent of the manpower and resources of a police department.[1] On that basis, in 1969 there were approximately 4,670 intelligence agents in local police units across the country.[2] The actual number assigned to the left is a little smaller; some energy goes to track a token number of right-wing groups and some goes into background and security checks on potential police personnel.

The few figures available on the actual strength of local units substantiates this approximation. BOSS, now Security Investigation Section (SIS), the New York police department's intelligence unit, had seventy regular and sixty undercover members in 1967–68—slightly less than 1 percent of the total N.Y. police force.[3] Senate committee hearings for the same period showed that the intelligence unit in Nashville, Tennessee, consisted of a police lieutenant and seven men, or 1½ percent of the force.[4]

The group that raided and analyzed the FBI documents from Media, Pennsylvania, estimated from the distribution of documents that the Bureau devotes 40 percent of its energy to political investigations, with another 14 percent divided equally between individual draft and army fugitive cases.[5] Of the 200 documents the group found in the political category, 95 percent pertained to left, liberal, or black groups, 5 percent to right-wing ones.[6]

Extrapolated to the national level, these figures suggest that the FBI effort is equivalent to the full-time work of 3,000 of its staff of 8,700[7] Special Agents. My own study of the documents suggested that three out of ten squads, accounting for about 25 percent of the regional staff, work full time on left and black surveillance. This would suggest a national equivalent of 2,000 full-time Special Agents.[8]

In reviewing the evidence, I came to the conclusion that the Bureau is not the foundation of the surveillance apparatus. Police units, especially those working in large cities, are its true underpinnings.

In the major political trials of the last decade, the government has often centered its case on the testimony of undercover sources. The most obvious evidence is that, in the great preponderance of cases, police units, not the FBI, have been responsible for these agents. Here are some examples:

1964, September:
The indictment of Progressive Labor leader Bill Epton rested on the testimony of New York City cop Abe Hart.[9]

1965, February:
Members of New York CORE were indicted for plotting to dynamite the Statue of Liberty on the evidence of New York City undercover cop Ray Wood.[10]

1967, June:
The alleged plotters of Roy Wilkins's assassination were indicted on the word of undercover cop Edward Lee Howlette.[11]

1968, August:
The indictment of the Chicago 8 for the demonstration at the 1968 Democratic National Convention depended on the testimony of two Chicago cops (Irving Bock[12] and William Frapolly[13]) and one undercover operative for the Cook County district attorney. FBI agents did testify, but even the evidence of FBI informer Louis Salzberg[14] was marginal to the prosecution's case.

1969, April:
The indictment in New York of the Panther 21 was based on New York police department undercover work, principally by Gene Roberts, Ralph Wood, and Carlos Ashwood.[15]

1969, November:
The indictment of "*RAT* bombers" (Melville, Alpert, etc.) in New York City was the result of undercover work by volunteer FBI informant George Demmerle.[16]

1970, June:
Fifteen members of the Weather underground were indicted in Detroit for conspiracy to bomb police installations around the country. Undercover agent Larry Grathwohl supplied the necessary grand jury testimony. First in contact with Cincinnati police, he was next passed on to the FBI and then put in direct contact with Weatherman prosecutor Guy Goodwin.

1970, December:
The case against the Berrigans *et al.* for the alleged plot to kidnap Kissinger depended on information from Boyd Douglas, apparently recruited by the FBI on the promise of an early parole for a previous conviction.[17]

FBI sources are central to only three of these eight cases.

These (and other) cases also illustrate a major contrast between police and FBI operations. Police units place regular staff members in undercover roles, while the FBI relies on volunteers. The police sources who testified in these major trials were all regular police officers assigned to undercover work. George Demmerle, one of the two FBI sources, said he was a willing volunteer. He seemed to have hoped to become a real G-man someday. Boyd Douglas, the other FBI source, made a living as a con man and became an informer when faced with the possibility of prosecution for contraband letters.

This pattern is repeated everywhere. Every FBI source I can find seems to have been either a volunteer or an untrained, solicited informant, sometimes recruited under pressure. Robert Hardy, who informed on the Draft Board raiders known as the Camden 28, volunteered himself to the Bureau;[18] so did William DiVale, who originally made public Angela Davis's connections to the Communist party.[19] Charles Grimm, an FBI informer at the University of Alabama in Tuscaloosa, seems to have been an unwilling volunteer, recruited by the local police by threats of a narcotics prosecution.[20]

The importance of this procedural difference is that the Bureau must rely on luck, threats, or local police to get inside sources in particular places. The police, on the other hand, lay careful plans.

On April 17, 1964, for example, BOSS inducted Gene Roberts and sent him to penetrate Malcolm X's organization.[21] On the following day, BOSS swore in Ray Wood and sent him to Bronx CORE. Wood surfaced in twenty-two months to turn in three co-conspirators in a plot to dynamite the Statue of Liberty.[22] Roberts remained undercover for six years, surfacing in April, 1969, to become the state's chief witness against the Panther 21.[23]

In 1971, David Burnham, a reporter for *The New York Times*, estimated that there were sixty-eight detectives and commanding officers at BOSS and fifty-five patrolmen assigned undercover.[24] It is a reasonable conclusion that each of these officers was assigned with the same care as were Roberts and Wood.

This systematic approach is an indication that local police collect more original material and know more firsthand information than does the Bureau. There is other evidence:

Boston: A Boston paper reported that the Bureau gets most of its information on blacks there from the city police.[25]

Philadelphia: According to the FBI documents from Media, Pennsylvania, when Philadelphia agents participated in the national campaign to step up surveillance of black ghettos, the FBI list of places to watch contained only obvious locations, such as CORE, Black Home, The Ghetto Training Center,[26] and black bookstores; the detailed list of restaurants where leaders ate came from the Philadelphia red squad.

New York: Anthony Bouza, a former member of the red squad, wrote that FBI intelligence was never as thorough as that of the local police because the Bureau spread limited personnel throughout the whole country.[27] According to its published procedures, the New York City red squad shares its files with at least thirty-two other agencies, from the FBI and IRS on the federal level to the Board of Education and the Waterfront Commission on the city level.

The Nixon White House may have shared this assessment of intelligence outfits. Tony Ulasewicz, bagman for payoffs to Watergate defendants and special investigator into Chappaquiddick and other political matters for the White House, was a veteran not of the FBI but of the New York City red squad. When he testified at the Senate Watergate hearings, he claimed some credit for that agency's thwarting of the "Statue of Liberty" plot in February, 1965.

Big-city police departments, through their red squads,

conduct systematic undercover surveillance. They also keep detailed files on people and organizations. Anthony Bouza said that the New York City files contained about 1 million cards and that the police unit also collected volumes of leaflets, newspapers, and clippings and kept reports on all people arrested at political demonstrations. (In early 1973, two days after the disclosure that the CIA had trained fourteen New York City police officers in the organization of intelligence files, Police Commissioner Patrick Murphy announced that the files had been purged of almost 1 million names.[28] The card file of names was cut back from 1,220,000 to 240,000; that of organizations was cut from 125,000 to 25,000. Index folders were reduced from 3,500 on individuals to 2,500, and from 1,500 on organizations to 200.) Figures on the size of BOSS and other big-city red squads, and comparative figures for the FBI and army, where available, can be found in *Table 1.*

A good picture of the day-to-day life of an FBI agent can be pieced together from the files stolen from the Bureau's office in Media, Pennsylvania. The following information is taken from the Media documents.

Thomas F. Lewis was the head of the Media, Pennsylvania, office of the FBI when the Citizens' Commission to Investigate the FBI (CCIFBI) removed all of its files. His position and his activities as they are revealed in the stolen documents give an idea of the life of an agent in an area with substantial left and black activity.

He was a Senior Resident Agent (SRA), head of one of the more than 500 field offices that were then satellites to the central FBI offices in the continental United States. Four other Special Agents worked under him.[29] A total of 205 Special Agents worked in eastern Pennsylvania.[30] One of his subordinates, Special Agent Jim O'Connor, specialized in the New Left.[31]

The file shows these activities for Tom Lewis between June, 1970, and March 8, 1971, the day of the raid:

Table 1   Major intelligence agencies:
Estimates of field staff assigned to
political intelligence

	FBI	Police Unit	Army	TOTAL
National	2–3,000[a]	4,500[b]	1,500[c]	
Boston		40[d]	20[e]	
Chicago		120–500[f]		1,000[g]
Detroit		70[h]		
Denver			48[i]	
Houston		14[h]		
Los Angeles		84 *(1969)*[h]		
		167 *(1970)*[h]		
New York City	125–165[j]	123 *(1968)*[k]		
		160 *(1971)*[k]		
		361 *(1972)*[l]		
Philadelphia	45–80[a]	42[m]		
Washington, D.C.		70[h]	100[n]	

[a]The Bureau has roughly 8,700 agents. Based on quantity of documents, possessors of the Media FBI documents estimate 35 percent of the Bureau's time is spent on politics; extrapolated nationally, that figure suggests 3,000 agents working on politics. Analysis of the Media documents shows in Philadelphia a New Left Squad, an Old Left Squad, and a Racial Squad, with an average squad strength of 15, or 45 total. Distribution directions show total Philadelphia office strength of 205, or 22 percent of force assigned to left, or 2,000 nationally.

[b]Total LLEA force in nation was 456,000 in 1968, according to U.S. Bureau of the Census, *Statistical Abstract of the United States, 1970* (91st ed.), Washington, D.C., 1970. The figure 4,500 represents 1 percent on intelligence, according the police department rule-of-thumb cited on page 16.

[c]U.S., Congress, Senate, Committee on the Judiciary, *Federal Data Banks, Computers, and the Bill of Rights, Hearings*, before the Subcommittee on Constitutional Rights, U.S. Senate, 92nd Cong., 1st sess. (hereinafter referred to as Ervin Hearings). USAINTC had 1,000 field staff, CONARC had fewer than 300, and ASA, OSI, and ONI had tiny numbers.

[d]Vin McLellan, *Boston Phoenix*, 8 June 1971.

[e]Mike Kenney, *Boston Globe*, 1 Feb. 1971.

[f]The lower figure is from testimony of Christopher Pyle in Ervin Hearings. The higher figure is from Frank Donner, "Theory and Practice of American Political Intelligence," *New York Review of Books*, 22 Apr. 1971, and is also cited in Richard Harris, *Justice: The Crisis of Law, Order, and Freedom in America* (New York: E.P. Dutton, 1970), pp. 135–36. The larger figure probably includes all casual undercover sources.

June 18:

He interviewed a bank cashier and an executive officer of the bank computer center and obtained copies of the bank statements of Muhammad Kenyatta (an officer of the National Black Economic Development Corporation) and photocopies of individual checks.

September 16:

He initialed and circulated to his subordinates a copy of a memo that instructed the Philadelphia region to separate its "security" details into "Old Left" and "New Left" sections.

November 12:

He went to Swarthmore, Pennsylvania, and interviewed the head of the campus police, the switchboard operator, the chief of the town police, and the postmaster. He had been ordered to see if subjects wanted in connection with the Stanley Bond case—the hold-up and murder at a Waltham, Massachusetts, bank—had visited Daniel Bennett, a Swarthmore College professor. He found no evidence.

November 13:

He typed and filed with the Philadelphia office a report of his efforts.

December 2:

He initialed a xeroxed letter from the Philadelphia office to the national office. The letter reported that surveillance of all Black Student Unions in the area had begun, as ordered one month before. Lewis's copy indicated that he was responsible for surveillance at Worcester State.

---

gHarris, *Justice.*

hDonner, "American Political Intelligence."

iFrom testimony of agents Lane and Pierce, in Ervin Hearings. The headquarters of Region 4 of the 113th MI detachment was Denver. It had a dozen agents. This was USAINTC's operation. There were three more agents in Colorado Springs. CONARC had an unusually large detachment there: thirty-three or more agents in the summer of 1969, attached to the Fifth MI detachment of the Fifth Mechanized Infantry Division of the Fifth Continental Army.

jAssumes that New York City has the same ratio of FBI agents to population as Philadelphia; range is proportionately the same as that of national FBI.

kThe New York Times, 1 Dec. 1970. Figures for 1971 are estimated from data there.

lDavid Burnham, *The New York Times,* 11 Mar. 1973. This is the figure for the total staff, not just field staff.

mJoseph Daughen, *Philadelphia Bulletin,* 23 May 1971.

nRon Weber, former member of the Army Security Agency, in interview by NBC-TV, aired on "First Tuesday," 1 Dec. 1970.

February 4:

Lewis received one of the nineteen copies of the report for February 1, 1971, from the tap and bug of the Black Panther Party Philadelphia headquarters. Lewis received a copy because Kenyatta had been mentioned on the telephone as speaker at a proposed meeting, and Lewis had Kenyatta's file. He marked the report 157–1567–354 (category 157 for "racial"; number 1567 for Kenyatta's file; item in file, number 354).

February 8:

He received from agent Halterman, assigned to the Philadelphia office, a report on a meeting of the National Black Economic Development Council (NBEDC) that Halterman had gathered from PH–307–R (Philadelphia informant 307, Racial). The report gave only the time and place of the meeting and the names of some participants. Lewis made this item 355 in Kenyatta's file. Elapsed time, informant's notification to file: thirteen days.

February 9:

Lewis added to Kenyatta's file item 357, a report from informer PH–897–R (by way of agent Edward Cole). It reported in some detail the planned reorganization of NBEDC's executive board.

February 19:

Lewis received and filed a report originating in Baltimore in December concerning the remarks of a high-level administration official of the University of Maryland to an FBI agent about a black student who was a "constant source of agitation."

February 23:

Received and filed for future action a request from the Newark office to check the background of a Rutgers University student, whom Rutgers campus police had identified as a resident of Drexel Hill, Pennsylvania (near Media). Newark, in turn, was acting on a report from the Portland, Oregon, FBI office about the Panther's Revolutionary People's Constitutional Convention.

March 8:

CCIFBI removed all files from Lewis's office. Subsequently, Thomas F. Lewis was transferred to Atlanta, Georgia.[32]

Here is an operation more substantial than the army's, but not as thorough as that of the police or as omniscient as it is often thought to be. This chronology indicates that Bureau research is not particularly penetrating. The Bureau's sources are scattered and not systematic. Its agents spend much of their time pushing paper and collecting information that is either public to begin with or trivial in its implications. If, for example, the other 353 documents in Kenyatta's file are like the ones Lewis submitted, the totality is as unilluminating as it is extensive.

Nonetheless, the Bureau is not a paper tiger. It is in a position to round up many activists, should the government order such a step in a national "emergency." Jack Levine, an FBI agent who quit the Bureau in the early 1960s, wrote in 1962 that the Bureau could round up all the people on the lists it kept within hours of the order to move.[33] Documents taken from Media, Pennsylvania, refer several times to a list of activists called the SI, and once directly to the "Security Index."[34] The FBI and Justice Department are tight-lipped about the Index. The most carefully researched report about it comes from William Greider of the *Washington Post*.[35] According to his interviews with former Justice Department personnel, the list has three categories for people considered to be dangerous to different degrees. Names are placed on the Index through special forms and reports filed by Special Agents and reviewed by the Bureau in Washington. Greider quotes a former Justice Department lawyer as saying that the names were kept in a "big green book" in the Internal Security Division of the Justice Department. Greider said estimates on the number of names varied, but that a conservative guess put the total at 10,000. There may also be, according to Greider, an "agitator index" with a similar purpose. (There is an ambiguous abbreviation in the Media documents that may refer to this index.[36]) Greider quotes the same Justice Department lawyer referring to the Security Index: "When I was there, there wasn't any secret about it. Those were the people they would grab." Compared to the "enemies list" revealed by John Dean during the Watergate hearings, this list is serious business. Relatively speaking, Dean's list was the disinvitation to a tea party the White House said it was.

Until that order goes out, the Bureau can use its files to keep people out of jobs for being political activists or for refusing to inform on activists; and the FBI does win court cases despite the insufficiencies of its technique.

The Bureau's main strength, the area in which it surpasses police intelligence, is in the collation and redistribution of political intelligence reports. Exchange of information, even between police intelligence units, often takes place through the medium of the FBI. Police give the Bureau reports from their jurisdictions, and when they in return want information on outsiders, they get it from the Bureau. As the head of the Nashville, Tennessee, intelligence unit told a congressional hearing on riots: "The FBI contributed a greal deal to our knowledge of the situation, particularly in identifying people in from out of town that we could develop surveillance photographs on, or from informant reports."[37]

A slow but accelerating growth in direct interunit police cooperation has taken place in the last decade. Since the mid-fifties, intelligence sections have had a national organization, the Law Enforcement Intelligence Unit (LEIU). In 1967, it had 200 member units and met only semiannually; its meetings consisted mainly of shop talk and tales of derring-do. At the October, 1967, meeting (held in Toronto, some Canadian units being members), the Philadelphia red squad set the tone with a report of a foiled plot to poison city policemen with cyanide.[38] At that time, LEIU had no permanent staff and provided little besides ideological support.

Since that time, local intelligence units have begun

more routine interchanges. When militants from one area travel, the intelligence unit of their home city may telephone its counterpart at their destination to give warning.[39] In the last few years, regional alliances have been undertaken. *The New York Times* reported a meeting of representatives from nine midwestern cities to arrange "to share information and undercover agents."[40] The *Times* indicated that representatives from several neighboring small cities were meeting to start similar cooperation.

The aspect of interunit cooperation that is likely to show the most dramatic growth in the next five years is the exchange of warrant information. Computers are the new tool. Many systems are in the planning stage. One in Los Angeles is already working: from a patrol car, a name or a license or car number can be fed directly to data files in the Los Angeles city hall, in Sacramento, the state capital, and in the wanted persons center in Washington D.C. The police can know within seconds whether anyone they stop to check is wanted anywhere in the country.[41]

Operation of the interstate components of this system is in the hands of the FBI, so that the Bureau retains, at this time, control over all the principal means of national dissemination of political intelligence.

The explanation for the Bureau's specific place in the intelligence community—weaker in the field, stronger in dissemination and filing—is in its history. The Bureau is a Johnny-come-lately to the police field. There was little federal police authority other than the army until after the beginning of this century. Since then, in the face of growing federal authority, local police units have used the ever-present well of states' rights sentiment in the country to retain for themselves the place of first line of defense against disorder and disruption.

Smaller city intelligence units, county and state police, and district attorney's offices form a third part of the ci-

vilian network. They employ the same techniques as big-
city units, but their scale is smaller, their approach less
systematic, and their impact less profound. I recently had
the chance to examine a file copy from an intelligence unit
in a small city near the eastern seaboard. It showed the
same distance from targets, the same dependence on
secondary sources, and the same preponderance of irrelevant material as do the Media, Pennsylvania, FBI files.
It contained:

—Scores of xeroxed toll tickets subpoenaed from the local phone
  company, listing calls from the homes of four subjects, attached to voluminous notes of the agent's attempt to track
  down the owner of the called phones. The final list showed
  some friends, some predictable retail stores, and no pattern.
—A report on a national black nationalist organization, prepared
  by the Special Services Unit of the Los Angeles police department. It appeared without explanation although Los Angeles
  was more than 1,000 miles away.
—The minutes of a recent meeting of the local Policemen's
  Benevolent Association.
—A memo concerning a coordinating committee of intelligence
  units for several neighboring cities.
—A field report from another officer about a local public political meeting. It summarized the speeches and gave the agent's
  conclusion that the meeting had done much to promote dis-
  content and friction in the community.
—A reply from the state's motor vehicle registration unit giving
  owner and address information on cars used by the subjects
  and others.
—A carbon of the agent's progress report to his superiors. It
  contained neither conclusions nor information.

Three other agencies further augment the work of red
squads and the FBI. They are the Secret Service, the
Bureau of Narcotics and Dangerous Drugs, and the CIA.

The Secret Service has a total staff of about 2,500 of
whom roughly 1,000 are investigative agents.[42] Their
assigned mission is the protection of high-ranking govern-

ment officials. I have come across a few reports that political activists have been hassled by Secret Service agents supposedly checking out threats to the life of the president.[43] The agency does maintain files. They do not have their own widespread collection network, but rely on other agencies. One Media FBI document, for example, talks of passing information on to the Secret Service. Part of the Secret Service file is built up from "threatening" phone calls and letters received at the White House.[44] More than 50,000 names are now encoded and cross-indexed by this agency's computers.[45] Staff time is not generally spent in field investigations. In election years, for example, two-thirds of the entire staff may be assigned as bodyguards for campaigning officials.

The Justice Department's Bureau of Narcotics and Dangerous Drugs (BNDD) has approximately 1,200 field agents.[46] I have found no cases in which these agents have been charged with major acts of political harassment or surveillance. In several cases local narcotics agents have investigated political groups; they may receive long-term aid from BNDD. Local vice squad officers ran part of the investigation of the Fall River, Massachusetts, organizing effort in 1970.[47] Local narcotics agents, using an informer, staged a major raid on the hip political community in New Haven in 1970. BNDD agents have made menacing raids on people who had no connection to drug traffic. These seem to have been appalling mistakes by fanatic agents, not political raids.

The CIA does not figure prominently in the evidence available about domestic political surveillance. According to the logic of fear, its low profile is a product of skill, not an indication of noninvolvement. Were there no evidence at all, that argument might be convincing. Perhaps the sample available is not representative, but I know of no reason that leaks in the CIA's security should underrepresent any facet of its work.

On the basis of these leaks, it is reasonable to assume that most domestic CIA operations are not aimed at groups based in the United States. Allegations about CIA involvement in the Watergate affair made headlines, but large-scale domestic involvement is not revealed when the substance of the charges is examined. CIA domestic operations are, primarily, backups for foreign intrigue. Despite the possible interpretation of its name, the Domestic Operations Division of the CIA, established in 1964, has concerned itself chiefly with logistical support for foreign operations.[48] It is, for example, closely tied to Interarmco, an international arms dealer that covers international CIA gun-running,[49] and with Air America, the CIA-supported airline in Southeast Asia. The Domestic Operations Division may also run CIA recruiting, one of the few open CIA activities; there are CIA recruiting offices in thirteen cities.[50] It also recruits and routinely interviews informants in firms with international dealings. Herbert Itkin was one of these, but the CIA turned him over to the FBI when he lost his job and fell into Mafia circles (indicating that at least sometimes the CIA honors its prohibition from internal security involvement). Itkin became a chief government source in the New York City water department scandal known as the Marcus affair.[51] These and similar dealings are the substance behind rumors of domestic CIA involvement. In almost every case, they point toward an operation concerned with foreign intelligence gathering and international dirty tricks, not with domestic surveillance.

In three areas, the CIA has been involved in shaping the policy of domestic political groups and in one case it has trained law enforcement personnel. It has funded social science research at major universities. For example, the Center for International Studies at MIT was begun in the early fifties with CIA connivance and was supported by it until 1967.[52] In this and other ways the agency has impressed its assumptions on institutions where policy alternatives are formulated; as such, it may have influenced decisions.

The CIA controlled many officers of the National Student Association at least into the late 1960s. Most of the CIA's involvement with NSA, however, was part of its cold war, international mission. NSA delegations were used (often unwittingly) to collect information on foreign student groups and leaders. The CIA used NSA's votes in international conferences to bolster a liberal but pro-United States position in the cold war. This work sometimes led back home. Michael Wood, who first broke the NSA-CIA story to *Ramparts,* reported that the CIA played a very active role lobbying against a strong antiwar stand at the 1965 national NSA convention.[53]

The CIA has also evidently worked within emigré groups in the United States. Besides its work with exiled Cubans, primarily in Florida, it has worked with Arab student organizations and Estonian groups in the United States.[54]

Particularly in these last two areas, the CIA has engaged in exactly the kind of sophisticated political manipulation that is mistakenly attributed to police and FBI work within the left.

The evidence shows no instance of CIA penetration of left-wing organizations or small groups.

As of this writing, the Watergate affair has added little concrete knowledge about the extent of CIA domestic involvement. The agency did supply documents, a camera, a wig, and other paraphernalia to the burglars who entered the office of Daniel Ellsberg's psychiatrist. It does appear, from reports on the same incident, that the CIA maintains "safe houses" in the United States. These are points at which agents can meet surreptitiously to exchange information and equipment. And the CIA does admit conducting a psychiatric profile of Ellsberg himself. The CIA offers as a defense that it was misled in the case of equipment and made its first and only domestic mistake in the profile. It contends that White House officials represented that the equipment would help stop international drug traffic and that this was a proper use for CIA resources. As for the psychiatric profile, it was, according to the agency, the first time that one had been done on a U.S. citizen, and the mistake will not be repeated. It is not a defense that removes all doubt, and there are so many other points at which the CIA's name crops up in Watergate that it is hardly a sufficient defense. Even if, as the agency contends, the men who carried out the Watergate raid were only former CIA employees, and the equipment was obtained on false pretenses, the argument misses the main point. The expertise and equipment existed because of the CIA, and the men would not have been available and seasoned without it. Whether its involvement was willing or not, its operations have to be included in the picture of domestic surveillance.

The one documented case of CIA involvement on the level of policy in domestic surveillance concerns the training of approximately fifty city and county police officers in the use of wiretap detectors and explosive detectors and in the organization of intelligence files. The training, which reportedly consisted of a series of briefings, took place during 1970 and 1971, and was given to men from police forces in New York; Washington, D.C.; Boston; Montgomery County, Maryland; and Fairfax County, Virginia; as well as other undisclosed places.[55]

I know of only one other incident linking the CIA with the domestic left. It is, like the training of city police, involvement at one remove from field investigations. Word of it comes from former army intelligence agent Ralph Stein:

I went to the Central Intelligence Agency at McLean, Virginia, in the company of my immediate supervisor, I believe it was late in 1967, to deliver a briefing on underground and student newspapers. Mr. Jim Ludlum of the CIA had requested the briefing several days before. . . . Although the ostensible purpose of my briefing was to acquaint them with the financing for the purpose of determining if there was foreign support (there wasn't; most of the papers were going broke anyway), the questions asked suggested a deep interest in the beliefs of the students who published those papers. I think an inquiry in the CIA's involvement in domestic intelligence is called for. I made a number of remarks after the briefing . . . regarding my confusion about their interest, and I was then told that I would not have to deal with Mr. Ludlum in the future. I noticed Mr. Ludlum at our office on several subsequent occasions.[56]

The position of the CIA within the intelligence community suggests that domestic manipulations on its part are in fact rare. The CIA is not a law enforcement organization. It has nothing to gain from subverting a particular plot or capturing political fugitives. And it has a lot to lose. Were it not for the FBI's jealousy, the CIA could violate its charter's prohibition of internal security involvement without much fear of recrimination. Who would know, or who in any position of power would care? But the Bureau's jealousy of its bailiwick has grown in direct proportion to its incompetence. Particularly now that the CIA is openly criticizing the Bureau,[57] the FBI would love to catch the Agency with its fingers in the forbidden domestic pie. The CIA must watch its step, and, after all, its reputation does not depend on the domestic situation.

The picture that emerges is of an agency basically concerned with international intelligence. Its domestic operations are designed accordingly. The agency becomes most involved in those domestic groups that have direct roots (like emigré groups) or direct uses (like NSA) in the international arena. It keeps up on the left by debriefing people like Stein who work in surveillance programs focused on domestic concerns and by watching for links between foreign and domestic groups. In this way it undoubtedly updates its files on key people and organizations. During the Watergate affair reporter Seymour Hersh discovered CIA reports that seem to be based on just this kind of information. According to Hersh's article in *The New York Times* of May 25, 1973, the CIA conducted two studies of alien-radical ties at the end of the 1960s and found no significant connections. To judge from Hersh's report, the CIA study came much closer to the truth than the FBI hypothesis of international conspiracies, which was dominant within the Nixon Administration at the time. This substantiates an often quoted assumption that the CIA provides the most accurate and sophisticated reports of any unit in the intelligence community. With its edge on accuracy, its huge budget, and its dabblings in domestic politics *à la* Ellsberg case, anti-Castro movements in Miami, and training of police officers, it would be easy for the CIA to become more deeply involved in domestic affairs in the future.

The civilian collection apparatus, as it emerges from this review, is an aggregate of discrete parts. Big-city red squads do the spade work, backed up by the FBI, which also does most of the collating and intercity dissemination. Other agencies, including state and small-city intelligence units, the Bureau of Narcotics and Dangerous Drugs, the Secret Service, and the CIA play ancillary roles. All of them together give to the military much more than they get in return.

Electronic Surveillance

No telephone can be trusted. Even calls between coin telephones can be traced by the police and immediately tapped. Any room can be bugged. Laser beams can bounce off window panes and reveal to their sender conversations within the room. From a properly equipped speeding car, the authorities can eavesdrop on a whispered conversation in the car ahead. Police infiltrators carry bugs in the heels of their shoes. In basement rooms of telephone exchanges recorders monitor hundreds of telephone calls.

These are only some of the things people believe about the great extent and skillful art of electronic surveillance. The evidence concerning these and other forms of space age surveillance is spotty and questionable; it produces no precise conclusions even at its best. It proves to be worth marshaling, however, because it does indicate the upper limit of the technology, and it sets guidelines for guessing the probable extent of its application.

Elsur, to use the FBI's acronym for this practice, has unquestionably been conducted at a quickening pace in recent years. The devices are getting smaller and more powerful, and the state of the art has taken some quantum leaps. But the daily practice of the art is mundane compared to the fantasies about it.

The Justice Department has admitted that 113 elsur installations were used in 1970 for national security purposes.[1] That category is customarily used to cover surveillance of both foreign embassy personnel and domestic political groups. In making the figures known to Senator Kennedy's office, the department indicated that the average use of each device was between 54 and 200 days.[2] If the figures are accurate, they represent a ratio of less than one installation for every million adults in the country. (The Kennedy figure is larger than those released by the FBI or the White House for that year. If there is any basis of truth to the lower figures, it must be assumed that the Justice Department referred only to the actual number in use on the day of the statement, or else they took advantage of public ignorance of elsur terminology and referred only to *taps*—telephone connected devices—and excluded *bugs*—devices that monitor any conversation in a room.[3])

On June 19, 1972, the Supreme Court ruled that the national security argument could not be used to put domestic groups under electronic observation. It required that the government make application for such surveillance to the courts, as the Omnibus Crime Control and Safe Streets Act of 1968 demands for all other elsur installations.[4] In the following week, published reports said the Justice Department removed a dozen installations and claimed, then, to have only two operating against domestic groups for political purposes. These, it said, were groups tied to foreign governments and so, it implied, were not protected by the Supreme Court's new ruling.[5] If the Justice Department is to be believed, there are only two elsur installations now being used against domestic political groups. What can be said about the published figures?

Could the federal government be concealing the extent of political wiretapping by reporting political taps as criminal ones? The Omnibus Crime Control Act makes any law enforcement unit that wants to tap a phone or bug a room go before a judge, present probable cause that a crime is involved, and get a signed warrant before proceeding. In 1972, only 855 such applications were reported.[6] Most were said to be for surveillance of organized crime; none were labelled in a way that could be construed as political. It seems reasonable to believe that law enforcement agencies did conduct surveillance of organized crime and other criminal activities. Moreover, the geographical distribution of the 855 reported applications corresponds to locations cited in well-documented investigations of organized crime. New York authorities made 294 of them, and New Jersey 235. (All the other states combined made only 120 and federal authorities made 206.)[7] Then, too, little comes of the assumption that

every application for a nonpolitical warrant was in fact a
deceit practiced on a judge in order to undertake political
eavesdropping. The warrants would be pointless until
used, and they would be useless afterwards, since the
fraudulence of their authorization would then likely be
obvious. If one sets all this aside, on the good grounds that
the government is not known to be always rational, one
encounters a more important flaw in the line of speculation: even 855 additional applications for political purposes means only a rate of at most six per million adults.
It isn't sufficient cover for the extent of political espionage
often suspected of the government.

Could it be that the federal government knowingly fails
to report the number of national security taps installed by
federal agents? Only the Justice Department is in any
position to verify the number used in a year. Since it is
both principal perpetrator and sole watchdog, it is certainly in a position to engage in misrepresentation. One
of the few things that can be said about this possibility is
that the Justice Department does not seize every opportunity to misrepresent the extent of political electronic
surveillance. In the Pentagon Papers case, for example,
the department twice produced records of conversations
by principals in the case apparently overheard on national
security elsur installations. Each time, the trial was de-
layed, and, in addition, a jury to which the prosecution
had no particular objection had to be dismissed. The revelations did not appear in any way to help the government's
case. The department contended, in fact, that the conversations had no bearing on the litigation. If the government
reported national security installations in that case, when
it had nothing to gain and a trial to lose, is it reasonable to
believe that it would not report them when it is simply
engaged in publishing annual summaries?

Revelations in the Watergate affair touch ambiguously
on this point. On the one hand, the government does seem

to have made admissions damaging to its case like those noted above. On the other hand, in the normal course of operations the government did not reveal the tap on Morton Halperin in which Ellsberg was overheard. Only when newspaper reports prodded Richardson, the newly appointed Attorney General, to undertake a special investigation was an FBI agent who recalled the interception uncovered.

There is one explanation that fits both cases. If the government's guiding principle is fear of exposure, then it might well be honest in individual cases and devious in summaries. The people who overheard someone in the Pentagon Papers case would have known if the government failed to mention their reports in court. In the wake of all the leaks, in view of the Ellsberg case itself, the government certainly has grounds to fear that evidence of its perfidy will be smuggled to the press. Evidence of an undercount of installations might be thought to be safer. If records are in the main decentralized, then only a few of the highest level Justice Department bureaucrats know for certain of the misrepresentation. Their loyalty, it could be argued, is still taken for granted. (It was just such a centralized operation that was uncovered by the Watergate hearings: the seventeen Kissinger taps, including the one on Halperin, were handled by high-level FBI personnel.)

Such a scheme would only cover an underestimation of modest proportions. Employees in one of the fifty-odd field offices of the FBI would know if the devices they installed accounted for too large a percentage of the published national total. No leak concerning such a skewing of figures has been forthcoming. If there had been no leaks at all, it might be presumed that disaffection had not spread that high in the bureaucracy. But weight must be given to the leaks that have, in fact, occurred. Former FBI Special Agent Robert Wall has said, for instance, that he knew of very few political elsur installations in the Washington, D.C., area in the mid 1960s.[8] He worked inside the Internal Security unit in Washington, just the unit that would have been responsible for political surveillance. He personally conducted an investigation of the Institute for Policy Studies because his superiors thought that the organization was the mechanism through which foreign powers controlled and subsidized the New Left.[9] He has made no reference to the use of electronic listening devices in that investigation.

In a more dramatic leak, former Atlanta FBI agent Arthur Murtagh has disclosed that he knew of fewer than a dozen electronic surveillance operations on the same scale as the one aimed at Martin Luther King, Jr., in the mid-1960s. Murtagh made the disclosure in an interview with WBAI radio on May 21, 1973, the day *The New York Times* broke Murtagh's story on the wide scope of the King surveillance. Murtagh told the *Times* that 5,000 of King's calls were intercepted over a period that started in 1963 and ran for at least three years. The taps first became known in news accounts in 1968, but at that time reports said the FBI tapped only King's office and home telephone and the phone of a New York associate. According to Murtagh, the Bureau also tapped telephones at hotels where King stayed when he traveled. According to *Times* reporter Wallace Turner, Murtagh said: "The surveillance was massive and complete. He couldn't wiggle." Murtagh would not identify the subjects of the other elsur operations.

Another former agent, William Turner, has written about similar work in the San Francisco–Oakland area in the early 1950s.[10] He, too, writes of a relatively small number of installations—a dozen taps constructed of special telephone lines running from the tapped phone to one of two disguised offices in the city where agents listened with earphones.

Columnist Jack Anderson has also done some checking into the question and he believes the federal figures.[11] His evaluation may not be definitive, but, to judge from his reputation, his predilections would produce error on the high side if they produced any error at all.

Could it be that the official figures released to the Kennedy subcommittee are not conscious fabrications but still underrepresent the extent of electronic surveillance because the Justice Department officials who compile them do not know what goes on in the field?

Bill Turner has written that FBI personnel on the West Coast did make unauthorized installations. They were called suicide taps because of the consequences for an installer who got caught. Turner's account emphasizes the danger of their use.[12] One can infer from his account that their number would not bring the total number of political installations to a different order of magnitude from the official figures—at least not in his day. Suicide taps do not turn up in Robert Wall's account, nor are there any open references to them in the large sample of documents taken from the Media FBI office.

There still remains the possibility that agencies other than the FBI make wide use of unauthorized taps. Thus, at the same time that he verifies the FBI's figures for its own installations, Anderson acknowledges the possibility of arrangements with local agencies to install elsur devices.[13]

In the case of the army, many sources have come forward. Only one has given any testimony about telephone taps or room bugs used by the army against domestic civilian targets. The one source is Ronald Weber, former Specialist Fourth Class for the Army Security Agency and now a deserter living in Canada. He told Bruce Garvey of the *Toronto Star* that he had been in a unit assigned to give electronic support to army units stationed in Chicago for the 1968 Democratic National Convention. The unit

totaled 150 men; half of them, Weber told Garvey, actually
dealt with information. "The plan," according to Garvey,
"called for the Army Security Agency company to locate
in rooms or storefronts and tour the city in vans equipped
with radio receivers, monitoring police radios, 'certain
telephone communications,' and shortwave radio transmissions." Garvey quotes Weber:

We got one series of reports about a by-play between some of
Senator [Eugene] McCarthy's workers. We actually intercepted
a message from McCarthy headquarters to various radical organizations which had long been connected to the Communist
party in the United States. . . . We got in over our heads and did
not know what to do about it. Obviously that information, if it
were ever thrown back or over the air or anything like that, it
would have had to be documented. Before they (the army) could
have done anything in documenting it, they would have questioned a lot of constitutional rights like wiretapping, things like
this. . . . If the media ever got hold of the fact that there was an
army intelligence unit—operating in Chicago for the sole purpose of reading the telephone messages of both delegates and
people in the streets, I am sure they would have had some interesting by-play back and forth and a lot of people would have
had to answer a lot of questions.[14]

The army has been directly linked to only one other
type of electronic surveillance, but it is not the kind that
concerns us here. One source reported that the Army
Security Agency (ASA) had been called on to monitor
shortwave radio communication between amateur radio
operators in the Southwest. These hams were thought by
the authorities to be carrying on a coded conversation
about a revolutionary plot. The outcome of the investigation could not be learned.

If the army is not regularly engaged in domestic electronic surveillance, it is not for want of skill, equipment,
or practice. The army seems to be routinely engaged in
surveillance of international communications. Ralph

Stein, the former Military Intelligence agent whose testimony has been quoted elsewhere in this essay, mentioned
seeing reports that could only have come from surveillance of telephone conversations made by Dave Dellinger
when he was in Europe in 1967 meeting representatives
of the DRV and NLF.[15] In the same vein, a former employee of the National Security Agency (NSA) has been
quoted in *Ramparts* as saying that every transatlantic
telephone call entering or leaving the United States is
recorded by that agency.[16] The agency draws a principal
share of its operating staff from the ASA and the rest from
ASA's counterparts in the navy and Air Force.

In passing, it ought to be noted that the army appears
to be engaged in routine surveillance of another major
form of international communication—the mails. As with
electronics, there is no evidence yet that the army practices this art domestically.

Fourteen-year-old Norman Shore was sent, during the
summer of 1970, to a camp in East Germany run by the
youth division of the East German Communist party. All
summer long, letters written by Norman's parents, who
were in the United States, and sent to Norman and to
officials at the camp were recorded and summarized by a
unit known as the U.S. Army Operations and Research
Detachment (USAO&RD) in Frankfurt. The unit wrote,
when it passed on the information, that its source was the
Confidential Intercept Service. Frankfurt—the address
of this unit—is also the location of NSA headquarters for
Europe. USAO&RD sent along extracts of these intercepted letters to the U.S. legal attaché in Bonn. He passed
them along to FBI headquarters in Washington, where
they were routed to the Philadelphia field office of the FBI.

Nothing in the memos with the letters indicates that
they were the result of a special investigation requested
by the Philadelphia Bureau. Everything, in fact, suggests
that the FBI investigation was prompted by information

from routine army surveillance of mail going to East Germany. Is monitering of East German mail the exception or the rule for Eastern bloc countries?

Local police intelligence units have not produced numbers of disaffected agents as the army and the FBI have done. Glimpses of their inner workings have come from testimony of former army agents who claim to have known well the police intelligence personnel in their areas. Their testimony gives the impression that in each area there is a fraternity of domestic intelligence gatherers. They know each other on a first-name basis and visit each other's offices. They frequently exchange information on an informal basis, as often as they do through bureaucratic channels. Former army personnel made no mention at the Ervin hearings of extensive—or even any—electronic surveillance by the police units with which they worked.[17]

The only direct evidence that has come to my attention is similarly inconclusive. The police intelligence file mentioned earlier—it belonged to a police intelligence officer of a medium-sized city—showed that the agent was making extensive use of toll-call records gathered from the telephone company. He was apparently attempting to find some pattern to the calls or some contact among black insurgents in his area. It does not seem reasonable that he would have resorted to such obviously tedious attempts at cross-correlating toll sheets and hunting in phone books if he had had access to the contents of the calls. But then the absence of one bug doesn't rule out others.

These are very thin reeds on which to hang a judgment on the extent of illegal (unwarranted) electronic surveillance by local police units. In the absence of other, harder data, some useful deductions about the possible scope of political elsur can be made from official figures on the costs involved.

According to federal figures, authorized taps operated for an average period of two weeks each. The cost was

$5,435 for state and local authorities and $9,795 for federal authorities; or, on a daily basis, local units spent $388 and federal units spent $700.[18]

At these rates, 100 taps operating for only a year in New York City would cost one and a half times the entire budget for the New York City Intelligence Unit (using last known figures).[19] Those 100 taps would take three times the estimated current staff of the unit to install,[20] operate, and transcribe if, as common sense suggests, former Attorney General Ramsey Clark's estimate of two to six people per tap is accurate.[21] A tap seems to require three people working eight-hour shifts and another person to transcribe and log the conversations. Another well-qualified source estimates at least two people working full time.[22] In addition, by his estimate, it takes a team of three to make the installation—one inside and at least two lookouts. (If one calculates on the cost figures supplied by federal units, the cost of 100 installations jumps to four and a half times the last known budget of the New York City red squad.)

Confronted with these approximations, one can maintain a belief in innumerable elsur installations only if one believes in the existence in each city of a force of hundreds of people monitoring hundreds of taps and consuming hundreds of thousands of dollars in wages. One must further believe that their ranks have given up not one defector in spite of obvious temptations. Their pay scale cannot be great enough to quiet misgivings of conscience about the activity or to eclipse payment for selling the story to a magazine. Others have quit the FBI over issues of less principle than tapping telephones illegally. One must also believe that countless other people found ways to finagle the money out of state and local budgets to pay for these operations.

The best available guide to commonly used electronic surveillance equipment is a commercial catalogue published by Sirchie Fingerprint Laboratories of Moorestown, New Jersey, a firm that makes and sells a full range of equipment exclusively to law enforcement agencies. The catalogue is supposed to be distributed only in response to inquiries that arrive on the letterhead stationery of legitimate authorities. A xeroxed copy of it has come into my possession.

The catalogue illustrates dozens of systems. At the heart of each is a tape recorder. Each recorder is too large to be either easily hidden in the room under surveillance or readily concealed on one's person.

Each system also requires a microphone. The smallest of these was one-quarter inch square—the size of a collar button. Most were much larger. One could be driven through the baseboard of a room to pick up conversations in the room adjoining. Others could be concealed in furniture. A few could be fitted within a telephone or substituted for one of the regular parts of a telephone.

There were three methods for connecting the microphone and recorder. The telephone microphones used the regular telephone cables. In this case, the recorder also had to be connected to the telephone line. This connection could be made anywhere between the bugged room and the central telephone exchange. No equipment in the catalogue was suitable for use inside the exchange. The designs indicated that the recorder would be connected at a junction box in the basement, or in a nearby apartment. Many pieces of equipment are specifically advertised as being "undetectable by telephone company." Other microphones had to be connected to recorders by their own pairs of wires. All the wires offered were large enough to be seen by the unaided eye, although they could be concealed beneath floors, behind walls, or within cracks.

The most sophisticated gear connected a mike to a recorder by radio transmitter. In this case there was no physical connection at all, and even if the mike and transmitter were found, the recorder, tapes, and listener could remain securely hidden. Even the smallest transmitter had a volume of several cubic inches and required an antenna at least a foot long to transmit for any useful distance. All the transmitters operated within the 175 to 200 MHz (megahertz) range and sent a frequency modulated signal. Anyone wanting to hunt for such a device could easily purchase a suitable radio receiver. Only one of the devices could be turned off by remote control. It is unlikely that any of the devices could send a clear signal more than several blocks in a high-rise city environment.

The cost of equipment for each installation came to roughly $600.

The catalogue did feature some equipment designed for monitoring calls on multiple lines simultaneously. The devices were of desk size and were capable of recording sound from up to fifty sources. The ad spoke of uses in prisons and detention rooms.

Newspaper reports on police equipment actually used in the field bears out the contention that the catalogue is a good index. In the case of the Panther 21, a New York City intelligence unit agent wore a microphone and transmitter with parameters like those advertised.[23] Conversations were monitored by two agents in a car that stayed within a few blocks of the transmitting agent. Investigators for the Knapp Commission, investigating corruption among New York City policemen, used a similar device.[24] Both investigations were important enough to warrant the best equipment available to the department. Yet the police were not using heel-of-the-shoe transmitters and pin-sized microphones. Their equipment could be detected by a careful search.

Other sources suggest that more sophisticated devices are becoming available for agencies with the money and desire to use them. A recent press dispatch noted that someone did in fact place a microphone and transmitter in the heel of a U.S. ambassador's shoe when the shoes were sent to be resoled. Some idea of the current limits of elsur technology can be deduced from the fact that even that device could not transmit more than 300 yards. Other articles indicate that it is actually possible to decipher a conversation within a room by bouncing laser beams off the window panes.[25] Major U.S. embassies are said to have had to construct, on this account, windowless soundproof rooms for discussing and typing classified material.[26] But the equipment is still of such intricacy and bulk that it is not likely to be common, even in international espionage applications, for some time, and its expense puts it out of the question for local law enforcement groups for the time being.

A number of feats seem still to be beyond the capabilities of the art. Transmitters are getting smaller, but at a tiny scale their range is still measured in yards, not miles. And cars, although they can be bugged in the same fashion as a room, cannot be bugged unless there has been some physical installation made within the car itself.

The last bit of evidence on the state of the art doesn't quite vitiate all the others, but it does mean that any conclusions have to be transient. The state of the art is developing rapidly. In the early 1950s, elsur meant hooking up a telephone line from the room or phone in question to some other listening room. Concealable transmitters were as rare as laser listening devices are today. Now miniature transmitters are a growing over-the-counter industry, and cheap imitations are available for sale to anyone in many parts of the country. The industry has grown large enough to become the subject of a recent federal law. Eavesdropping devices can no longer be sold in interstate commerce except to law enforcement agencies.

One device in particular illustrates the edge of technology coming into widespread use. Until recently it was necessary, if one wanted to use a telephone to hear conversations within the room—that is, to convert a telephone into a bug—to make a physical and therefore detectable change in the wiring of the phone. It is now possible to send a radio frequency signal over the telephone and use it to activate the telephone's microphone even when the receiver is on the hook. This can be done without making any change in the telephone or ever getting closer to the phone than the pair of wires running to a nearby basement or pole.[27]

You call a friend and say: "Go to a pay phone and call me back at the number I'm giving you, which is the pay phone where I am now." Will anyone be able to tap the pay-phone-to-pay-phone call you then make?

It isn't likely. If the pay phone is in the drugstore opposite the national headquarters of Revolution Now, perhaps it already has attached to it one of the 113 national security taps or a suicide tap placed by the local police. If, on the other hand, it's just an ordinary phone, the following things have to happen in order for your conversation to be overheard:

—Your friend's phone must be tapped or his room bugged.
—Someone must be listening to your friend's phone at the moment you happen to call. If there is no tap, or if it feeds a recorder and the tapes are reviewed later, knowledge of the pay-phone-to-pay-phone conversation will come too late if at all.

—The eavesdropper must want to hear the next call and have the connections to act on it.
—He must find someone to race to your friend's house, follow him to the pay phone of his choice, and then find a way to tap the phone line. Finding the right pair of cables near the phone is a tedious job and requires a knowledge of the color coding of the particular phone if it's to be done with any speed. Perhaps a call to a contact in the central office could have the

phone monitored there. But it would take a good connection, and it is a method for which there is not one documented example.

There is another possible way: the eavesdropper could call some authority in your area, give him the number you gave your friend, and convince him to go through the routine of finding the phone, its cables, or someone in the central office to tie into it.

A news account that at first appears unrelated may demonstrate that equipment to trace calls quickly is not yet available. On November 7, 1971, *The New York Times* reported that local police had taken four hours to trace a call in order to locate a man trying to commit suicide. The person had called WBAI's Bob Fass and told him and his radio audience that he had taken a huge quantity of drugs. Fass kept him talking and notified the police. They eventually traced the call and took the caller, who had by then passed out, to the hospital.[28]

With any luck at all the two of you engaged in your hypothetical phone call would be back home long before the calls are traced. Technical and organizational machinery for doing the whole thing faster is conceivable, but there is no evidence that it now exists.

Not too long ago a friend of mine attended a meeting to discuss the problems of security that political groups encounter. As the group was beginning its discussion, someone suggested that the meeting room offered poor security. It had large, unshaded windows that faced many apartments. It was part of an office known for the radical politics of its regular users. It was also relatively open to the public. Someone who wanted to plant a bug in it could have done so, they pointed out, with relative ease. The meeting therefore adjourned to a private house.

That brief episode sums up a great deal that is misguided about most attempts to deal with security. It is much easier for people to confront the possible dangers from electronic eavesdroppers than from human spies. The group reacted quickly to the possibility that the room was bugged, but it made no effort to ascertain if all the people present were actually trustworthy. In fact, few people there knew and were known by all the others, and certainly some people there assumed others were all right only because no one else raised a question about them.

The reasons for that unbalanced reaction are not hard to guess. To ask after someone's credentials invites a personal confrontation; at the least, it invites embarrassment. To raise the possibility of a bug does not. Yet, to judge from the record of recent court trials, prosecutions are built around informers, not bugs: the Panther 21 (in which a bug was useful only because it backed up an informer's testimony); the Chicago 7 (no taps); and the Berrigan Harrisburg case bear witness to that point. Whether informers are inherently more effective, or whether they have been more effective only because inhibitions about searching for them are stronger, the result is the same: they survive longer and get more people in serious trouble.

The Uses of Political Intelligence

When J. Edgar Hoover made his congressional appearance to ask for funds for the FBI for 1970, he spoke at length of an upsurge in violent acts by the political left. He referred specifically to eleven attacks, including bombings, against ROTC buildings in Berkeley, Seattle, Oregon, and Connecticut, against a building in Michigan, and against power pylons in California. He reported obtaining indictments for three groups covering six of the eleven incidents. He successfully conveyed the impression of a rapid outbreak of violence met by diligent police work and implied that more manpower was needed to finish the job.[1] What he conveyed, however, was not the truth.

He left out at least ninety-seven damage-causing bomb or incendiary attacks that had occurred during the same period. Not all these attacks made national headlines, but neither did those cited by Hoover.[2] The FBI chief had to omit a large part of the left's activity in order to seem effective against it. Bombings are not the only area in which all this surveillance produces very few criminal proceedings. Concerning raids on draft and FBI offices, for example, the government has ferreted out fewer than twenty prosecutable cases. There have been more than forty successful draft raids across the country.

Because of the huge financial and psychological costs to political activists of any one prosecution—as, most recently, the New Haven, Harrisburg, and Angela Davis trials prove—it is hard to realize that the government's program to use prosecutions to interfere with political activists has been, relatively, a failure. Surely, the government cultivates confusion on the point, as Hoover's testimony illustrates. It needs myths of effectiveness to achieve by fear and intimidation what it cannot accomplish through the courts. It might be argued that it makes little difference whether the government stops political acts by prosecution or by fear of prosecution. No countermeasure exists for effective prosecutions except to refrain from the prosecuted acts. But fear that is based on an overestimation of the government's effectiveness at prosecuting could disappear with a marshaling of the facts. To catch and prosecute violators of the law is the purpose that provides a public justification for surveillance. It has not led to many successful prosecutions. Electronic surveillance in particular has thwarted prosecutions more than it has aided them. The Ellsberg case was dismissed because of it, and

the White Panther case never made it to trial because of
the possibility of evidence tainted by illegal surveillance.

The nonforensic uses of intelligence are never entirely
open. They fall into two categories: offensive and subversive.

News leaks are the method in the not-quite-legal offensive use of police intelligence. Their number is exceeded
only by the number of assurances issued about the sanctity of intelligence files. Sometimes information passes
directly to the press from the agency that collected it.
Former FBI agent Robert Wall gave WNDT-TV this
example of FBI techniques in the D.C. area.[3]

Wall: Among blacks who were competing for office, Julius
Hobson was a particular thorn in our side. Somewhere along the
line he made a statement that "I am a Marxist." He was working
for the government at one time. I guess it was HEW.

We wrote up a press release about the guy, saying all true
things. For instance, we would take his statement—on such and
such a day he said "I am a Marxist" and we'd throw it into a little
biographical sketch. And then you would throw into the same
article the implication that being a Marxist was a bad thing, or
you'd phrase it in such a way that it would come out derogatory.

And it would go over to the Bureau and they would contact
their friendly press man, and they'd say: "Here's the guy.
Here's the story. Here's the information we want to put in."
Generally a paragraph out of our press release would show up in
a story about the individual we were reporting on.

Questioner: It was clear to the Bureau that doing that stuff
was not just investigating or interviewing or watching but
actually trying to affect American politics?

Wall: Absolutely.

In an incident reported by the ACLU, police in a California town used the same technique in attempting to
defeat a candidate they opposed.[4]

A former FBI agent has now come forward to confirm

that one of the most widely publicized tapping operations of the 1960s was repeatedly used for political purposes. Former agent Arthur Murtagh, who worked in the FBI's Atlanta office, told *The New York Times* for a May 21, 1973, story that many newspapermen were urged to write stories on Martin Luther King's private life, based on Bureau information gathered from wiretaps. Murtagh said he knew the agent who had gone to visit the editor of the *Atlanta Constitution* to suggest such a story.

When information is given in this manner, its source is not revealed and so, from the police point of view, it loses the benefit of official attribution. When congressional committees act as intermediaries, the loss is recouped and the transgression of releasing police information outside the courts is disguised. The conduits for such information are three congressional committees—the Internal Security Committee of the House (HISC, formerly HUAC), also known after its chairman as the Ichord Committee, the McClellan subcommittee of the Senate Government Operations Committee, and Eastland's subcommittee of the Senate Judiciary Committee.

Many states have their own versions of these committees. They all get their information by calling police intelligence personnel to testify at hearings. Officials from police department intelligence units in Los Angeles, Chicago, Nashville, and other cities testified at the McClellan hearings on riots. Alcohol and tobacco tax investigators for IRS testified before the Eastland Committee about radical activity in Fall River, Massachusetts. Such witnesses draw on their files, prepare tables and charts, sometimes place entire reports in the official record, and turn over leaflets and other items they have collected. Many pages of one committee report are devoted, for example, to a facsimile reproduction of Weatherperson Bernadine Dorhn's diary.[5] Congressional committees also have access to police intelligence through the intelligence officers they hire to prepare and run their hearings.

There are other routes from police investigation to congressional files. Major General Ralph Van Deman was head of army intelligence until 1929. After he retired he went right on collecting information on subversives in the U.S.[6] His files contained the names of 115,000 people and organizations by the time of his death in 1952. An army investigation into his files, undertaken in the late 1960s, said, in part: "He regularly received classified domestic intelligence reports from the army and the navy. . . . The number of FBI summaries, reports, and photographs indicates that he could, upon request, obtain information from the Bureau."

Richard Halloran of *The New York Times* reported that these files were used during the 1960s to screen applicants for state jobs in California; and the politicians in southern California claimed the Van Deman files had been the source of the "pink sheets" distributed during Richard Nixon's 1950 Senatorial campaign against Helen Gahagan Douglas.[7] The files, including the FBI and army material, are now in the possession of the House Internal Security Committee.

It may take the press and conduits like congressional committees to broadcast political intelligence, but the FBI and police can do little hatchet jobs themselves. A friend of mine learned that the police had given one landlady a ride to the station house and a look at an intelligence file to convince her not to rent my friend an apartment. The Los Angeles police, according to the ACLU, gave dossiers on liberal, OEO-funded groups to congressmen to bring about an adverse vote on continued funding for the groups.[8] Bob Wall, in the TV interview quoted earlier, explained that it was a regular practice to threaten reluctant sources with visits to their employer: "If the guy wouldn't cooperate with us when we interviewed him or agree to be an informant for us, we'd be likely to go out to talk to his employer about it and drop the fact that this guy was an activist and might be in contact with Communist party people and should be watched. Of course the object of this was to get the guy fired."[9]

Publicity is the whole point of news leaks, congressional hearings, and other offensive uses of police intelligence. The other nonforensic use is the subversive one, designed to change the outcome of political plans without the knowledge of the planners. It is made as invisible as possible. The government's arsenal of weapons for this end consists almost entirely of two kinds of tricks: to cause confusion or to provoke violence. Wall gave this example of confusion:[10]

National Mobe was having a big march in Washington, and we decided that we were going to try to disrupt the march and keep down the participation. So someone hit upon the idea of saying: "Well, the blacks in Washington aren't going to participate in the march because they get the short end of the stick— the police always come after them and tear gas them after every march."

So we composed a letter saying in effect that the blacks in Washington aren't going to participate in the march by the National Mobilization Committee unless the National Mobe pays $20,000 as a security bond to a black organization in the city. Then we forged the name of a black leader in Washington to the letter. I think it was Doug Moore's name we signed on it.

We sent this letter off and we learned through an informant who was in NMC headquarters out in Wisconsin that this caused quite a bit of difficulty in their planning.

They were not sure exactly what tack to take because if they came down and got real hard resistance from Carmichael and other black groups in Washington, they'd have real problems with their demonstration. [A later] meeting between Hayden and Carmichael was to straighten this out. I think they knew by that time that they had been taken.

Examples of such provocation are numerous. A former FBI Special Agent, David Sannes, has testified that he was urged to foment a bomb plot in Seattle and to arrange a misfire that would kill one of the bombers.[11] Charles Grimm, a police informant from Tuscaloosa, says he was tacitly encouraged to promote violence there.[12]

Fantasies to the contrary, nowhere in the histories of agents I have checked, and I have researched the activities of eighty or more, is there evidence of a more sophisticated police strategy. Nothing to create a split or tendency in order to shape the left differently (unless the split leads directly to a crime), and nothing to turn a group from confrontation to cooptation.

An explanation for this relatively crude approach lies in the ideology that imbues the surveillance apparatus. The apparatus is so committed to the proposition that conspiracies lie behind all social unrest that it can see nothing but conspiracies and can originate only such counterstrategies as might frustrate them.

Ralph Stein's description of his army superiors fits all the intelligence hierarchies:

There was a great preoccupation on the part of many general staff members with the background and activities of David Dellinger. There seemed to be a belief that he controlled so vast a segment of dissenters that he could initiate violence at his pleasure. I prepared a briefing on Mr. Dellinger, drawing heavily from classified files, which reflected his life's work, philosophy, travels, and future plans as well as activities and associations. It was evident to my coworkers as it was to me, that whatever opinions one might personally hold of Mr. Dellinger, and mine were negative, he was not behind any riot anywhere at any time nor did he ever hope to cause a riot. Yet requests to be briefed on Mr. Dellinger were numerous. I last briefed on this subject in the summer of 1968 to Lieutenant General George Mather, then chief of what was then called the Directorate of Civil Disturbance Plans and Operations. An Air Force major general also attended the briefing. The fascination and interest by these generals, as well as by many others in the Pentagon, is indicative of the counterproductive paradigm verbalized by the general staff that key men were behind the disturbances.[13]

The military is not unique or even pre-eminent in this respect. The most celebrated formulations of the great conspiracy explanation of dissent came from Hoover's writings and his congressional testimony. Congressional hearings on riots and "subversion" contain similar postulations by intelligence experts from the police apparatus.[14]

Stein's presence in Military Intelligence might suggest that only some people inside intelligence have such a stereotypical perspective. But Stein quit because he could not make any changes. The conspiracy paradigm is so well fastened into the ideology of the surveillance network that it is one of the strong determiners of who does and who does not make it to command-level positions. That political movements could be the result of social conditions or could produce leaders rather than be created by them is a theory that is not allowed to exist inside the apparatus.

In this context, only counterstrategies aimed at conspiracies, like provocation and confusion, seem directed at the cause. Except perhaps within the CIA, where marginal involvement in domestic affairs has already been suggested, countermoves like cooptation are as unthinkable as the political movements to which they might be applicable.

Many different forces acting on the intelligence apparatus assure that when conspiracies are hunted, the most sought-for will be those that plan violence, and that when people are provoked, the aim will be violent destruction of one kind or another. The simplest and most important reason is that the letter of the law requires it. Intelligence units are geared to the needs of law enforcement agencies. When action is taken, it must be to prosecute for a violation of law. The laws that are available today are laws that ban violence. In the late forties and fifties, the law forbade *advocacy* of violent overthrow of the government and interpreted the teaching of Marxist doctrine to be advocacy. Conspiracies to foment violence were not as important to the police. But today, the police must use the conspiracy law joined to other statutes: the law against interstate travel to promote riot, the law against destruction of federal property like Draft Boards, and the laws against kidnap. "Violence" also tends to be found where police training centers and police fantasies come together. Successful police action against violence can quickly enhance the reputation of district attorneys, police departments, and undercover operatives.

For all these reasons it is to openly violent plots that police intelligence and police-intelligence operatives are most often attracted. Ray Wood, the New York BOSS agent planted in CORE in 1964, drifted out of CORE and into a succession of splinter groups until he found one that had within it the makings of a violent conspiracy.[16] Even then he had to work hard to bring out the violent tendency. He did, then he surfaced. Gene Robert's BOSS career was similar and of even longer duration.[17] He drifted for five years before he found his Panther targets. An agent named Tommy the Traveller worked for police authorities in upstate New York for at least a year before he succeeded, after countless tries, in fomenting a bomb plot. There is no evidence that the police used Tommy's reports for any purpose before the bomb attempt. They did not try, so far as can be learned, to disrupt, discredit, or otherwise divert SDS organizing in the New York region during that time. The one use of his talents and his information, and the one circumstance that justified ending his undercover career, was the hope of gaining a conviction for a violent act.[18]

In sum, courtroom testimony, the justification for domestic surveillance, is only one of the uses of political intelligence. The apparatus maintains a readiness to round up dissidents. It spreads fear through leaks and hearings, with the conscious, although seldom acknowledged, goal of discouraging what it sees as dangerous activity. It attempts to direct dissent toward violent action. The uses of intelligence are restricted, however, by the apparatus's deep preoccupation with violence and by its inability to see social movement as anything other than conspiracy.

Dealing with Infiltration

On a number of occasions during the several years I spent studying police surveillance and infiltration, people who had heard of my interest approached me for advice. "Someone we work with is doing thus and so," they said. "Should we take that as a sign that the person works for the police?"

One woman, for example, had come to think that a former companion of hers was an agent. When she heard reports, based on congressional hearings in the spring of 1971, that the army had been following Jane Fonda, she took it as one more bit of suspicious evidence against her friend, for he had recently gone out of his way to talk to Ms. Fonda. She reasoned that her friend—let him be referred to as "Dee"—could be working for the army or the CIA and was part of a network of agents who shifted from target to target to avoid detection and coordinated their movements and reports at a national level.

She was in a frightening, unresolvable, and increasingly common dilemma. Her fears might be justified and they might not be; there seemed no way to tell for certain; yet the courses of several people's lives depended on certainty.

After collecting information on some eighty infiltrators who have surfaced or have been uncovered in recent years, I came to several conclusions about agents. One was that it was difficult to deduce an answer on the basis of only one or two actions. A few things, of course, are tantamount to proof: when one campus militant already under suspicion by his fellow radicals was seen entering the local police station shortly after the firebombing of a campus ROTC building, there should have been little doubt that he was a provocateur. But many things that could be taken as suspicious—from interest in Jane Fonda to lying about one's past—are far from proof. Few people's lives are open books; people have had many reasons, besides police control, for example, for hiding or disguising a part of their past.

People have frequently urged me to prepare a mugbook of known agents. I decided it would be a waste of time. Although narcotics agents frequently return to old haunts after they have been identified through their court testimony, cases of *political* undercover operatives who resubmerge after being publicly identified are undocumented. (I did, however, hear rumors of this kind of behavior.) Mug books are, at best, only a minor harassment to the police, who are in a position to hire new faces as often as old ones become well known.

I found also that with words I could make pictures of the common features of undercover operatives that were more helpful than photographs of the particular ones, but not, in the end, terribly helpful either.

A large number of the agents had been recruited into activist groups and were respected by the members because they had a special skill the group needed. Agents were frequently, but not always, the only people in the group who held their position mainly by virtue of such a skill. In the case of Boyd Douglas, the Harrisburg informer, it may well have been his claim to expertise with explosives that initially attracted Phil Berrigan to him. It was certainly Douglas's special position—on study release from prison, which gave him opportunity to smuggle letters in and out of Lewisburg—that assured him a place in the Catholic left's "inner circle." In the correspondence between Berrigan and McAlister, Douglas was at times referred to as "the courier" and also as "a resource." Steve Weiner, who infiltrated the Piggybank 6, a New York City group that planned the firebombing of a local bank, was the only member with a car and a driver's license, both necessary for the plot.[1] Robert Hardy alone among the Camden 28 had both the technical skills to enter the Camden Draft Board without tripping the alarms, and the money (from the FBI) to keep the group in food while it practiced its plans. David Sannes, who surfaced in Seattle in 1971 to accuse the FBI of using him to provoke violence, said he used his knowledge of explosives to form a group for a bombing plot.[2]

Several agents seem to have led lives that trained them in the skills of keeping secrets about themselves even before they came to work for the police. As Barbara Herbert argues in her sketch of Jack Weatherford (p. 227), he seems to have learned the art of dissembling in order to conceal homosexual leanings and then to have used the skill to conceal his police connections when they developed. The art of dissembling requires the ability to disguise the art. That capacity is not likely to be visible before the entire masquerade is itself revealed.

Almost all the informers and all of the regular police operatives with political assignments whom I studied were men. One of the few women I heard of was reporting

not to the police but to a political science professor, and
it is not clear whether the information wound up in government hands. Another reportedly worked for a narcotics squad.

The most common trait among the agents I checked out
was that they had all been endowed by the groups they
infiltrated with some special privilege by virtue of their
background. A person of working-class background in a
largely middle-class group is protected. The shield may
sometimes be made of condescension and pity ("What
can you expect from someone who . . ."), but most often
it is from ideological reverence. Philip Berrigan wrote
to Elizabeth McAlister about Boyd Douglas and other
working-class prisoners:

The local minister with portfolio has emerged as the best
thing hereabouts since polio vaccine. His ministrations have
been no less than providential—and given the setting here—
very nearly heroic. Later on, I consider he'll be a bee in the
saddle for many of our people, for already he's paid up the price
and kept the taxes in proper shape. As he might have told you,
there are guys here with comparable potential. One must break
through Little Brother's net of informers, spy glass, and omni-
presence to get them looking beyond themselves. To feed a
regular influx of ingenious and reliable ex-cons into the ranks
would make a resounding blow for public integrity. Some would
have a bit of bad education to shuck off, but they would help
with some of the bad education of our people. And they do know
the law and order people as we'll never know them.

Although these traits may show up frequently in case
studies of informers and infiltrators, they also show up
among the innocent. They are not sufficient, therefore, to
pinpoint an agent. I was not often a direct help when questions arose about people like Dee. I could not name acts
that would be proof positive or patterns of behavior that
would be conclusive. I could say these few things, and I
could say what I knew of the apparatus that plants and

controls agents. Such talk was helpful because sometimes suspicions had grown from nothing more than fantastical assumptions about the controlling apparatus.

This was the case, for example, with the woman, call her Dolores, who suspected Dee. I knew that if Dee or anyone else were a professional operative, he worked for the police; that if he were an undercover volunteer informant, he worked either for the police or for the FBI. The chances that he worked for the military or the CIA seemed, on the basis of what I knew and have written elsewhere, remote; suspicions based on those assumptions were probably unfounded. What led Dolores to suspect the CIA and FBI more than the police?

Ignorance was not the root of her mistake; it does not explain why she had a predisposition to suspect some agencies rather than others. Part of the explanation lies in stereotypes. The police have an image: flying nightsticks, screeching sirens, smirking redneck faces. Dee did not fit that image. Nor did he match the sniggling character given to police stoolies in gangster movies. He did not have an expressionless face or a trenchcoat; he was not humorless; in short, he did not fit the image of an FBI agent either.

Suspicion had to come to rest elsewhere. Army intelligence functions had only recently been uncovered. The CIA's image is built on its actual history of political intrigue and subterfuge and has been reinforced by spy novels and James Bond and "Mission Impossible." The National Student Association affair made it impossible to rule out domestic CIA involvement. The absence of an image let suspicions include the army; the nature of the CIA's image let suspicions center there.

There is another cause, one that is more painful to admit. If any of us are being fooled, we have to think—for the sake of our self-esteem—that the person responsible is very brilliant and very evil. Given our image of them

(never mind, for a minute, the reality), it is not quite so
shameful to be duped by the CIA as by the local red squad.
The game of revolutionary status-seeking leads in the
same direction. To think oneself the object of CIA scrutiny
is, in a backhand way, to rank oneself with Latin American
revolutionaries, with the NLF, and with other heroes of
white American revolutionaries. Class prejudice may
contribute something too, at least in the case of middle-
class groups. It is easier to admit vulnerability to the
white-collar CIA than to the blue-collar police.

In these ways undercover operatives are assumed to be
so evil and so skilled that real agents seem pale and harm-
less by comparison, unnoticeable and therefore more
effective.

William DiVale, who volunteered to infiltrate the
southern California Communist party for the FBI, illustrated this point in an interview in which he was asked
what he had thought when his cell discussed infiltrators
in his presence. He answered that they were talking about
people so evil and so crass it didn't seem as if they were
talking about him at all, and he was not greatly troubled
by it.[3]

The difficulties presented by the concurrence of ignorance, cultural stereotypes, class prejudice, and re-
quirements for self-esteem might be overcome in other
circumstances. But a conspiracy such as Dee, Dolores,
and their friends contemplated—breaking a friend out of
jail—sets up just the conditions to make surmounting those
obstacles very hard. Dolores was hardly in a position to
think about Dee's possible connections in a detached
manner. They lived together. They were bound together
by their relationship and by the nature of Dee's plan. The
man to be freed was the lover of Dolores's roommate.
The plan was at the same time a part of Dee's attraction
and a basis for suspicion. Between rescuer and provocateur there was no easy distinction.

Looking back, or perhaps looking in from outside at the time, one can conclude that Dee's acts were undoubtedly suspicious. He had little caution and an unseemly haste to contact people underground who might have had experience in that kind of planning. But all the suspicious acts were bound up with the plot. And he was friend and confidant and lover. He had at times a shy and gentle way that counterpointed his frequently *macho* manner.

It was impossible to go to someone outside the group to talk over doubts, for that would have violated group discipline and sensible security. Everyone inside, meanwhile, was subject to the strains of furtive behavior. That is the time when any cop's curious look seems like a knowing leer; when a caller on the other end of the line saying, "Sorry, I've got the wrong number," seems like the police finding out if the occupants are home. Everyone knew they were on edge, suffering from a state of nerves. The capacities that, in other times, would have discriminated reasonable from unreasonable fears did not function well, and all fears were endured and discounted as the result of an occupational hazard called paranoia.

When suspicions are voiced in such an atmosphere, they breed other suspicions. Others become suspect because of their response or nonresponse to the original misgivings. All political discussion becomes contaminated with the possibility that each proposal might be part of a conspiracy to trap the group or to throw suspicion upon the wrong person. Personal relationships become tinged with uncertainty. A friendship develops strains over unbroachable doubts; another relationship is entered on too quickly and with willful blindness to some of its faults. And in the quagmire of muddled thought and slipping relationships, self-doubts surface: "If he is an agent, what does it mean about me that I felt affection for him?"

This amalgam of ignorance, egoism, nervousness, and isolation, together with suspicion and tension, the by-products of their commingling, is the lens through which the substantial reality of surveillance appears larger than it is.

The tensions that produce this distortion have their roots deep in our culture. In the story of Larry Grathwohl's infiltration of a Weatherman cell in Cincinnati, the route from early tensions to final distortion is easily traced. The story of Larry Grathwohl was carried in the *Berkeley Tribe* of August 21, 1970. Its outline can be seen in the following excerpts.

Larry Grathwohl began hanging around the Cincinnati Weather collective before the National Action in October, 1969. He came on as a greaser, a poor Cincinnati working class street kid. He said he was an ex-GI. . . . People didn't quite trust him and tried to run security checks on him. . . . He never got flustered or contradicted himself. The best example of how Grathwohl handled himself in the collective is the story of an "acid test" of him they did in January. For the first six hours of the trip people laid into him hard about their suspicions, questioning, accusing, and pressing for information. He wouldn't say anything at all. Finally he looked up at them. "You're right," he said slowly, "I am a pig. I'm a pig because of what I did in Vietnam . . . because I stood by and watched Vietnamese women being raped by GI's and didn't try to stop it. . . .

[Later] Grathwohl was in another city, supposedly sick with malaria. . . . When his friends called the hospital to check on how he was, they were told he had never been there. At the same time he was seen outside the Federal Building in Cincinnati in a coat and tie. . . . Because of communications fuck-ups this information didn't get through to the people who could put it together until much, much later. . . .

Larry met up with Dianne in New York City shortly before the April bust [of Dianne Donghi, Linda Evans, and Grathwohl]. . . . His sexual uptightness had returned once again, he was incapable of fucking. He demanded to meet with other Weatherpeople who were underground, and refused to tell Dianne why. He said he had his own reasons and he didn't trust her enough to tell her what they were. She grew suspicious of him again;

she was sick, pregnant, and fucked up by the contradiction of caring for him and thinking he might be a pig. She tried to make sure he didn't know much about anyone but her.

The day of the bust, Larry went out to meet with Linda Evans. As they walked down the street they were surrounded by FBI agents. "Linda Evans," the pigs announced, "You're under arrest." They said nothing to Larry (or Tom Niehman, the alias he was going under). Larry took off down the street. He says that when they caught him, he pulled a knife and hit one of them. He and Linda were taken to jail, and the pigs went for Dianne. Twenty agents busted into her hotel room at once. "Where's your boyfriend?" they demanded.[4]

Even in this sketchy account the stresses active within the group are suggested. "Communications fuck-ups" could indicate—and it does here—debilitating strains in the internal organization of the group. The sexual strain is obvious; and there is a third stress around the question of class. Each of these pressures limited the group's ability to pool and act upon the misgivings that, at one time or another, each member had felt about Grathwohl.

The first stress developed around the question of leadership. Weathermen were engaged in militant street demonstrations—the Days of Rage in Chicago and the Pittsburgh school episode—and had developed democratic centralism as a mode of operation in and out of combat. Once leadership was chosen, its decisions had to be accepted. Many members, including people in the Cincinnati cell, were not comfortable with the arrangement. Part of the tension was manifested and channeled into the golden circle—an informal group that included the formal leadership and their acquaintances. Some tensions within the Cincinnati collective were not resolved. Looking back, members could see times when they had resisted raising uncertainties because they seemed to violate the accepted structure for decision making.

The collective felt the second strain when they elected

as "leadership" a woman, Dianne Donghi, at a point when, looking back on it, they "had not completely dealt with their male chauvinism." Since she was leadership, and since it was correct within the framework of their ideology and culture for a woman to be leadership (the same virtue-by-dint-of-oppression argument gave a vanguard position to the Vietnamese, blacks, and working-class youth), misgivings about her judgment had to be interpreted as personal failings. Such misgivings were, therefore, seldom converted to actions or objections.

The third strain involved class, or at least class-rooted cultural issues. Dianne, by her own account, had never felt comfortable in the highly intellectual atmosphere created by the discussions among most of the other group members. She had attended Columbia University but had never been central to the activities or the group there that later formed the core of Weatherman, and, coming from a less advantaged background, she had had only enough money for one semester of school. In Cincinnati she felt somewhat isolated, and the differences stemming from her style were exacerbated by the distances created by leadership. Larry was one of the few people she felt close to, and, after a time, a relationship developed.

There were the barriers created by an unfamiliar leadership structure, barriers created by a leadership choice in which the head's desire to end male chauvinism out-paced the heart's ability to change, others created by cultural differences, and now the difficulties caused by Dianne's intense emotional involvement with Larry.

Strains like those are not limited to small groups like the Cincinnati Weatherman collective. Problems of leadership, male chauvinism, and class-biased behavior run throughout the forces of dissent in this country. They are basic features of the culture against which the movement is rebelling, yet they plague the very groups that are trying to eliminate them. In this instance they did more than make a group vulnerable to infiltration. The group's blindness to its own faults made it attribute its vulnerability entirely to the agent's powers. He became, as the *Berkeley Tribe*'s headline put it, ". . . One of the Most Dangerous Police Agents Ever to Infiltrate the American Revolutionary Movement." The myth of Grathwohl's expertise spread on the movement grapevine and contributed to the exaggerated image of police efficiency and skill; in so doing, it set the stage for more fear, more mistakes, and more infiltration.

The carrying over of debilitating tensions from bourgeois culture into the surveillance syndrome is doubly illustrated in the case of Vee. She is their victim, but so are her accusers. The circular that follows was distributed in the Northeast in early 1971 by people who had worked with her and knew her well.

SECURITY RISK

```
[Name omitted]
Ht. 5'5" Wt. 135 Age 30 birthday 4/4/41
Brown eyes, dark brown hair (thin), slightly
heavy set, olive complexion, glasses
```

SUMMARY:
1. We know there are 500 female agents in our movement trained in 1969 (NY Times).
2. Vee has sought out the heaviest political people above ground since she first came to RAT (May 1970) to present (April 1971) deliberately collecting names and phone numbers—her address book looks like who's who on the attorney general's list altho warned this was suspicious.
3. Her politics are externally inconsistent with who she hangs out with—and internally inconsistent because her line changes as she moves from group to group. In addition when pushed about her politics, she can't go beyond certain

rhetorical phrases and general raps about collectivity, love, and life style. Never gives
an indication of where her commitment and
views are coming from—any real understanding
of what she claims to believe is missing.
4. She has travelled extensively seeking out
heavies. Altho maintaining that collectivity is
most important to her, she operated always
alone—independent of the decisions of her collective—moving from group to group and city to
city. Always split when intense revealing relationships or participation were demanded.
5. There is no one who can vouch for her anywhere in the movement before January 1970, and
everyone she has given as a personal and/or
political reference has doubts about her.

MOVEMENT BEHAVIOR
From the time she first entered the women's
movement (Jan. 1970) to April '71 she has
moved in and out of a large number of movement
groups in rapid succession. She uses the names
of specific people and groups to give herself
legitimacy—claims she is close to the people or
very involved in the groups when in fact she is
on the fringes. She has consciously sought out
well-known ex-Weatherpeople, Yippies, White
Panthers, and Conspiracy people and made a point
of collecting names and addresses of people she
didn't even know.
Her career in the movement began in Jan. 1970
in Radical Feminists, went to Gay Liberation
Front, to RAT, to Radicalesbians, to organizing
a revolutionary women's convention, to a woman's
collective in NY, to Washington D.C. for the
RPCC where she stayed on and moved from one
woman's collective to another. When in DC she
eagerly involved herself in situations involving
big demonstrations including planning for March

8th, April 10th (Woman's march on the pentagon),
the Laos demonstration and May week, all independent of the collective she claimed to belong
to at the time.

In the last 6 months she has contacted Weatherpeople as soon as they surfaced and traded off
her contacts with well-known people to get tight
with them. During this time (Jan.-April '71) she
travelled to NY, Boston, Ann Arbor, Madison,
Milwaukee, Kent State, Cleveland, Detroit, Chicago, Baltimore.

Women on the RAT as early as June 1970 were
suspicious of her because of inconsistencies in
her story and her irresponsible pushing for
violent actions. An inconclusive security check
was done at that time.

THINGS THAT ADDED TO OUR SUSPICIONS:
1. she comes across with a line about lesbianism,
   love, sisterhood, unity, sensuality, sexuality
   —and initially appears to be very open and
   warm—but then does not develop any intense
   relationships with women in which love and
   sexuality get beyond this superficial level
2. she has no grasp of the women's movement or
   of women-identification (though she says she
   is a lesbian). In consciousness raising she
   consistently backed out when any discussion of
   politics including woman's politics came up.
3. always made a point of being very physically
   affectionate to people she did not necessarily
   know well in front of large groups of people,
   creating the impression that she was tight
   with those people.
4. picking up the current line of the group she's
   into, and in conversation always reflecting
   back ideas someone else has said, almost verbatim.
5. passes herself off as close to people who she

thought would give her an in with the group or
person she was currently trying to get into
e.g. telling RAT she was from LNS and LNS that
she was from RAT; telling people in the midwest that she was sent by weatherpeople
6. she is persistently divisive—never was up
front, but consistently trashed, gossiped,
questioned other people's motives and trustworthiness always behind their backs. In this
way she frequently played one group off against
another or one individual against another.
7. inability to commit herself to any politics or
people—was only interested in certain people
and heavy actions. Floated around looking into
groups, always moving into increasingly heavier
movement circles. Although she met many people
on her travels, she only related to and took
the names and addresses of heavy people.
8. in regard to work going on around MayDay, her
behavior seems to be typical of ways that she
has acted throughout the past year. . . . During the couple of months before May, she was
living in D.C. (although she was gone alot of
the time, to talk to people in other cities.)
For most of this period of time, she was relating to a D.C. women's collective as "her collective," saying she wanted to live and work
with them. At times she would agree with the
D.C. collective women about the sexism of
MayDay politics and of the men working on it.
But other times, almost arbitrarily, she would
be into May: she worked at the MayDay office;
she considered travelling around the country
with MayDay men to talk to women about May; she
eagerly accepted a ride to the Ann Arbor conference with male MayDay heavies, instead of
waiting to go with women from the collective;
she considered moving into the MayDay collective house; she told women less concerned
about MayDay's sexism that she did not agree

with the D.C. women, and encouraged them to
organize May women's actions; in Boston, about
two weeks before May, while she was centrally
involved in planning a militant women's march
for May, she told lesbians at a gay meeting
that they should sabotage May—that they should
not let it happen because it was male dominated and had terrible politics.

IDENTIFYING TRAITS
   working class background, lesbian, films,
travel in Africa, smokes dope and trips with
ease, smokes cigarettes heavily, talks about
youth culture and freaks, extraordinarily good
at ripping off, warm and affectionate, photog-
rapher, lived in London, talks about her sister
who is having trouble with her child and family,
knows New York and Chicago well, talks a lot
about life style and collectivity, is very
likable, picks up reflects back what others say

CONCLUSION:
   This investigation was initiated by gay women
in Boston, New York and DC. Many of her close
friends and lovers from her movement "career"
have participated in this security check. In
addition to the information here, we are still
completing an investigation of [her] past history. A longer article dealing with this will be
prepared for underground papers. While we are
trying to deal with the situation seriously
before harm is done we also know that paranoia
and witch-hunting can be just as destructive to
our own community. Out of doing this whole thing
we can understand in very human terms what could
have led [her] to become an agent. The process
of our deciding about her was painful, because
we know her humanness so well. But, understanding the contradictory nature of every human
being, we also know that her humanness cannot,

by itself, prove her trustworthiness. We know
that she is a real person—but this does not
lessen how dangerous she is to the lives of many
in our movement.

Without a bust or a confession we cannot prove
conclusively that she is a paid police agent. We
realize that any one aspect of this description
by itself might not be suspicious, but taken al-
together with all the inconsistencies it is hard
to account for her behavior in any other way.
Regardless, she is an incredible security risk
and must be treated as dangerous. She cannot be
trusted.

Collecting an address book filled with the names of
"heavies"? At a loss for words when pushed to the limits
of the current rhetoric? Afraid of deep personal relationships? Attracted by both the women's movement and the
male-dominated segments of the movement? I know in
myself all of these tendencies. My own address book once
read that way. As for my arguments, now I listen to memories of earlier discussions and feel ashamed at the trans-
parency of some of my contentions; I know few people
who don't feel the same. And only a handful of all the
people I know are unafraid of deep friendships.

I can see a sad but not sinister person, a social climber,
a person to whom "heavy" connections are an antidote to
self-doubts. For in fact within the social fabric of the
movement, name-dropping is effective, and heavy connections are a main line of entry into esteemed circles.
These parts of Vee's actions might be the result of in-
security, abetted by a counter culture that has not challenged the status-dependence of bourgeois culture as well
as it has countered some of its political beliefs.

Not every charge in the leaflet, it is true, can be explained psychologically, but those that cannot are foolishly
flimsy. One charge, for example, is that no one in the

movement can vouch for her before January, 1970. It's
hardly surprising or incriminating since, as the leafllet
elsewhere explains, she first found movement circles that
spring. The only other is: "We know there are 500 female
agents in our movement trained in 1969 (NY Times)." I
have heard that rumor from several other sources. Never
has it been more fully elaborated and never has the date
of the *Times* article been passed along with it. I cannot
find the article, or any other source. Even were it true, it
is hardly an argument against any particular woman. It is
as much an argument, in fact, against the authors of the
leaflet as it is against their subject.

Vee may have had revolutionary politics, but she behaved like many people in the unrevolutionary society.
No one of the things mentioned should have been initial
grounds for suspicion of police connections. If there was
a real basis for suspicion, it is not enumerated in the circular.

Vee's accusers show in this leaflet that they are as bound
up in old culture ways as is Vee. Faced with the choice of
two explanations, one assuming human failings and no
malicious, conspiratorial purpose, and the other presup-
posing a conspiracy, they chose conspiracy. In this respect,
although certainly not in others, they behaved like the
police. They chose a conspiracy theory over a sociological
one. It is a habit of our culture that we have not over-
thrown.

If the circular's description of Vee is accurate, I would
not want to trust her with any dangerous secrets. They
might prove to be good currency for her passage into other
circles, and she might be tempted to pass them on. To say
that someone should not be given certain trusts is not at
all the same thing as to say that she has conspired with
the police.

There are no perfect safeguards against infiltration.
Knowledge of the apparatus helps, particularly knowledge

of its preoccupations and its style of work. And anything
that works to facilitate honest transactions within groups
reduces the tension, ignorance, and blindness that can
be an agent's best cover.

Dealing with Surveillance

There is no ultimate countermeasure either for the overall
apparatus or for the particular weapon of infiltrators. It
would be surprising, in fact, if the well-funded efforts of
so large a machine could be completely nullified by one
or even any combination of measures. But there are some
defenses.

Exposure is an antidote. The Ervin hearings did help
to curb army operations. The Media raid embarrassed the
Bureau and gave heart to its victims by stripping the FBI
of its reputation for invulnerability.

Better laws are another countermeasure. Judicial warrants could be required for the use of infiltrators. Such a
law might pass Congress, but doubt that warrants would
be any more effective in restraining infiltration than they
have been in restraining wiretapping. And laws that might
have some clout—such as laws permitting public access
to police files or barring police unequivocally from political surveillance, with effective provisions for external
audit—seem to me to have little hope of passing. Nothing
is lost, however, by attempting to get such measures enacted. Such attempts create pressure for change even if
they fail, and some pressure is better than none.

One lesson that can be learned is that legislative attempts to curtail surveillance have chosen the wrong targets. Those most visible targets, the FBI and the military,
have been attacked and the police, whose work is nearer

the heart of the intelligence operation, have gotten away scot-free.

Destroying the myths about surveillance is a counter-measure of particular importance because it is more possible than the other steps. Such a setting-straight of the record is not always to the point—it could be simply an exercise in scholarship, satisfying a penchant for historical accuracy. But these particular myths are still doing their damage, and their dissipation can be effective. For, large and skilled as the apparatus is, its image in the popular mind is larger still. Guesses about its size are very high off the mark. The expertise of its agents is overrated. Its technology is clumsy compared to the fantasies about it. The FBI's infiltration system is much more an amateur affair than it is thought to be. And the intelligence of the intelligence apparatus is overrated. The data is generally of poor quality; in large part, it is publicly available. Ability to reason from the data—intelligence in another sense —is also more limited than generally presumed. It cannot transcend the preoccupation with the search for a violent, conspiratorial center to social unrest.

By seeming larger than it is, the apparatus becomes an effective damper on political activity. The larger it is thought to be, the greater is the presumption that it has its ears at any particular meeting or on any one phone line. The more intelligent it seems, the more numerous are the things that might be manifestations of its deceits and plots. Almost any political proposal can be interpreted as a police plot by people who want to discredit it and by people who are fearful.

I have already described the result of these exaggerations inside small groups. In the wider movement, they have at least two other effects. One is to destroy the ability to reason soundly about the few bits of definite evidence that do become available about the apparatus. When, for example, the Citizens' Commission to Investigate the FBI

began circulating the papers it had obtained from the
Media, Pennsylvania, FBI office, one of the few passages
to receive wide circulation was the order to "enhance the
paranoia endemic in these circles and . . . get the point
across that there is an FBI agent behind every mailbox."

That passage was widely taken as evidence that the FBI
had a conscious strategy of using its agents and resources
to terrify the New Left. Taken in context, the passage does
reveal some things about the Bureau, but not that. In 800
pages of documents that often deal with FBI tactics, the
mailbox passage is the only reference to creating paranoia,
or any remotely related scheme. One memo, in documents
that seem by every available measure to be representative, is hardly evidence of a strategy. Moreover, and despite common presumption, the memo's author, Special
Agent James O'Connor, was explicitly referring to interviews between coverless Special Agents and members of
the New Left. If it does signify a strategy, then the strategy
is strangely limited. These agents are the least feared
members of the Bureau's staff. Allowing undercover
agents to surface, allowing phone taps to be discovered
would heighten paranoia much more precipitously.

The other result of the myths is to discredit the major
means of attacking the myths. One myth-influenced conclusion, for example, is that it is dangerous to describe our
vulnerability to the FBI or police in print. The police, so
this line of reasoning goes, will then use what is said to
improve their deceits. But police actions are determined
by the pressures upon them, their organizational histories,
the ideologies they spring from (and, at the same time, are
trapped in), their centralized structures, and the habits of
mind and ideologies of the people who are attracted to
service. Their world view is not shaped by the intelligence
they collect, but rather the reverse: their intelligence,
structures, and practice are shaped by their world view.
Their response to essays like this one is more apt to run to

tracing its sources. They are no more equipped to use our criticisms than to use constructively any other piece of intelligence. A farfetched comparison seems worth the clarification it might bring: the theory of people's war is no trade secret of the Third World, and for the same reason. Open promulgation tells colonial powers nothing they can use, and it is the only way for separated groups to share and profit from each other's experience.

Notes

Several of the notes that follow contain prime sources that were cited in government hearings; in such cases, parenthetical references to the specific hearings have been added.

The Overall Dimensions

1 Frank Donner, "Theory and Practice of American Political Intelligence," *New York Review of Books,* 22 Apr. 1971, p. 27.

2 "Of Note," *American Libraries,* July 1970, pp. 633, 658. A good summary article by Judith F. Krug and James A. Harvey appears in *American Libraries, Oct. 1970, pp. 843–45.*

3 U.S., Congress, Senate, Committee on the Judiciary, *Extent of Subversion in the New Left, Hearings,* before the Subcommittee to Investigate the Administration of the Internal Security Act, U.S. Senate, 91st Cong., 2nd sess., 11 June and 9 July 1970, part 5, pp. 811–81. (Hereinafter referred to as Eastland Hearings.)

4 Robert Wall, former FBI Special Agent, in interview with author, 12 May 1972; corroborated by the Internal Revenue Service, as reported by Robert M. Smith in *The New York Times,* 13 Jan. 1972.

5 Testimony by Christopher Pyle, former instructor for the U.S. Army Intelligence School, in U.S., Congress, Senate, Committee on the Judiciary, *Federal Data Banks, Computers, and the Bill of Rights, Hearings,* before the Subcommittee on Constitutional Rights, U.S. Senate, 92nd Cong., 1st sess., 23, 24, and 25 Feb. and 2, 3, 4, 9, 10, 11, 15, and 17 Mar. 1971, part 1, pp. 147–245. (Hereinafter referred to as Ervin Hearings.)

6 John S. Lang, *Boston Herald-Traveller,* 19 Apr. 1970 (Ervin Hearings, part 2, pp. 1792–96).

7 Robert Wall, WNDT-TV telecast, 11 Apr. 1972, 10:30 P.M.

8 Lang, *Boston Herald-Traveller.*

9 Seymour M. Hersh, *The New York Times,* 24 May 1973.

10 Robert Sherrill, *The New York Times,* 14 Mar. 1971.

The Military Collectors

1 For a detailed history of the army operation, see the testimony of Christopher Pyle in the Ervin Hearings. The entire hearings, which include the personnel accounts of some half a dozen former agents, provide the fullest available inside account of an intelligence agency.

2 Official figures cited by Richard Halloran, *The New York Times,* 19 Dec. 1970; other estimates from testimony of former FBI agent Quentin L. Burgess, Ervin Hearings, part 1, p. 288, and from former FBI agent Ralph Stein in interview with author, 15 Mar. 1971.

3 Stein testimony, Ervin Hearings, part 1, p. 267.

4 *The New York Times,* 4 Oct. 1969, p. 10; interview by author with staff of coffeehouse, 15 Aug. 1970.

5 Diane Schulder, an attorney for the Fort Jackson 8, in interview with author, 14 Jan. 1971.

6 Pyle testimony, Ervin Hearings, part 1, p. 198.

7 Ron Weber, former member of the Army Security Agency, in interview by NBC-TV, aired on "First Tuesday," 1 Dec. 1970.

8 *New York Post,* 22 Dec. 1970.

9 Mike Kinney, *Boston Globe,* 1 Feb. 1971.

10 Stein interview.

11 Joseph Hanlon, *Computer World,* 11 Feb. 1970 (Ervin Hearings, part 2, p. 1635).

12 Pyle testimony, Ervin Hearings, part 1, pp. 185–86.

13 *Ibid.,* part 1, p. 201.

14 See pp. 11–13.

15 Stein interview.

16 *Ibid.*

17 Stein testimony, Ervin Hearings, part 1, pp. 263–64.

18 Weber, on "First Tuesday."

19 Stein interview.

20 See, for example, Tad Szulc, *The New York Times,* 29 Jan. 1971, where an issue of the Air Force's publication *Significant Counter Intelligence Briefs* (SCIB) is described and its cover reproduced.

21 *United States* v. *David T. Dellinger et al.,* Docket 69CR180, U.S. District, Northern District of Illinois (Chicago: Commerce Clearing House, 1970), microfilm. For more information of Pierson's activities as an employee of the Cook County State Attorney's Office, see U.S., Congress, Senate, Committee on Government Operations, *Riots, Civil and Criminal Disorders, Hearings,* before the Permanent Subcommittee on Investigations, U.S. Senate, 90th Cong., 1st sess., part 10, p. 2004 (hereinafter referred to as McClellan Hearings); U.S., Congress, House, Committee on Un-American Activities, *Subversive Influence in Riots, Looting, and Burning, Hearings,* U.S. House of Representatives, 90th Cong., 2nd sess., 1, 3, and 4 Oct. 1968, part 1, pp. 2391–2438 (hereinafter referred to as Ichord Hearings); Jason Epstein, *The Chicago Conspiracy Trial* (New York: Random House, 1970), pp. 200–03; Jerry Rubin, *Do It!* (New York: Simon and Schuster, 1970), pp. 181–85.

22 Senator Ervin, opening statement, Ervin Hearings, part 1, p. 300.

23 Testimony of Laurence Lane, former agent for Military Intelligence, Ervin Hearings, part 1, p. 326.

24 Laurence Lane, in interview with author, 25 Feb. 1971.

25 Testimony of John O'Brien, Ervin Hearings, part 1, p. 116.

26 *Ibid.,* p. 115.

27 Vin McLellan, *Village Voice,* 11 Nov. 1971.

28 Jared Stout, *Staten Island Sunday Advance,* 19 July 1970 (Ervin Hearings, part 2, pp. 1660, 1804).

29 Richard Halloran, *The New York Times,* 2 Apr. 1971 (Ervin Hearings,

part 2, pp. 1782–83, where it is mistakenly dated April 13).

30 Morton Kondracke, *Chicago Sun*

Times, 9 May 1970 (Ervin Hearings,
part 1, p. 619).

31 Halloran, *The New York Times*.

Civilian Collectors

1 "The Intelligence Unit," *Law and
Order* 14, no. 6 (June 1966): 68; see
also Anthony Bouza, "The Operation of a Police Intelligence Unit"
(M.A. thesis, Baruch School of the
City College of New York, 1968),
p. 28.

2 Estimated from the *Law and
Order* formula given above and from
figures for total law enforcement
agency officers given in U.S. Bureau
of the Census, *Statistical Abstract
of the United States, 1971* (92nd
ed.), Washington, D.C., 1971, p. 148.

3 *The New York Times*, 1 Dec. 1970.

4 Testimony of Captain John Sorace,
in McClellan Hearings.

5 Unsigned, open letter from the
Commission to Investigate the FBI,
3 May 1971.

6 *Ibid.*

7 "Applications for Jobs in the CIA
Have Declined," *The New York
Times*, 4 July 1973.

8 See p. 22.

9 Adolph (Abe) Hart, of the New
York police department, infiltrated
the Progressive Labor Party in Harlem in 1963. See Ichord Hearings,
part 2, pp. 929–64; Bouza, "The
Operation of a Police Intelligence
Unit."

10 Raymond Wood, of the New
York police department, infiltrated
CORE, East Harlem Revolutionary
Action Unit (RAM), and the Black
Liberation Front in 1964–65. See
Susan Brownmiller, "View from the
Inside: I Remember Ray Wood,"
Village Voice, 3 June 1965, p. 3;
Claudia Dreifus, "Boss Is Watch-
ing," *The Nation*, 25 January 1971,
pp. 106–07; Bouza, "The Operation
of a Police Intelligence Unit";
Ichord Hearings, pp. 929–64, 1031–
48.

11 Edward Lee Howlette, of the New
York police department, infiltrated
the Black Brotherhood Improve-
ment Association in 1967. See Dreifus, "Boss is Watching"; Paul Chevigny, *Cops and Rebels* (New York:
Pantheon, 1972), p. 254.

12 Irving Bock, of the Chicago police
department, infiltrated the Veterans
and Reservists for Peace and the
National Mobilization Committee
in 1968. See the transcript of the
trial of *United States* v. *David T.
Dellinger et al.* Richard Lyons, of
the New York police department,
also infiltrated the Veterans and
Reservists for Peace, in 1967. See
Dreifus, "Boss is Watching."

13 William Frapolly, a Chicago po-
lice department trainee, infiltrated
SDS at Northeastern Illinois State
College in 1968. See the transcript
of the trial of *United States* v. *David
T. Dellinger et al.*; Jason Epstein,
The Chicago Conspiracy Trial (New
York: Random House, 1970), pp.
239–43.

14 Louis Salzberg, an FBI agent, infiltrated the National Mobilization
Committee in New York City and
testified at the trial of the Chicago
8. See Maury Englander, "Double
Exposure," *Win*, 1 Dec. 1969, p. 26.

15 Carlos Ashwood, of the New York
police department, infiltrated the
Black Panther Party (BPP) in 1968–
69. See Edith Evans Asbury, *The
New York Times*, 6 Mar. 1971. Other
infiltrators into the BPP: Wilbert
Thomas (see Paul G. Chevigny,
"New York's Red Squad: The Ver-
dict is Entrapment," *Village Voice*,
11 Feb. 1971), and Ralph White (see
Edith Evans Asbury, *The New York
Times*, 17 and 19 Feb. 1971).

16 George Demmerle, an agent of

the FBI in New York City from 1965–69, infiltrated the Veterans and Reservists for Peace, the Crazies, and the "RAT bombers." See *The New York Times*, 14 Nov. 1969; *RAT*, Spring 1970, pp. 7–8. According to these two sources, Steve Weiner, of the New York police department, also infiltrated the "RAT bombers," in 1970.

17 Boyd Douglas, volunteer informer for the FBI in Lewisburg, Pennsylvania, infiltrated the Berrigan-McAlister "Kissinger kidnap plot." See Paul Cowan's essay in this book, pp. 236–247; John Kifner, *The New York Times*, 21 Feb. 1971; Jack Nelson and Ronald J. Ostrow, *The FBI and the Berrigans* (New York: Coward, McCann & Geoghegan, 1972), pp. 237–81; William O'Rourke, *The Harrisburg 7 and the New Catholic Left* (New York: Thomas Y. Crowell, 1972), pp. 141–215.

18 Robert Hardy's affidavit is reproduced in this book on pp. 222–227.

19 William Tulio DiVale, an FBI agent, infiltrated the Communist party at the University of California at Los Angeles from 1965 to 1969. See William Tulio DiVale with James Joseph, *I Lived Inside the Campus Revolution* (New York: Cowles Books, 1970), pp. 143–86.

20 Charles R. Grimm, Jr., an FBI agent, covered the Tuscaloosa campus of the University of Alabama in 1970. See *Tuscaloosa News*, 13 Sept. 1970; also mentioned in WNDT-TV telecast.

21 Gene Roberts, of the New York police department, infiltrated the organization of Malcolm X from 1964 to 1969, and the Black Panther Party and other black organizations from 1965 to 1968. See Edith Evans Asbury, *The New York Times*, 17 Nov., 8 and 9 Dec. 1970.

22 Brownmiller, *Village Voice.*

23 Asbury, *The New York Times*, 8 and 9 Dec. 1970.

24 *The New York Times*, 1 Dec. 1970.

25 Vin McLellan, "Boston Red Squad," *Boston Phoenix*, 8 June 1971.

26 FBI document from the Media, Pennsylvania, files, dated 26 February 1968, p. 3.

27 Bouza, "The Operation of a Police Intelligence Unit," p. 23.

28 David Burnham, *The New York Times*, 9 Feb. 1973.

29 Media FBI documents dated 16 Dec. 1970 and 26 Feb. 1971.

30 *Ibid.*

31 O'Connor's name appears in the Media files only on security items: he covers a black action at Swarthmore College (document dated 27 Jan. 1969), he handles the investigation of the daughter of Congressman Reuss (document dated 19 Nov. 1970), he receives informer reports on the Philadelphia Labor Committee (document dated 26 Feb. 1971), and he is the author of the FBI's *New Left Notes* and goes to New Left conferences.

32 *The New York Times*, 29 Mar. 1971.

33 Jack Levine, "Hoover and the Red Scare," *The Nation*, 20 Oct. 1962, pp. 232–35.

34 Media FBI document dated 19 Jan. 1971.

35 William Greider, *Washington Post*, 13 June 1971 (Ervin Hearings, part 2, p. 1778).

36 *Ibid.*

37 McClellan Hearings, p. 661.

38 *Ibid.*, pp. 661, 662, 700.

39 *Ibid.*, p. 700; also mentioned in a speech by Thomas J. Lyons of the Chicago police department Intelligence Unit, before a meeting of 600 police intelligence experts at Palm Springs, California, as reported in *Justice: The Crisis of Law, Order, and Freedom in America* by Richard Harris (New York: E.P. Dutton, 1970), pp. 135–36.

40 Anthony Ripley, *The New York Times*, 5 Sept. 1970. The cities listed in the intelligence coordination plan were Omaha, Des Moines, Minne-

apolis, Tulsa, Sioux City, Lincoln, Madison, Denver, and Kansas City.

41 See Norda Z. Trout, *New York Post*, 8 Nov. 1971, for an account of the Los Angeles system. The establishment of these systems was one of the major recommendations of the President's Commission on Law Enforcement and Administration of Justice Task Forces.

42 U.S., Congress, House, Committee on Appropriations, *Departments of Treasury, Post Office, and Executive Office, Appropriations for 1971, Hearings,* before a subcommittee of the Committee on Appropriations, U.S. House of Representatives, 91st Cong., 2nd sess., part 2, pp. 840, 949.

43 *Ibid.*

44 *Ibid.*

45 Ben A. Franklin, *The New York Times,* 28 June 1970 (Ervin Hearings, part 2, pp. 1667–70). This article, based on an interview with Thomas J. Kelley, assistant director of the Secret Service, gives most available material on Secret Service files, including the criteria now used for accepting entries into the file.

46 U.S., Congress, House, Committee on Appropriations, *Departments of State, Justice, and Commerce, the Judiciary, and Related Agencies, Appropriations for 1970, Hearings,* before a subcommittee of the Committee on Appropriations, U.S. House of Representatives, 91st Cong., 1st sess., part 1, p. 935. (Hereinafter referred to as Appropriations Hearings 1970.)

47 Eastland Hearings, part 5, pp. 761–881.

48 David Wise and Thomas B. Ross, in *The Espionage Establishment* (New York: Random House, 1967), devote twenty-five pages to a study of domestic CIA operations without finding more than is recounted here. See pp. 142–68.

49 Wise and Ross, *The Espionage Establishment,* pp. 167–68.

50 *Ibid.,* p. 142.

51 *The New York Times,* 2 June 1968 and 15 Dec. 1969.

52 Harry Howe Ransom, *The Intelligence Establishment* (Cambridge: Harvard University Press, 1970), p. 224.

53 *The New York Times,* 27 Feb. 1967.

54 *Ibid.;* Wise and Ross, *The Espionage Establishment,* pp. 147–52.

55 David Burnham, *The New York Times,* 6, 8, 9, and 11 Feb. and 6 Mar. 1973.

56 Ervin Hearings, part 1, p. 269.

57 Robert M. Smith, *The New York Times,* 10 Oct. 1971.

Electronic Surveillance

1 Juan M. Vasquez, *The New York Times,* 19 Dec. 1971.

2 *Ibid.*

3 For more discussion of these and other ruses, see Fred P. Graham, *The New York Times,* 5 May 1971.

4 *The New York Times,* 30 June 1972.

5 *Ibid.*

6 Warren Weaver, *The New York Times,* 6 May 1973: Figures quoted therein were compiled by the Administrative Office of the U.S. Courts.

7 *Ibid.*

8 Robert Wall interview.

9 WNDT-TV telecast.

10 William W. Turner, *Hoover's FBI: The Men and the Myth* (Los Angeles: Sherbourne Press [1970]), pp. 315–16.

11 Jack Anderson, *New York Post,* 4 Dec. 1970.

12 Turner, *Hoover's FBI,* pp. 315–16.

13 Anderson, *New York Post.*

14 Bruce Garvey, *Toronto Daily Star,* 5 Sept. 1970 (Ervin Hearings, part 2, pp. 1717–19).

15 Stein interview.

16 "U.S. Electronic Espionage: A Memoir," *Ramparts,* Aug. 1972, pp.

37-50. At a later date *Ramparts* identified the person interviewed for this article as "one Winslow Peck."

17 There is testimony of frequent contact between local Military Intelligence personnel and civilian intelligence agencies from many parts of the country. Former agent John O'Brien has already been quoted to this effect about the Chicago area (Ervin Hearings, part 1, p. 116). An unidentified agent told the counsel for the Ervin Hearings and Gordon Yale of the *Twin City Sentinel* (Winston-Salem, N.C.) that his unit met monthly with the FBI, the State Bureau of Intelligence, and representatives from many of the region's police forces (Ervin Hearings, part 2, pp. 1487-88). According to the *Kansas City (Mo.) Times* (21 Jan. 1971), similar meetings occurred in Kansas City. And from Texas, the *San Antonio Express News* (1 Mar. 1970) quotes the city's

police chief about similar contact there (Ervin Hearings, part 2, p. 1644).

18 Weaver, *The New York Times.*
19 Burnham, *The New York Times,* 8 Mar. 1971.
20 *Ibid.*
21 Harris, *Justice,* p. 39.
22 Ronald Kessler, *Washington Post,* 25 June 1972.
23 Edith Evans Asbury, *The New York Times,* 2 Dec. 1970.
24 James M. Markham, *The New York Times,* 21 Oct. 1971.
25 Benjamin Welles, "Helms of the CIA," *The New York Times Magazine,* 18 Apr. 1971, p. 44. See also Kessler, *Washington Post.*
26 Welles, "Helms of the CIA."
27 Kessler, *Washington Post.*
28 James F. Clarity, *The New York Times,* 7 Nov. 1971; confirmed by Bob Fass, the subject of that article, in interview with author, 19 Feb. 1973.

The Uses of
Political Intelligence

1 Appropriations Hearings 1970, part 1, pp. 527-29.
2 "Guerrilla Acts of Sabotage and Terrorism in the United States, 1965-1970," *Scanlon's* I, no. 8 (Jan. 1971): 29-32.
3 WNDT-TV telecast.
4 Frank Donner, "ACLU Fights the Spies," *Civil Liberties,* Feb. 1971.
5 McClellan Hearings, pp. 243-96.
6 Richard Halloran, *The New York Times,* 7 Sept. 1971.
7 *Ibid.*
8 Donner, "ACLU Fights the Spies."
9 WNDT-TV telecast.
10 *Ibid.*
11 Testimony at Conference on the FBI, 29-30 Oct. 1971. The conference was held at Princeton University and called jointly by the Com-

mittee for Public Justice and the Woodrow Wilson School at Princeton. The testimony of Sannes was omitted from the book that came out of the conference, *Investigating the FBI,* edited by Pat Watters and Stephen Gillers (New York: Doubleday, 1973).
12 *Tuscaloosa News.*
13 *Ervin Hearings,* part 1, p. 209.
14 See, for example, testimony of David C. Myer, former head of the Michigan State Police Intelligence Section, in McClellan Hearings, pp. 3600, 3644, 3638, and testimony of William Olson, a Chicago police lieutenant, pp. 4455-60.
15 *The New York Times,* 3 Oct. 1971.
16 Brownmiller, *Village Voice.*
17 Asbury, *The New York Times,* 8 and 9 Dec. 1970.
18 Ron Rosenbaum, "Run, Tommy, Run!", *Esquire,* July 1971, pp. 51 *et*

seq. For more information of Thomas Tongyai's activities as an employee of the Ontario County, New York, Sheriff's Office, see Charlie McCollum, "Tommy and the Trashers," *Boston Phoenix,* 4 July 1970; Frank Donner, "The Agent Provocateur as a Folk Hero," *Civil Liberties,* Sept. 1971.

Dealing with Infiltration

1   *RAT*, no. 17, 6 Jan. 1971, p. 18.
2   Testimony of David Sannes, Conference on the FBI.
3   See DiVale's book, *I Lived Inside the Campus Revolution,* for background.
4   "Unsettled Accounts," *Berkeley Tribe,* 21–28 Aug. 1970, pp. 8–9. When this article appeared, Grathwohl vehemently denied that he worked for the authorities. Acknowledgment did not come until May 20, 1973, when Seymour Hersh of *The New York Times* reported that government sources told him Grathwohl worked for the FBI and gave information to Guy Goodwin, the Justice Department's Weatherman prosecutor.

Inquisition in the Courtroom

PAUL COWAN

For the past two years, five working men of Irish extraction from the New York area have been in and out of Fort Worth, Texas, jails because they refused to answer a grand jury's questions about an alleged IRA gun-running plot. None of the men (a nurse, a janitor, a bus driver, a construction worker, a real estate agent) has been charged with any substantive crime. Their only crime is silence: the refusal to answer questions put to them in secret and before an institution that they consider unjust.

Two of the men have lost their jobs. One has a son who nearly died of malnutrition, the result of his extreme fears about his father's safety. During one long stint in jail, the wives of several were threatened by neighbors and forced to move in with relatives for psychological and material survival.

The agony of the Fort Worth 5 is by no means a novelty in recent American legal history. Their experience in front of grand juries has been shared by hundreds of witnesses, who have been subpoenaed because they might supply fragments of information, not because they have been suspected of any crimes. Indeed, over the past decade the grand jury, which was written into the Bill of Rights as a shield for defendants, has been transformed into an indispensible tool for prosecutors. It is a legally sanctioned way of making the courtroom into an arena for inquisitions.

Grand juries first emerged in eleventh-century England; by the seventeenth century, they had developed into what one eminent English legal theorist, John Somers, described as "our only security, inasmuch as our lives cannot be drawn into jeopardy by all the malicious crafts of the Devil unless such a number of our honest countrymen shall be satisfied by the truth of the accusation." In the United States, Thomas Jefferson and James Madison included grand juries in the Fifth Amendment of the Bill of Rights in order to provide for a "people's panel" that would protect potential defendants against overreaching prosecutors and unwarranted prosecutions.

The panels usually consist of eighteen to twenty-three laymen whose terms last from one to eighteen months. They have traditionally carried out two functions. The first has been to sift through evidence a prosecutor has amassed and decide whether it is sufficient to force a man to undergo an expensive trial in front of a petit jury. The panel members met in secret to spare innocent people painful publicity.

The juries have also possessed a second, more complex power: that of carrying out investigations. In pre-Revolutionary America and during the Republic's first century, they were composed of ordinary citizens who used their considerable authority to investigate delays in bridge construction, for example, or the efforts of large business interests to hoard lucrative frontier land. In the nineteenth century, it was not unheard of for a grand jury to fire a prosecutor the local political machine had assigned to work with it, so that it could have a free hand in investigating corruption.

By the twentieth century, however, legal theorists had

decided that the law was too complex for ordinary citizens. To make sure that the grand juries behaved responsibly, they evolved a "key-man" system, whereby ex-grand jurors, city officials, and law enforcement authorities selected future panelists. Soon the institution became a kind of select Rotary Club for middle-aged, middle-class white men who enjoyed each other's company and rarely challenged a prosecutor's decision. Of equal consequence, the juries' powers of independent investigation atrophied. Sometimes they made pro forma trips to local prisons or hospitals, but their recommendations were rarely taken seriously. Instead, an inverse relationship was developing: as the influence and authority of the juries diminished, the relative might of the prosecuting attorney steadily increased.

The juries' powers of investigation and indictment have recently grown indistinguishable, and both have become strong weapons in the arsenals of the prosecutors whose powers they were intended to check. But because of the juries' exotic and technical aura, and because the cases they investigated in the past few decades generally concerned white collar crime or organized crime, the decay of their independence was barely noticed by the activists, journalists, and scholars they now work against.

Indeed, as long as prosecutors were using such potentially powerful tools as contempt of court citations and immunity grants to investigate organized and white-collar crime, civil libertarians ignored the possibility that those tools could also be used as techniques to intimidate reporters and scholars. Thus, the increasing and changing use of grants of immunity and contempt of court citations in the 1960s went, at first, relatively unnoticed. Rarely used in federal cases before 1965, they have now become the grand juries' most common and effective weapon.

It was in 1965 that two assistant U.S. attorneys from Chicago, Sam Betar and David Schippers, effected a major change in the operation of the grand jury. The two were trying to break up an organized crime outfit they suspected was headed by a man named Sam Giancana. When they convened the grand jury, they—and their quarry—thought the panel would play its traditional role of subpoenaing peripheral witnesses in order to amass enough information to indict more prominant suspects. Betar and Schippers were aware that if they subpoenaed Giancana, he'd surely invoke the Fifth Amendment and refuse to testify; traditionally, such central figures were not given immunity from prosecution, since the point of the investigation was to indict them. Within a few weeks, however, the two attorneys came up with a relatively novel way of trapping Giancana. They would indeed get him court-ordered immunity since, they were quite sure, he would still refuse to testify (as he'd have to, in order to preserve his credentials with the rest of his colleagues). At that point, they would jail him for contempt of court. And they would keep him in jail for the duration of the panel's life. That device had been used in state courts—Alfred Scotti, of the Manhattan district attorney's office, estimates that he has obtained more than 100 contempt citations in the past twenty years—but Betar and Schippers, and Nicholas Katzenbach, who was then Attorney General, agree that the technique had never been used in a major federal case. "Prosecutors were always afraid that a witness who was granted immunity would come out looking as innocent as a lamb," Betar says. In Katzenbach's mind, there was a principled distinction between granting a witness immunity in order to encourage him to testify, and using immunity as a device to imprison people who were certain not to talk. After much thought, he decided that Giancana fell into the first category, not the second.

Nevertheless, the use of immunity "was such a new technique that other law enforcement people treated us as if we were freaks at first," says Betar, who is now in private criminal practice in Chicago. "We realized that we'd better do our homework on Giancana, in case he decided to bluff us out by testifying to some lies. So we took six months surveilling him, putting things together."

The device worked well, Betar says. "Giancana went to prison. And jailing him created a state of chaos and fear in the minds of his associates. At first, they had thought we were just trying to grab some headlines with the grand jury. But once the lesser lights learned that we'd found a way to put the head of the whole show in jail, they didn't know how to cope." One of them decided to testify, lied, and was cited for perjury. Others talked and produced information that led to indictments and convictions of several important mob figures.

Giancana remained in jail for a year, until the grand jury disbanded. Then, Betar and Schippers and their superior, U.S. Attorney Edward Hanrahan, tried to bring him before the next panel to imprison him for its full session—eighteen months. But Ramsey Clark, who had replaced Katzenbach as Attorney General, vetoed the idea. "I just couldn't accept the method of coercing testimony," he said when interviewed later.

Giancana left town for Cuernavaca, where he still lives. Meanwhile, Betar and Schippers had provided law enforcement officials with an effective new tool. "I don't want to brag," Betar says, "but I know we laid the groundwork for the way immunity provisions have been used in the past few years."

The tool remained dormant until Richard Nixon's election as president. Then, the Justice Department, under John Mitchell, devised what came to be known as the 1970 Omnibus Crime Act, whose first two titles expanded the powers of federal grand juries. Title I empowered the Justice Department to convene special investigative grand juries that would last for eighteen months and could be reconvened for eighteen more. And Title II allowed prosecutors to go beyond the all-encompassing "transactional immunity" that Betar and Schippers had granted Sam Giancana. "Transactional immunity" would have provided sufficient legal basis to imprison any witness who refused to testify. But now, for the first time, the law also provided for a narrower "use immunity," which could, in certain instances, allow witnesses to be indicted for the substantive crimes the grand jury was investigating.

Traditionally, lawmakers and the courts had adhered to a strict construction of the Fifth Amendment in cases involving grand jury witnesses. When Sam Giancana was granted "transactional immunity," it was tantamount to assuring him that he'd never become a defendant in the case about which he was testifying. "Use immunity" affords the prosecutor more leeway. Giancana, if he'd been granted it, still couldn't be indicted on the basis of his own testimony. Nor could the information he supplied be used in such interrogations of other witnesses as might be used in turn to trap him. But if the government obtained incriminating information from an independent source—from a witness whose name he hadn't mentioned or a question his testimony hadn't suggested—then he could be included in an indictment.

Many civil libertarians view a statute that allows a witness to be jailed under any circumstances as a dangerous breach of the Fifth Amendment. And, as a practical matter, given the sophistication of the government's investigating techniques, there is always the possibility that the testimony of a Giancana can be subtly transmuted into apparently unrelated questions applying to apparently unrelated witnesses, and thus be used to indict him. (Congressmen John Conyers, William Fitts Ryan, and Avner Mikva were members of the House Judiciary Committee at the time the 1970 Omnibus Crime Act was passed out of committee. In a blunt dissenting report they called the special grand juries, and the powers of use immunity with which they

were newly equipped, "a frightening version of 'I've Got
a Secret.'")

From their very different perspectives, civil libertarians
and law enforcement officials agree that the special grand
juries play a crucial role in the government's antisubversive police apparatus. They agree that the intelligence
needs of the FBI or local police units often dictate decisions as to what witnesses to summon and what questions
to ask. And they agree that requests for information are
relayed to prosecutors who then use the jury's extraordinary powers to gain the necessary information.

Thus, two experienced defense lawyers, Frank Donner
and Eugene Cerruti, contend (in *The Nation,* January 3,
1972) that the Internal Securities Division (ISD) of the
Justice Department is trying to establish a "grand jury
network," the point of which is not so much to solve
specific politically motivated crimes as to compile a dossier on as many movement activists and activities as possible. Donner and Cerruti assert that the ISD is in charge
of a computer that contains all domestic political intelligence. And they say that the computer, which has un-
limited filing and cross-filing potential, sometimes deter-
mines what witnesses are called and what questions are
asked.

Officials of the Justice Department deny the Donner-
Cerruti charges about computers and dossiers, but they
firmly endorse the idea that the juries should be used to
extract information the FBI can't obtain. In a recent interview, A. William Olson, then head of the Internal Securities Division,* saw nothing wrong with the use of the
grand jury as a tool to develop broad information for the

---

*The Internal Security Division's function was recently transferred to the
Criminal Division of the Justice Department, and Olson was replaced by his
deputy assistant, Kevin Maroney. Spokesmen for the department assert that the
shift does not indicate any change in policy, but is instead the result of the new
White House desire to "streamline" the federal bureaucracy. Some independent

government. I asked him how he felt about agents threatening people who would not divulge information voluntarily with grand jury subpoenas. (Such a situation is not a mere possibility. It happened to the well-known New York lawyer Arthur Kinoy when he refused to reveal his daughter's whereabouts. Burton Caine, a Philadelphia lawyer, told *The New York Times* that the Bureau had threatened to bring a client of his before a Harrisburg grand jury "and prosecute him for perjury thereafter" if he didn't tell all he knew about the thefts of documents from the FBI's branch office in Media, Pennsylvania.) I also asked him about the propriety, during grand jury proceedings, of government prosecutors consulting FBI agents in regard to what questions they should ask witnesses.

In Olson's view, such behavior is proper. As he sees it, traditional intelligence techniques are often ineffective when used to probe into the affairs of today's activists. "These people," says Olson, "have life styles that are very hard to infiltrate. And they're very distrustful of outsiders." So it's often necessary to convene a grand jury to investigate crimes like the bombing of the U.S. Capitol. And once such proceedings are under way, Olson says he is "sure that the prosecutor would work closely with the FBI agents during the time the grand jury was convened so that he'd be able to ask the witness the proper questions and to evaluate his answers. In conducting a grand jury, the Attorney General and the FBI are part of a team

observers of the department speculate that the shift also resulted from declining administration interest in domestic subversion; however, the new Internal Security unit of the Criminal Division has the same budget and same staff (except for Olson) that the ISD had as a separate entity, and Maroney confirms that his group will continue to investigate politically motivated crimes and to use grand juries as it has in the past. Most recently, the unit's lawyers have been holding grand jury sessions on the West Coast to develop information about the Weatherman faction of SDS.

solving a crime. They're organs of the Justice Department."

Olson's description of the way witnesses are selected reinforces the contention that the grand jury is an extension of the FBI. "In many cases you go into an investigative grand jury with only a suspicion that criminal laws have been violated. And sometimes as the grand jury progresses you get bits and pieces. And sometimes they fit in not with what you started out to investigate, but with other crimes, not necessarily in the same jurisdiction." This arbitrary, haphazard process—which often results in substantial prison sentences for contempt—resembles nothing so much as a fishing expedition.

Most of the juries that investigate politically motivated crimes are directed by a cadre of about a dozen Justice Department lawyers headed by Guy Goodwin, a controversial ex-Democrat from Wichita, Kansas. Despite its size the group has performed a Herculean chore. Between 1970 and January, 1973, it had presented evidence to more than 100 grand juries in thirty-six states and eighty-four cities. It had subpoenaed between 1,000 and 2,000 witnesses (not people charged with substantive crimes, but simply those who might know a fact or two that could lead to an indictment) and compelled them to testify under oath. Hundreds have chosen to stand mute. About thirty have been cited for contempt of court. The juries have produced an estimated 410 indictments. Since many of their cases haven't come to court yet, it's still too early to tell the proportion of indictments to convictions.

One such case, headed by prosecutor Guy Goodwin, involved five young activists from Venice, California, who were subpoenaed in 1970 to testify before a Tucson grand jury about an alleged illegal purchase of dynamite. The subpoenas were issued *after* an indictment had been issued against the man who had supposedly bought the dynamite. Goodwin justified that by saying he was con-

tinuing the grand jury investigation with the intention of
bringing a second, superseding indictment. But his questions had nothing to do with dynamite. Their sweep was
reminiscent of the broad, provocative questions Joseph
McCarthy had asked in the 1950s. Since witnesses are not
allowed copies of their own testimony in the jury room
(though prosecutors get those transcripts immediately),
these samples of Goodwin's questions come from rough
notes the witnesses made:

Tell the grand jury every place you went after you returned
to your apartment from Cuba, every city you visited, with whom
and by what means of transportation, and who you visited at all
of the places during the time of your travels after you left your
apartment in Ann Arbor, Michigan, in May, 1970.

I want you to describe for the jury every occasion during the
year 1970 when you have been in contact with, attended meetings that were conducted by, or been any place where any individual spoke who you knew to be associated with or affiliated
with the Students for a Democratic Society, the Weathermen,
the Communist Party, or any other organization advocating the
overthrow of the United States, describing for the grand jury
when the incidents occurred, who was present, and what was
said by all members present there, and what you did at the times
you were in those meetings, groups, associations, or conversations.

At first, all of the witnesses refused to talk and spent
five months in a Tucson jail for contempt of court. They
were freed when the jury's term expired. But as soon as
a new one was convened, Goodwin subpoenaed them
again (as Betard and Schippers had sought and failed to do
in the Giancana case when Ramsey Clark was Attorney
General). They were asked the same questions with the
same threat of imprisonment. At that point, three of them
buckled and testified.

Witnesses, then, are "bits and pieces," people branch-
office agents have fingered as potential leads. A witness

may be the friend of a suspect, or someone whose name has bubbled into the consciousness of an erratic informer like Boyd Douglas, or someone whose name was mentioned in a wiretapped conversation. Someone, in other words, who is only peripheral to most movement activities —like Susan Susman, an Oberlin graduate who had been working with the Harrisburg defense committee in New York for several months when the Bureau began to suspect that a coworker whom she scarcely knew had been involved in an abortive raid on an FBI office in Garden City, Long Island. She was summoned to testify and had to spend six weeks sitting in Manhattan's federal building day after day before the investigation was blocked by a technicality involving the legal definition of theft. And though she didn't have to make the difficult decision to testify or risk contempt, the experience did give her some serious thoughts: to her the price of a chance friendship with a resister turned out to be potentially very high. She has continued her friendships with members of the resistance community, but she can see how fear of the grand jury might make others wary of forming such friendships in the future.

Sometimes freak accidents can cause a lode of names to cascade through FBI offices and into the Internal Securities Division files. For example, in April, 1971, twenty-five people were subpoenaed to appear before the grand jury in Harrisburg. The witnesses, who came from as far away as Boston and Chicago, couldn't figure out what relationship they had to one another or to the case. A year later, during the trial, it became clear that the Justice Department thought they might yield "bits and pieces" because they had all been mentioned in the Berrigan–McAlister correspondence that Boyd Douglas had turned over to the FBI. Most of their names came up in the context of gossipy, marginal comments.

As illuminating as their reason for being called was their

reaction once in front of the grand jury. Most refused to testify, and four were cited for contempt. Given their marginal connection to the case, it is clear that self-protection was not the source of that reluctance. The source was the grand jury proceeding itself. There's a terrible choice that confronts people like the Harrisburg witnesses or the Fort Worth 5 or Sue Susman, people who suddenly, unaccountably find themselves in the terrifying confines of the grand jury room. Often they don't know anything that would incriminate themselves or anyone else—or at least they think they don't—but they don't want to jeopardize their friendships, or compromise their principles, or provide the scrap of information that might wrap up an indictment they consider vindictive. So they refuse to participate in a process that seems illegitimate. A. William Olson considers that attitude antisocial. Nevertheless, hundreds of witnesses have chosen to risk contempt of court citations by standing mute. And, though most witnesses are only jailed for the life of the grand jury (or until they agree to testify), that crime has recently been redefined as a felony, which can bring sentences of up to four years.

One of the most frustrating things for witnesses who refuse to testify is the power the prosecutor has to manipulate them into looking like criminals in front of the jurors. The witnesses are very much at the mercy of the prosecutor. They are not even allowed to have a lawyer accompany them. If they wish to consult their attorneys in the corridor, they must ask the prosecutor's permission to leave the room—an obligation that, many feel, makes them appear even more suspect to the jurors, who rarely understand their principled reasons for standing mute. Here is how Harvard scholar Samuel Popkin recalls his experience with the Boston grand jury investigating the Pentagon Papers distribution. (In reading his description, it is crucial to recall that never, from the day he was sub-

poenaed to the day he was jailed, did he know why he was
called to testify. He knew Daniel Ellsberg but was out of
the country during the Pentagon Papers controversy. He'd
always been a scholar, not a political activist.) During his
hours in the jury room, Popkin says,

I was very concerned with the whole power of insinuation the
prosecutor had, and with the way he would influence the jury
with that power whenever I tried to assert my constitutional
rights. For example, I had to keep taking the Fifth Amendment
to protect the immunity I was trying to establish. And there were
times when I didn't know how to respond to questions, so I had
to ask if I could leave the room to talk with my lawyer. Whenever I did something like that on questions that must have
seemed very trivial to the jurors, the prosecutor would snicker
and say something like, "Oh, so you're afraid to answer a little
question like that." And there was nothing I could do but sit
there and take it. I felt paralyzed from defending myself by the
law. I felt intimidated and manipulated in that room. The whole
thing was humiliating.

During the past year, reporters and academics like
Popkin have joined members of organized crime and political activists in the roster of those who are forced to decide whether to testify or risk jail. It has always been true
that reporters and academics may be able to find out more
about the doings of criminals or the radical underground
than government agents can—they do so by guaranteeing
absolute anonymity to their sources of information, and
for years that right has been respected in practice.

But in June, 1972, in a 5–4 decision, the Supreme Court
ruled that reporter Earl Caldwell would have to answer
questions before a San Francisco grand jury investigating
the Black Panthers. (Since the grand jury in question had
disbanded while Caldwell's case was in the courts, he was
never actually imprisoned.) A few months later, in line
with the Caldwell decision, Samuel Popkin was cited for
contempt. Peter Bridge of the now defunct *Newark Eve-*

ning News and John Lawrence of the *Los Angeles Times* are only two of the other reporters who have been jailed on similar grounds.

For many journalists and scholars, the issue is plain: to obey the Supreme Court decision is to violate crucial professional ethics and to jeopardize not only one's livelihood but also the public's right to know. For, a reporter or scholar who betrays one source to the government runs the risk that all his other sources will refuse to confide in him because they perceive him as a spy or, at least, as a bad risk. And so many journalists and scholars have agreed to resist the juries. But it's suddenly clear that a good story can now lead to prison rather than a Pulitzer.

Still, if the current controversy over the Justice Department's grand jury strategy is understandable, its focus is also somewhat limited. For those who criticize the political use of the juries speak mainly in terms of an administration attack on dissent. If it is outrageous to subpoena, immunize, and imprison journalists, scholars, and political activists, then aren't the same methods outrageous when they are used against the Mafia?

Some of the activists who complain most insistently about a "grand jury network" will argue, in private, that the panels should have unrestrained right to investigate the Mafia. Is it legitimate to jail people who refuse to answer questions about people who might be smuggling drugs into Harlem (or to give G. Gordon Liddy an eighteen-month prison sentence because he refuses to tell a grand jury about the Watergate episode), but wrong to pursue the same strategy as a means of discovering who was responsible for the bombing of the U.S. Capitol? The current critics of the grand jury system have simply refused to face this issue. They have no consistent answer to the argument that the social benefit of powerful grand juries—the increased potential for fighting crime—is worth the loss of some individual freedom.

The week that Peter Bridge went to jail for contempt of court, Eugene Gold, Brooklyn's district attorney, sub-poenaed 600 witnesses to testify about the Mafia in front of a Brooklyn grand jury. That day a "high police officer close to the case" was quoted in *The New York Times* as threatening that hundreds of those witnesses would go to jail for contempt. Editorials abounded about Bridge's jailing; silence greeted the policeman's threat.

The day that Samuel Popkin went to Norfolk prison for contempt, another federal judge in Boston jailed Joseph Itrato, a Cambridge nightclub owner, also for contempt. There was no more published evidence that connected Itrato to organized crime than Popkin to the Pentagon Papers. Popkin's sentencing was a front-page story in the *Times* and the subject of an anguished Thanksgiving day column by Tom Wicker. Itrato, who was the fifth witness in his grand jury hearing to go to prison, rated a four-paragraph article in the back of the *Boston Globe*, and no editorials. An extraordinary amount of pressure from Harvard and the rest of the academic community convinced the government to discontinue the jury that had heard Popkin. The scholar was released after only three days in jail. Itrato and the other witnesses in his case served out their full term.

In 1933, Britain abolished its grand juries, choosing instead to weigh the validity of each indictment in open court. Since then, there has been considerable sentiment that the United States should follow suit. Indeed, some states, most of them in the West, never adopted the panels as part of their system of criminal justice. (Decisions to proceed in criminal cases are made on the basis of pre-liminary hearings before a judge.) In 1965, New Jersey judge Melvin P. Antell kindled considerable controversy when he wrote an article in *The American Bar Association Journal* calling the juries a "benighted supergovernment," archaic at best, tools for the prosecution at worst. Furthermore, it's not yet clear that even reforms that seem to be crucial will have much effect. In 1968, Congress passed what seemed to be a very important measure when it outlawed the "key-man" system of selecting panelists and stipulated that jurors must henceforth be drawn from the voter rolls. While this has meant a broader representation, it has not helped the institution regain its independence. Most jurors still don't know their duties. Federal judges take about thirty minutes to select the panels and instruct them about their obligations. ("Those instructions usually consist of a few very general sentences," according to Irwin Brownstein, a Brooklyn Supreme Court judge. "You know, 'welcome to the club,' something like that.") Then they send them up to the jury room, where the prosecutor instructs them about the case under investigation and begins to present his evidence. Spencer Klaw, a freelance writer who served on a county grand jury in Manhattan, remembers a sense of disorientation that persisted from the first day to the last. That was probably one reason, he says, "that once the district attorney presented a case, the jurors felt it was their job to process it into court, no matter what the facts. It was a struggle even to get them to discuss the evidence."

Nevertheless, many jurists have hesitated to press for the abolition of the panels, since that could be accomplished only by an amendment to the Bill of Rights. And some civil libertarians fear that the alternative to the juries—which at least enable some citizens to be present when witnesses are put under oath—is the expanded power of individual prosecutors to compel testimony in totally private proceedings.

Judge Brownstein believes that the issue of grand juries is so crucial and so unexamined that it should be the subject of major public hearings by state and federal judiciary committees. Meanwhile, he and other jurists have some suggestions for reforms.

Many people who have had dealings with grand juries agree that there should be some sort of adversary proceeding before an indictment is handed down. Lawyers like James Reif of New York's Center for Constitutional Rights, Senator Kennedy, and Judge Brownstein believe that witnesses should be allowed to take their own attorneys into the jury room, though some jurists insist that there should be some limits to prevent the proceeding from becoming a minitrial. Some also feel that many of the minor cases now heard by the juries (though not major investigations, which are usually the most controversial) should be transformed into pretrial proceedings that take place before a judge in open court.

James Reif argues strenuously that immunity provisions should exist only as a means of protecting frightened witnesses who want to testify. Its current role, as a gateway to jail, should be abolished completely, Reif contends.

Witnesses and their lawyers feel it's essential to have time to prepare themselves. Most feel that at least a week should elapse between the time a subpoena is served and their appearance before the jury. They also contend that if a number of witnesses live in one locale, they should be allowed to appear before a grand jury there instead of being whisked to an unfamiliar place, as the Fort Worth 5 were. They think it's imperative to tell witnesses why they've been subpoenaed.

In theory, grand juries are supposed to be part of the judiciary, which means that prosecutors have the unchecked right to subpoena anyone they want. However, since in most cases the juries serve as tools for the prosecution, Stephen Gillers, former director of the Committee for Public Justice, feels that judges should begin to play a more active, watchdog role. In some cases, he says, it may be necessary for them to require that grand jury subpoenas be subjected to the same scrupulous tests as court-ordered wiretaps and search warrants.

Finally, it's clear that the courts and the public can do a great deal more to restore the grand jury's independence. For example, when a jury is impaneled, at least half a day could be devoted to orienting it to its task. The talents of legal historians and scholars could supplement the instructions of sitting judges. Films and manuals could describe the role the juries have played in the past, emphasizing their independent nature and their traditional responsibility to protect citizens, not aid prosecutors. That way the citizens who are called to serve on grand juries might come to realize that, even with the limitations here proposed, the institution could once again become the guardian of individual liberties that the framers of the Constitution envisioned when they wrote grand juries into the Bill of Rights.

But if the grand jury system is to be reinvigorated, its critics and the prosecutors who use it must conduct themselves according to a single standard. At present, public opinion and a powerful institution like Harvard can protect a member of the Establishment like Samuel Popkin from jail. Journalists and politicians can express outrage at the seemingly endless anguish of the Fort Worth 5, but because those Irish working men lack the kind of institutional power a Popkin possesses, they can be shuttled back and forth from jail to nervous freedom for two or three years.

There are no reporters or politicians to protest the treatment of a G. Gordon Liddy or a Joseph Itrato, who were jailed for precisely the same reasons as were Popkin and the Fort Worth 5. By the same token, pundits and politicians express only fleeting, wistful disapproval when the supposedly secret grand jury testimony of a Watergate witness or a conservative candidate like Mario Biaggi winds up in *The New York Times*. There would, of course, have been widespread outrage if the Internal Securities Division lawyers had tried to use the testimony of grand jury witnesses in the Ellsberg and Berrigan cases in the same way.

The juries must not serve as meat grinders with which overzealous prosecutors—conservative or liberal—chop facts out of a powerless witness. They can only survive as part of a thoroughly independent judiciary, as a real shield for defendants.

II
SELECTIONS FROM
THE MEDIA PAPERS

ANNOTATED BY PAUL COWAN AND NICK EGLESON

On March 8, 1971, the FBI discovered that hundreds of documents were missing from its branch office in Media, Pennsylvania. By the end of March, reporters for such newspapers and news services as the *Washington Post,* *The New York Times,* the *Los Angeles Times,* the *Village Voice,* and Reuters had received parcels containing some of the documents, with a covering letter from a group calling itself the Citizens' Commission to Investigate the FBI. As soon as the first stories were printed many other newspapers sought to obtain the documents and to publish them at regular intervals. During the next several months, at two- or three-week intervals, reporters for those papers and others (like the *Philadelphia Bulletin,* the *Philadelphia Inquirer,* and *Newsday*) received new parcels of material. Each fresh batch of documents was treated as a new major story. Newspapers broadcast each successive story over their news services. The wire services sent the material to papers all over the country.

During the weeks when stories about the documents were appearing in the press, newspaper and television reporters interviewed a dozen or so of the people named in them. Those interviews appeared as newspaper or television features. CBS, ABC, NBC, and NET programmed special news clips or longer documentaries, which included material from the Media files, about the FBI and surveillance. In March, 1972, *Win* magazine published an entire issue devoted to the documents.

According to a letter mailed to the press on May 3, 1971, by the Citizens' Commission to Investigate the FBI, "30 percent of the materials in the Media files were manuals, routine forms, and similar procedural matter." The remainder included "40 percent political surveillance and other investigation of political activity. Of those cases, two were right wing, ten concerned immigrants, and over 200 were on left or liberal groups. Twenty-five percent bank robberies, twenty percent murder, rape, and interstate theft. Seven percent were draft resisters, including refusal to submit to military induction. Seven percent were leaving the military without government permission. One percent were organized crime, mostly gambling."

In this book, we are including extensive selections from the political documents. For reasons of space and relevance, we omitted some material. But we have preserved what seemed most significant or typical, and we have tried to summarize the omissions in the introductions to the different sections. In most cases we have printed the complete documents. Some documents arrived with pages missing. In a few cases, we have omitted long lists of such things as file categories. All omissions are noted where they occur. Although these are not facsimile reproductions, we have reproduced the documents in their original form. We have not changed spelling or syntax.

The documents are organized into nine categories, each of which we have described in a separate introduction. There are forty separate documents here. We have prefaced most of them briefly but have written lengthier introductions to those that seemed particularly instructive or complicated, or to those for which we possessed supplementary information.

The most complicated issue in editing the documents has been the use of names mentioned in them. Our desire has been to convey a clear sense of the process by which the FBI obtains information about people—to let the apparatus reveal itself through its own writings—without violating the liberties or sensitivities of individuals. Accordingly, in the cases of those who voluntarily used their official capacities to obtain information about people and relay it to the FBI, we have retained professional titles but omitted names. We have omitted the last names of all paid informers, except those who have freely and publicly acknowledged their work. We have left intact the names of all FBI and police employees. We have omitted the last names of all subjects of investigations, except public figures like Bobby Seale and Muhammad Kenyatta, or people whose acknowledgments that they were the subject of investigation have been published. When informers or subjects of investigations have commonplace first names we have preserved them; when their first names are unusual, we have used an initial of their first or last names. We have omitted all telephone numbers and addresses.*

Do not expect to find any isolated, staggering revelations in these documents. They record the workaday functions of America's secret police, and not their most sensational or scandalous cases. There are, however, a number

---

*In the interest of accuracy, a description of all the minor alterations we have made in the documents is in order. All documents that appear in memorandum form, with TO, FROM, and SUBJECT in the upper left, were originally composed on a form bearing, in the far upper right, these words: OPTIONAL FORM NO. 10 / MAY 1962 EDITION / GSA FPMR (41 CFR) 101-11.5 / UNITED STATES GOVERNMENT / MEMORANDUM. At the lower left was a picture of the colonial minuteman holding a gun. A line along the bottom of the page read: "Buy U.S. Savings Bonds Regularly on the Payroll Savings Plan." All of these documents also bore an imprint affixed when they were received by the addressee, bearing the date, the words "FBI—PHILADELPHIA," and the following words, each followed by a blank: SEARCHED____INDEXED____ SERIALIZED____FILED____. Some documents bore initials in one or more of these blanks, and some had a serialization number handwritten above the stamp. In this version, that number has been typeset and set flush right as at the end of the text of each document.

When original documents ran beyond one page, we have not indicated the separation and have removed the file number which appeared at the top left of the second and all following pages. This number still appears in parentheses following the word TO at the top of the first page of such documents. Routing information, the total number of copies, the initials of author and typist, and serialization number (if present) now appear at the very end of these multipaged documents. In the original this information was at the bottom of the first page.

of very disturbing documents here. Orders to watch all Black Student Unions; to scour the ghettos and set up a block-by-block network of informers; to find grounds to prosecute antidraft leaders; to talk with American businessmen about doing espionage work when they visit the Soviet Union; to consider evaluating a woman for the "Security Index" on the basis of a single informer's remark about her. There are instances when, by its own admission, the Bureau finds no evidence, and still keeps its surveillance files alive. There is a report based on one day's tapping of the Black Panther Party's phone. But most of this material is so diluted by the form—memos and routinized reports—and so debased by the language of bureaucrats that its impact may be blunted at first reading.

These documents show, more clearly than anything else the public has seen before, the machinery of the FBI's information-gathering apparatus, the style in which the apparatus talks to itself, and the rigid assumptions through which it filters the information it receives. The picture that emerges is fascinating, unsettling, and ominous.

Glossary

aka or AKA	Also Known As
ASAC	Assistant Special Agent in Charge (see SAC)
AX	symbol for Alexandria, Virginia, Regional Office
BUDED	Bureau Deadline (see Bureau)
Bureau	national headquarters of FBI (not the same as Washington Field Office)
COINTELPRO	Counterintelligence Program
CI	Criminal Informant
DEAD	When used with file number, refers to the inactive section of FBI files

DESECO	Development of Selected Contacts: name of program for interviewing US citizens who return from trips to the Soviet Union
EDPA	Eastern District of Pennsylvania (Division of Federal Court system)
ELSUR	Electronic Surveillance
FD 376	Federal form 376, used to pass information on to the Secret Service
FD 553	Federal form 553, used by army to tell FBI to watch out for AWOL
FNU	First Name Unknown
FUDE	Fugitive-Deserter
GILROB	label attached to the case of bank robbery-police murder in Boston in 1970, for which Stanley Bond is held and Linda Saxe hunted
IS	Internal Security
IS-C	Internal Security-Communist
IS-R	Internal Security-Racial
LDB	Local Draft Board
LHM	Letterhead Memorandum
LNU	Last Name Unknown
MDPA	Middle District of Pennsylvania (Division of Federal Court system)
OO	Office of Origin
PCI	Potential Criminal Informant
PD	Police Department
Ph or PH	Philadelphia
PH-(908)-s	(Number could be any number): Philadelphia informant with code number 908, for security matters
PH-(809)-R	(Number could be any number): Philadelphia informant with code number 809, for racial matters
PH-T-1	Philadelphia informant assigned the number 1 for purposes of this report only. (Could be any number)
PRI	Potential Racial Informant

(Glossary continues on p. 114)

A Guide to a Typical Document

SAC means Special Agent in Charge, or head of the Philadelphia ⌐
Regional FBI office.

IC probably means Investigative Clerk. —————————————

PH means Philadelphia. The number is the code number of this —
particular informant. Other informants (who may be taps and
bugs as well as agencies, but are most often people) have
different numbers. C means Criminal (S means Security, and
R means Racial).

This part of the page contains the instructions for distribution
of the memo. It provides, inadvertently, information on the
size of the Bureau.

This is a typical file number; 66 is the category. It happens to
mean "operating instructions." (Number 100 means left wing,
105 is espionage, 157 is racial militant, 170 is racial informant,
25 is Selective Service.) The rest of the number is the particular file.

This is the quantity of copies to go in each file.

This is the total number of copies to be made, in this case 190.
Since one went to file 66–3864, and the rest to all agents, there
must have been 189 agents in October 1970.

TO   : ALL AGENTS   DATE: 10/9/70
FROM   :(SAC)JOE D. JAMIESON
SUBJECT: RECORD CHECKS AT HARRISBURG, PA.

   The following record checks are now conducted
by Special Clerk JOHN VERESPY at Harrisburg, Pa.,
and any requests for record checks should be set
out accordingly. Many of these checks were previously handled by (I.C.) BRIAN MC LAUGHLIN:
Bureau of Vital Statistics—birth and death records
Bureau of Motor Vehicles—operator and vehicle
   information
(PH)237-C—Social Security check (not to be used
   to verify employment)
State Harness Racing Commission—race track
   employees
State Insurance Dept.—insurance agents, brokers
   and company license
Selective Service Headquarters—registrant check
Pennsylvania National Guard, IGMR—personnel files
Bureau of Traffic Safety—operator traffic
   violations
Corporation Bureau—corporation data
Pennsylvania State Police—Bureau of Criminal
   Identification—name checks and file reviews
State Board of Probation & Parole—record reviews
State Liquor Control Board—personnel checks and
   State liquor law violations, liquor licenses
Department of Military Affairs—Vietnam Bonus
   Bureau—possible aid in location of fugitives
Department of Justice—Bureau of Correction in-
   formation—location of state prisoners
Fish Commission and Game Commission—fishing and
   hunting license information
Department of Education—background information
   on certified public school teachers

1—66-3864
1—ALL AGENTS
JDJ:MMcG
(190)

Glossary (cont'd.)

PSI	Potential Security Informant
RA	Resident Agent: agent assigned permanently to one of the Field Offices
Regional Office	one of the fifty-nine major offices in the United States, Hawaii, and Puerto Rico
RM	Racial Militant
rotor	device used to sort memos at regional office
SA	Special Agent: title of most FBI investigative personnel
SAC	Special Agent in Charge: head of a regional office
SC	Special Clerk
SE	Special Employee
SF	San Francisco
SI	Security Index, also used for Security Informant
SM	Student Militant
SOG	Seat of Government (Washington, D.C.)
Squad	The basic subdivision within regional offices. In Philadelphia, about ten squads of fifteen to twenty men each.
SRA	Senior Resident Agent: in charge of one of the small field offices.
SSA	Selective Service Act
SSN	Selective Service Number
STAG	Student Agitation
Supervisor	in charge of a particular squad (q.v.)
UNSUB	Subjects with unknown names.
WFO	Washington Field Office: the field office for Washington, DC, not the same as national headquarters.

Sources of Information

Here are some documents that show the wide range of institutions with which agents maintain casual, routine contacts. One document instructed Bureau agents to maintain regular contact with 312 airports, hotels, corporations, banks, government agencies, police departments, and colleges. Also included was a list of the agents and of the institutions' file numbers. In later documents it will become clear how the "good will" that these liaisons are supposed to foster pays off in facts. In one case, the Bureau obtained its information through a passenger service representative of the KLM Royal Dutch Airlines. When the FBI wanted to know about the Black Student Union at Pennsylvania Military College, it used a newspaperman as a "Ghetto Racial Source." The Bureau learned about the bank records of the National Black Economic Development Conference through a cashier at a bank and an executive officer at the bank's computer center in Chester, Pennsylvania. And the Bureau found out about students through registrars, campus police, campus switchboard operators, and deans.

Here is the memorandum preceding the list of twelve airlines, seventeen banks, eight educational institutions, ten hotels, sixteen major companies, eighty-three outlying police departments, eighteen branches of the Philadelphia police department, eighteen state and local agencies, ten stockbrokers, eighteen trucking companies, fifty-eight government agencies, fourteen news media, and forty-four institutions (like the Philadelphia 76ers basketball team and Trailways bus system) that the FBI categorizes as miscellaneous.

```
TO      : ALL INVESTIGATIVE PERSONNEL (80-00)   DATE: 8/28/70
FROM    : SAC JOE D. JAMIESON
SUBJECT: LIAISON PROGRAM
```

Set forth on the attached pages are the current liaison assignments of the Philadelphia Office.

It is the responsibility of the Agent assigned to make a liaison contact with the agency at least once each six months and to record such contacts in the file. A contact made during the regular course of business by the Agent assigned

or another Agent may be counted as the liaison
contact, but should be recorded in the file.

The personnel to be contacted at each agency
should be recorded on a current basis so that in
the event the assigned Agent is not available
the appropriate individual or individuals may
be contacted by the Agent investigating.

The primary purposes of these contacts are to
create good will and to develop sources of new
cases so that we may be sure that all matters
within our jurisdiction are being reported to us.

It is realized that all of these agencies are
contacted frequently during a six-month period,
but no formal recording is usually made in the
liaison file. Please remember to record any
contacts in the normal course of business, as
this may save the assigned Agent the necessity
of making a special visit to do so.

```
1—80-00                        1—#1 Squad Rotor
1—66-6007                      1—SA JAMES W. GOING
1—Complaint Duty File          1—MARGUERITE RICHARDS
1—Chief Clerk                  1—Each Investigative
1—Assistant Chief Clerk          Employee (200)

JDJ:MMR
(208)
```

Bell Telephone allows agents to obtain names and addresses
of subscribers with unlisted numbers, a service that is not available to ordinary citizens.

```
TO     : ALL AGENTS                        DATE: 2/26/71
FROM   : SAC JOE D. JAMIESON
SUBJECT: BELL TELEPHONE COMPANY OF PENNSYLVANIA
         LIAISON MATTER
```

Arrangements have been made through the Bell
Telephone Company of Pennsylvania, Security
Office, Philadelphia, Pa., for maintaining alphabetical telephone listings in the FBI Philadelphia Office. These alphabetical telephone
listings reflect all individuals who possess

telephone service through Bell Telephone regardless of published or non-published telephones.
It is to be noted that a non-published (NP) listing will show only subscribers name and address,
no telephone number.

At present, in the Philadelphia Office are
alphabetical listings for the following:

> Delaware County   Lower Bucks County
> Philadelphia   Doylestown
> West Chester   Norristown

These alphabetical listings will be updated
monthly as new telephone subscribers commence
service.

In the near future, additional alphabetical
listings will be obtained for Lancaster,
Eastern Montgomery County, Harrisburg, Allen-
town, Reading, Wilkes-Barre and Scranton, Pa.,
as they become available.

Should information from alphabetical listings
be disseminated this source should be so concealed.

The alphabetical listings will be maintained
by SCs JAMES L. KNOTTS and EDWARD GALLAGHER,
telephone extension 217.

1—66-6041   1—IC GUNDERMANN
1—EACH AGENT (205)   1—EACH SC (8)
1—EACH SE (6)

JDJ:PNJ
(221)

Here is one way the Boy Scouts are used:

POSITIVE PROGRAM

Police-Community Relations
Rochester, New York

The Rochester, New York, Police Department is
deeply committed to Police-Community Relations

activity in an attempt to reduce crime and
create greater understanding between the police
and the total community that they serve.

"OPERATION S A F E"

The Boy Scouts of America, Otetiana Council,
Rochester, New York, in cooperation with the
Rochester, New York, Police Department has prepared a circular enlisting the support and help
of approximately 20,000 Boy Scouts in reducing
crime. Operation S A F E stands for Scout
Awareness for Emergency. The Scouts involved are
issued an identification card by their leader
which has the bearer's thumb print and emergency
telephone numbers on the reverse side. The
emergency telephone numbers include the Rochester
Police Department, Fire Department, Sheriff's
Office, State Police, Coast Guard, FBI, Poison
Control Center, and Civil Defense along with the
telephone numbers of the surrounding town police
departments.

Each Boy Scout participating in this program is
given instructions as to how he can assist the
police in making the community a safer place to
live. Each Scout is requested to observe and
report any suspicious act or unusual occurrence
that endangers the life and property of friends
or relatives. The Scouts are instructed as to
how to observe and report these incidents. "If
they see it—they will report it."

Particular emphasis is placed on the accurate
reporting of license numbers, addresses and locations, the number of people involved, and a
description of the incident. The Boy Scouts were
instructed to remain on the telephone until all
the information they have has been furnished to
the police.

The Scouts receive instructions on the types of

incidents or activities that should be observed
and reported, such as:
1. Criminal acts such as assaults, robberies,
   shoplifting, breaking and entering, vandalism.
2. Fires—in buildings, in vehicles, in wood
   areas, etc.,—youngsters playing with matches,
   dangerous fire conditions.
3. Accidents—involving automobiles, people,
   and animals.
4. Suspicious acts—persons loitering in
   secluded places, strangers loitering around
   schools, neighborhoods, and parks.
5. Unusual situations—faulty traffic lights,
   flooded viaducts, power lines down, youngsters playing in or around dangerous places,
   fallen trees, broken windows, and unusual
   activity or lack of activity in neighbors
   homes.
As a result of this partnership between the
Rochester, New York, Police Department and the
Regional Council of the Boy Scouts, the police
department has approximately 20,000 more "good
citizens" operating as extra eyes and ears for
the police department in attempting to reduce
crime.

Internal Bureau Matters

These documents show how the Bureau makes sure the
agents it hires are willing to conform to rigid standards
of dress and appearance and to obey orders.

Watch those pear shaped heads.

CLERICAL APPLICANT ROUTING SLIP NOT TO BE
SERIALIZED—DESTROY WHEN PURPOSE SERVED

In connection with Bureau applicant investigation, when you send a written communication be sure to reference prior communications either outgoing or incoming. In addition, be sure to include status.

I recently saw a photograph of a favorably recommended clerical application. This photograph reflected long sideburns and long hair in the back and too full on the sides. Please, when interviewing applicants be alert for long hairs, beards, mustaches, pear shaped heads, truck drivers, etc. We are not that hard up yet.

In connection with long hair and sideburns, where you have an applicant that you would like to favorably recommend, ask the applicant to submit to you a new photograph with short sideburns and conventional hair style. I have not had one refuse me yet.

1—67-7190
1—67-24790
1—ASAC
1—SA GWINN
1—SA SAVARD
1—SA CAPOZZELLA
1—SA MUZIK
1—SA J. O'CONNOR
1—SA C. T. ADAMS

1_SA CHRISTENSEN
1—SA RODGERS
1—SA BRAMLEY
1—SA HENDRICKS
1—SA HANNIGAN
1—SA JENKINS
1—SA DE BUVITZ
1—SA SPIVEY

JES:MS
(17)

Watch your weight.

TO   : ALL SPECIAL AGENTS, MALE CLERICAL   DATE: 1/4/71
          EMPLOYEES, INVESTIGATIVE CLERKS, &
          SPECIAL EMPLOYEES
FROM   : SAC JOE D. JAMIESON
SUBJECT: PHYSICAL EXAMINATION MATTERS—
          WEIGHT STANDARDS

By SAC Letter #65—39 dated 7/14/65, the

Bureau instructed that during the months of July, October, January and April of each year, each Special Agent must be weighed and the Bureau advised of the results by the last day of such months.

The next report will be due 1/29/71.

<u>HEADQUARTERS PERSONNEL:</u> All Headquarters City male personnel will be weighed beginning January 11th through January 22nd, and their weights recorded by Mrs. LEE LANDSBURG in the Nurse's Office. ANY MAN FOUND TO BE OVERWEIGHT WILL BE REQUIRED TO LOSE THE WEIGHT, AND WILL BE WEIGHED WEEKLY BY HIS SUPERVISOR UNTIL HIS WEIGHT IS BROUGHT WITHIN BUREAU STANDARDS.

<u>RESIDENT AGENTS:</u> Any Resident Agent coming into Headquarters City during any month must be weighed there and his weight recorded by Mrs. LANDSBURG. Those Resident Agents who have not been in Headquarters City during any month will be weighed by the Senior Resident Agent who will immediately furnish the results to me, Attention: Mrs. LANDSBURG. <u>ALL RESIDENT AGENTS' WEIGHTS FOR THE 1/29/71 REPORT MUST BE IN THIS OFFICE BY JANUARY 22, 1971.</u>

The Wellsboro agent must be weighed by Mrs. LANDSBURG when he comes in to Headquarters City, but no more than once a month.

I expect every Agent and male clerical employee to maintain his weight within the desirable limits at all times.

1—66-244   1—Each Male Employee as above
1—66-6135   1—Nurse

JDJ:MMR
(230)

Hire veterans: they're used to discipline.

DISCHARGED VETERANS PROGRAM

The Philadelphia Division has had excellent
success with a direct mail approach to persons
who have just been discharged from the military
services.

TECHNIQUE

On discharge, the military services complete a
form, DD-214, which gives an account of the
military service of the discharged person. This
is mailed directly to the Selective Service
Headquarters of the state where the discharged
veteran lists his permanent home address. At the
Headquarters, these forms are then "zoned" and
mailed to the various local draft boards.

Through liaison at the State Selective Service
Headquarters at Harrisburg, these forms have
been made available to us for review. After elim-
inating persons whose service has been other
than honorable, a letter describing the advantages of working for the FBI is mailed.

It should be pointed out this includes both
men and women, officers and enlisted personnel.

During a test period, September 24-27, 1968, a
GS-2 clerk was sent to Harrisburg, Pa. During
that time he was able to address approximately
950 letters. Twenty-one were returned because
the veteran had furnished the improper address.
Of the remaining 930, we have received 45 interested clerical replies and 10 interested
Special Agent replies. As of this date, we have
under investigation, nine persons who appear to
be fully qualified for clerical appointment at
SOG.

By extension it can be seen that a continuous
program at Harrisburg for Eastern Pennsylvania
could be expected to produce at least 30 clerical
applicants of worthwhile quality per month. Per-

haps half or more of these might receive appoint-
ments.

KEY ELEMENT
The key element in getting a response is a
letter to the veteran which is crammed with
facts, facts sufficient to make the receiver
think and to enable him to make a decision as to
whether or not this offer of employment is
genuinely of interest. A letter containing
generalities produces much extra work as it is
necessary to explain on an individual basis what
the facts are.

DISADVANTAGES
Because the discharged veteran is several years
further along than the current high school
graduate, some may have had a "wild oats" period.
The investigations may be more demanding. Educational qualifications sometimes present a problem
as many of these veterans did not graduate from
high school and have general equivalency diplomas.

ADVANTAGES
The cost of locating an interested applicant is
very low. Sending a GS-2 clerk from the Philadelphia office to Harrisburg two or three days a
week will take care of all discharged veterans
for eastern Pennsylvania and will average $350—
$400 per month; this opposed to the cost of
putting several Special Agents on the road at
$1,500 to $1,800 per month, with no certainty of
equal success.
From the outset, we have a genuinely interested
prospect. These persons are mature, have already
been relocated certainly at least once and have
no fear of living in Washington, D.C. They have
been subject to discipline and orders. We are

also offering a job to a veteran, someone who
has served his country.

By reviewing the DD-214 at the State Headquarters, you save up to two weeks and catch the
veteran almost before he is home. This plan saves
resident agents having to go to local draft
boards and work out individual liaison arrangements, an expensive, time consuming process.
When the interested veteran responds, the papers
are then turned over to the resident agent for
handling and he works the applicants into his
quota.

This program is especially timely now as there
is a great number of veterans being discharged
into Pennsylvania. For the first eight months,
there were:

January	4280	May	2972
February	5737	June	3977
March	4101	July	6352
April	4425	August	4730

Well over half of these are in the Philadelphia
territory.

CURRENT PROGRAM
This office has made two recent additional
weekly mailings since September. We have received
50 interested replies from these to date and they
are now coming in at the rate of 5 to 8 per day.

A sample copy of the letter sent the veteran is
attached.

Surveillance

The following three documents not only provide glimpses
into two of the FBI's most common means of obtaining
information—personal visits and electronic surveillance

—but they also show how far the Bureau strays from its own ground rules. For example, at first glance the form that agents often ask the people they visit to sign appears to be "Advice of Rights." It is only after reading half-way down the page that a citizen learns he's signing a "Waiver of Rights." Similarly, the restrictions on electronic surveillance that are so carefully delineated in the Omnibus Crime Control document are totally ignored in the summary of one day's tapping of Black Panther phones.

The Waiver of Rights

```
         INTERROGATION; ADVICE OF RIGHTS
                  YOUR RIGHTS

                        Place....................
                        Date.....................
                        Time.....................
```

Before we ask you any questions, you must understand your rights.

You have the right to remain silent.

Anything you say can be used against you in court.

You have the right to talk to a lawyer for advice before we ask you any questions and to have him with you during questioning.

If you cannot afford a lawyer, one will be appointed for you before any questioning if you wish.

If you decide to answer questions now without a lawyer present, you will still have the right to stop answering at any time. You also have the right to stop answering at any time until you talk to a lawyer.

```
              WAIVER OF RIGHTS
```

I have read this statement of my rights and I understand what my rights are. I am willing to

make a statement and answer questions. I do not
want a lawyer at this time. I understand and
know what I am doing. No promises or threats have
been made to me and no pressure or coercion of
any kind has been used against me.

                    Signed...................
Witness:..................
Witness:..................
Time: ....

The rules of the game for electronic surveillance (elsur, in the
Bureau's jargon).

TO   : SAC (92-2315)   DATE: 9/17/69
FROM   : SA FRANCIS J. GAFFNEY
SUBJECT: OMNIBUS CRIME CONTROL AND
         SAFE STREETS ACT OF 1968

   The following outlines contain pertinent Bureau
instructions relating to application for and
procedures to be followed in the intercept of
Wire or Oral communications under the above
Act:

              SAC LETTER 68-39, 7/9/68
       "OMNIBUS CRIME CONTROL AND SAFE STREETS ACT
              OF 1968" PUBLIC LAW 90-351

Federal Court Order to Intercept Wire or Oral
Communications in Specific Categories of Crime
requires:
1. Authorization of the Attorney General or
   designated Assistant Attorney General for
   filing an application by the FBI or other
   Federal Law Enforcement agency to a Federal
   Judge.
2. The application shall:
   a. Identify the officer making the application
   b. Identify the officer who authorized it
   c. Give complete statement of facts and cir-

cumstances relied on by applicant, including:

1. details of offense which has been, is being or is about to be committed.
2. nature and location of place of interception.
3. Type of communication sought
4. Identity of person, if known, committing offense or whose communication is to be intercepted.

d. Applicant must state whether other investigative procedures have been tried and failed.
e. Period of time for which interception intended.
f. History of previous applications involving same facilities, place, or individuals.
g. The Judge may require applicant to furnish any other testimony or documentary evidence he believes necessary.

3. Judge may issue order authorizing surveillance:
   a. If he finds probable cause for belief that person is committing an enumerated offense.
   b. That communications concerning such offense will be obtained through such interception.
   c. That normal investigative procedures have been tried and failed.
   d. Reasonably appear to be unlikely to succeed if tried.
   e. To be too dangerous.
   f. That the facilities where the interception is to be made are used, about to be used, leased to or listed in the name of the person named in the application.

4. Similar provisions are made for issuance of such orders to the Attorney General of a State

or the principal attorney of a political subdivision of a State by a State judge of
competent jurisdiction.

5. Order authorizing interception of any wire or
oral communications may be issued for no longer
than 30 days, with extensions, as needed, upon
reapplication.

6. Emergency situations involving conspiratorial
activities which "threaten the national security or are characteristic of organized crime"
enable law enforcement to intercept without
court order if:
   a. there are grounds upon which an order
   could be obtained through prescribed
   application.
   b. In this case application must be made
   within 48 hours after emergency interception has commenced.

7. A permanent recording must be made of all
conversations intercepted pursuant to court
order and shall be sealed under directions of
the issuing judge.

8. In reasonable time but not later than 90 days
after termination of surveillance
   a. Judge shall cause to be served on individuals named in the order and on other
   parties to intercepted communications as
   judge may see fit
      1. An inventory including:
         a. Notice of existence of the order
         b. Date of entry
         c. Period Authorized
         d. Fact that during the period wire or
         oral communications were intercepted.
   b. On showing of good cause, judge may post-
   pone the serving of this inventory.

SAC LETTER 69–36, 7/1/69

Absolute necessity that true copies of the
original logs be made in connection with the

program of furnishing logs to the Department for
possible use in court proceedings.

There must be no deletions whatsoever of any
type markings which appear on the original
logs.

BUAIRTEL 7/2/69, captioned "ELECTRONIC
SURVEILLANCE UNDER TITLE III OF THE OMNIBUS
CRIME CONTROL AND SAFE STREETS ACT OF 1968"

During tenure of any electronic surveillance
the name of each individual directly covered,
monitored or mentioned must be included in the
special indices at Bureau and each office maintaining the surveillance.

Handled by—

3 x 5 plain blue index card containing:

"Name (Last Name First)

Source

BUfile

Direct Coverage (date)

Participant   (date)

Mentioned   (date)"

These cards must be submitted,

Attention: Special Investigative Division,
   Criminal Intelligence and Organized Crime
   Section, each Friday

Only one of last three items on card should
   be utilized.

Bureau requires one card on an individual monitored or mentioned.

If the individual was monitored or mentioned
   by more than one installation submit a separate card on each individual for each installation.

It is not necessary to list all dates on which
   an individual was monitored by a particular
   source only the first date.

If an index card has been sent to Bureau show—

ing individual mentioned and this person is
subsequently monitored by the same device an
index card showing this coverage must be
sent to the Bureau.

Each source will be identified by judicial
district where court order was approved
followed by a number starting with number 1
for the first order and following in sequence
with each subsequent order. (Example,
Ph EDPA 1).

Handle these sources on a strict need-to-basis.
Insure that appropriate administrative procedures are established for such handling.

All electronic surveillance logs must be
indexed in accordance with instructions
listed in Part II, Section 3, page 4, Manual
of Rules and Regulations.

SAC LETTER 69–43, 8/13/69

Tapes which clearly contain no evidence or
leads to evidence:

A. Need not be retained after they have served
needs of office

The Department has pointed out the following:

a. Frequently must disclose to court and
defense counsel recorded conversations of a
defendant to refute allegation relevant
information obtained through elsur.

b. Department suggested when individual being
monitored is known by monitoring personnel
or the Special Agent preparing summation of
the conversation to be subject in Federal
criminal case, the taped recording or a
verbatim transcript should be retained
whenever possible.

c. When individual becomes defendant in
Federal criminal case, every effort should
be made to avoid monitoring his conversations.

d. Effort must be made to avoid monitoring

any conversations of anyone serving as an attorney for a defendant in Federal criminal case.

1. Therefore, when elsur is operated in which Federal prosecution may be involved, monitoring should be conducted by a Special Agent or Special Employee.

2. <u>Monitoring personnel must be instructed in writing</u> that they must immediately cease monitoring, both in person and by electronic recording any conversation as soon as it becomes clear that any party is either a defendant or an attorney of a defendant in a Federal criminal case.

3. Efforts must be directed at surviving test of whether our approach not to monitor defendants or their attorneys was logical, reasonable, and practical.

4. Monitoring personnel, to comply with above, must be provided with a list of such defendants and their attorneys.

5. Monitoring personnel should be instructed to be alert not to monitor other individuals who are defendants or their attorneys, in other than the substantive case, when there is reasonable basis for the contention that it was general public knowledge that such persons were involved in Federal prosecutive action.

6. Monitors in the above situations are to make a note in the log that the conversation was cut off and was not overheard after identifying the name of the defendant or attorney which occasioned the cutoff.

7. Above procedure should be followed with conversation relating to defense strategy or tactics as soon as the subject matter becomes apparent. The same should be

followed when it may be reasonably expected calls will be received from
defendants or attorneys in current or
future prosecution.

8. If conversation of a defendant or one of
his attorneys should inadvertently be
overheard and later comes to attention of
a Special Agent, that SA shall immediately
seal the record of the conversation,
attach a memorandum certifying he has not
and will not orally or in writing relate
the substance to any other representative
of the Government or to anyone else except
on order from the Attorney General. The
sealed log and the SA's certification
should be immediately forwarded to the
Bureau.

Elsur logs should be confined to:
   a. Basic entries of dates.
   b. Basic entries of time.
   c. Identification of individual monitoring.
   d. Notification made that monitoring ceased
      when one of the parties was recognized as a
      defendant in Federal criminal case or an
      attorney of such individual.
   3. Identity of reel number and location of
      conversation on the reel.

Summations of contents of conversation are to
be prepared only by Special Agents after reviewing tapes, notes, and logs except when a foreign
language is involved. In such instances summations are to be prepared by personnel handling
the translation.

Indexing of names is to be made from the summation rather than from the logs.

Proper indexing has become increasingly significant so that individuals or cases with great
public interest will be identified even though
only a nickname is used and because of the

possibility of close scrutiny by news media and
general public when introduced into court.

```
1—92-2315
1—Supervisor #5
1—Each Special Agent and Resident Agent
    Assigned to Supervisor #5 (38)
1—Each Special Employee (5)

FJG:bjt
(45)
```

In subsequent federal cases, some of the crucial safeguards listed
in the Bureau's regulations were clearly abandoned. In the
Pentagon Papers trial, the Bureau tapped the phones of two
defense lawyers. The trivial details in the Panther tapes that
follow (the sort of thing that probably constitutes the fruits of
most of the FBI's electronic surveillance) dominate what few
particles of political activities exist in the tapes. Since not a
single one of the discussions even hints at an illegal activity, a
discriminating agency, one that heeded its own rules, would
almost certainly have followed the injunction in SAC letter
69-43, 8/13/69, which says, "Tapes which clearly contain no
evidence or leads to evidence need not be maintained after they
have served the needs of the office." Of course, that mandate can
be interpreted so broadly that an agent could retain a laundry
list for a decade because it might contain a description of a shirt
a potential criminal might wear on the night of his crime. The
Panther tapes that follow suggest that is the type of rule by which
the FBI plays the intelligence game.

```
TO      : SAC, PHILADELPHIA (157-2004)        DATE: 2/4/71
FROM    : SA RONALD D. BUTLER
SUBJECT: BLACK PANTHER PARTY
          RM
```

The following information was excerpted from
data furnished on 2/1/71, by PH 1209-R*. Any
dissemination of this information outside the
Bureau must be adequately paraphrased in order to
protect this highly sensitive source.
During a conversation between SANDRA [——] and
RUSSELL [——], RUSSELL mentioned there was no

heat in the office and said that they had no
money.

During a conversation between DELORES [——] and
RUSSELL, DELORES stated her baby was due in four
months.

RUSSELL reached EILEEN [——] and left a message
for her to tell SMITTY [——] to tell M. [——] to
be at staff meeting tonight.

A representative of Western Union called for
RUSSELL [——] advising they had a money order for
him to pick up.

SMITTY mentioned during the day that TINA [——]
had not been around the office for several days
and that someone should go see her. He then mentioned BOBBY [——] currently had the responsibility for the Liberation School.

S. of the Free Press called for D. T. who was
not in. S.[——] advised RUSSELL that during the
convention, he had rented a truck in his name
for D. T. and another brother to haul food from
New York and Philadelphia to the convention. He
stated the truck was not returned for two weeks,
and that his father had received a call from a
collection agency and was advised that $400 was
owed on the truck and the agency has a three-
state alarm out for S. at this time. S. stated
he had talked to D. T. and had been advised the
Party had paid $90 for full payment on the truck.
D. T. was to call S. at [phone number omitted].

DOC reached D. T. at [phone number omitted] and
related the above story. D. T. instructed DOC
to have S. bring the bills into the office and
stated that the Panthers would deal with them.
The subject of the conversation then turned to
TINA [——] and DOC stated that TINA claimed she
was being treated cruelly by the Party members.
D. T. said she should attend a meeting, discuss
her griefs, and then make up her mind whether
she was going to stay in the Party or get out.

D. T. then confided to DOC that he would like to move out of "this place." DOC stated he had "already made his move."

GERALDINE called WILLIAM [——] regarding the vehicle belonging to the BPP and was told that the car was a 1964 Chevrolet and that the engine had completely stopped running. [William] stated that they were thinking of getting a VW bus. GERALDINE then stated she had just talked to her friend who gets cars from sherrif's sales in New Jersey, and that he expected to have something in a couple of weeks. GERALDINE stated the friend who obtains the cars name is Carter, and it was learned that the disabled 1964 Chevrolet is parked at 36th and Haverford, but was going to be moved in front of the Party Headquarters. GERALDINE stated that Carter would pick up the car and that if he could repair it cheaply, he would give it back to the Party so they can have two cars if they got the VW bus.

LORRAINE (LNU), telephone [phone number omitted] called RUSSELL to advise West Catholic High for Girls is having a Black Workshop 2/6/71, from 9 A.M. to 1 P.M., in Room 206 at 45th and Chestnut. LORRAINE stated they would like a Panther to speak at the event. It was indicated someone from the BPP would call LORRAINE by 2/4/71 to confirm the speaking date.

During the conversation between HERMAN [——] and WILLIAM [——], HERMAN stated the Party had a five day extension to pay a phone bill of $363. It was indicated the telephone service would be discontinued if the bill were not paid.

HERMAN called an unknown female at [phone number omitted], and mentioned that he was filling out income tax forms. HERMAN stated he was considering filling out two reports under different names from that address.

RUSSELL [——] placed a collect call to Wheaton,

Ill., telephone [phone number omitted]. [Russell]
talked to LIBBY and then N. and advised them he
was leaving Philadelphia and should be in Chicago in two weeks. [Russell] asked his mother to
send him $17 to get home which she agreed to do.
[Russell's] mother then tried to convince him to
get out of the Black Panther Party although she
was unsuccessful.

P. [——] called the office just to find out
what had been happening and was advised a
People's Tribunal would be held sometime in
March and that a rally was scheduled for February
28, in honor of BOBBY SEALE. The location of
these events was unknown to RUSSELL at the present time. P. requested that he be furnished any
further information regarding the matter.

RUSSELL called the Greyhound Bus Terminal to
obtain scheduling information for a bus to
Pittsburgh and was told he could catch a bus at
either 6:30 or 8:30 P.M. tonight.

DOC called V. (female) at [phone number omitted]
to ask what was happening at her school and to
inquire about student unrest. V. stated there
was no unrest and that nothing was happening at
all. DOC then mentioned a meeting for parents
and students of all schools which was to be held
at the Church of the Advocate, 18th and Diamond,
on 2/3/71, at 7:30 P.M. It was indicated MUHAM-
MED KENYATTA was to be the speaker. This meeting
is to show the parents and students what's going
on in the schools.

During the conversation between DOC and SMITTY,
it was indicated PAT [——] would handle the
Breakfast Program 2/2/71 for the North Philadelphia section. SMITTY then commented that they
couldn't give PAT the keys to the building because she was merely a community worker. DOC then
asked if SMITTY's section had been successful in
obtaining stock and SMITTY stated he had received

16 reams of mimeograph paper. DOC instructed him to be sure that he hid the paper away from the office because there couldn't be any stock piling at any of the offices. SMITTY mentioned that the "pigs" were starting to get "uptight" and that "Pig" WINCHESTER had been sitting outside the office all weekend. DOC commented that this was good and stated they would have to keep the pressure on the "pigs."

M. called DOC to advise he couldn't be present at the meeting tonight and was instructed to write a resume and send it into the office. During the conversation between HERMAN and SMITTY, HERMAN mentioned the Party was going to cut down the telephone expenses by having the buzzer system removed because it was to expensive. SMITTY stated he had put a lock on the phone upstairs but would keep the phone because they would need it for the Doctor if and when they get one.

D. T. called HERMAN to advise the neighborhood was saturated with "pigs" and was asked by HERMAN if the "machinery" was all set up for such things. D. T. said the machinery was ready and that they had "everything going for them."

ACTION: <u>INDEX</u>

S.

The White Left

For the sake of clarity, we have divided eleven documents pertaining to the white left into two categories. The first group of four documents contains general directives. The second group of seven documents contains individual investigations.

GENERAL DIRECTIVES

This document, and the ones that follow, are particularly interesting in light of the Domestic Espionage Security Plan that White House aide Thomas Charles Huston proposed in the summer of 1970. This plan, which Hoover supposedly rejected, involved intelligence gathering by means of burglary and forgery.

The White House plan was accepted and then abandoned in July, 1970, about six weeks before "The New Left Notes" that follow were written. The "New Left conference at SOG 9/10-11/70" that the memorandum refers to was not a meeting of student radicals at Berkeley; it was a meeting of FBI personnel at the Seat of Government (SOG)—that is, in plain English, the FBI headquarters in Washington.

The sentence about increasing radical paranoia by promoting the idea that there's "an agent behind every mailbox" is the most famous passage in the documents. But the news that follows—that the Director had okayed the use of Potential Security Informants (PSIs) and Security Informants (SIs) between the ages of eighteen and twenty-one—is perhaps more important. Was it the intricate White House negotiations over the Huston plan, and fears about domestic security in general, that freed—or pressured—Hoover to countermand his previous practice?

NEW LEFT NOTES—PHILADELPHIA

9/16/70

Edition #1

This newsletter will be produced at irregular intervals as needed to keep those persons dealing with New Left problems up to date in an informal way. It is not a serial and is considered an informal routing slip. It should be given the security afforded a Bureau serial, classified confidential, but may be destroyed when original purpose is served.

The New Left conference at SOG 9/10-11/70 produced some comments:

In disseminating reports recommending for the SI it is preferable to designate and disseminate to Secret Service immediately and put the FD-376 (the buck slip to Secret Service) on the second Bureau copy.

There was a pretty general concensus that more interviews with these subjects and hangers—on are in order for plenty of reasons, chief of which are it will enhance the paranoia endemic in these circles and will further serve to get the point across there is an FBI Agent behind every mailbox. In addition, some will be over—come by the overwhelming personalities of the contacting agent and volunteer to tell all—per—haps on a continuing basis. The Director has okayed PSI's and SI's age 18 to 21. We have been blocked off from this critical age group in the past. Let us take advantages of this opportunity.

In payments to informants, if the total of services and expenses to an informant is less than $300 in a lump sum payment or per month, our request for such payment is handled within division 5. If the lump sum payment or monthly authorization is $300 or more, it must be approached on a much higher level. Note: If an informant is to travel outside our division and we initially go in and request expense payment of less than $300, it can be handled simply while the services payment can be requested later based on what he has produced.

A New Left Events Calendar will be maintained by Squad #4 secretary. When from reviewing

underground newspapers, calls from outsiders,
complaints or informants we know of a demonstration gathering, educational, or similar event
planned by a New Left group, it should be given
to SA DAVENPORT who will coordinate this calendar. He will log it with #4 secretary. This will
enable us to project ahead what manpower needs
we will have and enable us to answer all kinds of
queries about the date we know a particular event
is scheduled. It will correlate the knowledge
of all.

Again on the subject of informants, there have
been a few instances where security informants in
the New Left got carried away during a demonstration, assaulted police, etc. The key word in
informants, according to Bureau supervision, is
"control." They define this to mean that while
our informants should be privy to everything
going on and should rise to the maximum level of
their ability in the New Left Movement, they
should not become the person who carries the
gun, throws the bomb, does the robbery or by
some specific violative, overt act becomes a
deeply involved participant. This is a judgment
area and any actions which seem to border on it
should be discussed.

"Armed and Dangerous." Remember that every case
which bears the Weatherman word in the caption
must include the armed and dangerous warning in
each communication just as armed and dangerous
is carried in criminal cases.

Anti-Riot Law on 176 classification matters are
now handled on desk #4. If they are racial in
nature, they will continue to be handled on #9
desk. The basic legal statutes for them are Title
18, Sections 231, 245, and 2101. The Manual of
Instructions should be referred to on this topic.

There are about 30 fugitive cases under investigation in this division where the basic

violation grew out of New Left activity. Most
are assigned to one agent. They will be re-
assigned in the near future so that each agent
on Squad #4 will have about two of these cases.
The

[remainder of document not available]

A memorandum on the difference between the New Left and
the Old Left.

```
TO      : DESIGNATED EMPLOYEES              DATE: 9/16/70
FROM    : SAC
SUBJECT: SECURITY INVESTIGATIONS
          OF INDIVIDUALS & ORGANIZATIONS
```

During the recent inspection this office was
instructed to separate security matter supervision to create a "New Left" and an "Old Left"
desk.

Squad #3 was designated to be the "Old Left"
desk. While retaining espionage and foreign
intelligence matters, it will handle the investigations of all organizations and individuals who
fall in the "Old Left" category. Generally, "Old
Left" means the Communist Party and the various
splinter and Trotskyite groups which have been
in existence for many years. The youth groups
and satellites of the Communist Party and these
splinter groups are also to be handled in the
"Old Left" category and on Squad #3.

Squad #4 was designated to handle "New Left"
matters which includes both organizations and
individuals. This is a relatively broad term
insofar as newly formed organizations with
leftist or anarchistic connotations. Among other
things, desk #4 will be responsible for such
matters as SDS, STAG, underground newspapers,
communes, commune investigations, the Resistance.

It is not contemplated that such organizations
as the Women's International League for Peace
and Freedom, SANE, AFSC, etc., which have long
been in existence and are now attempting to
polarize themselves toward revolting youth will
be considered within the investigative purview
of "New Left." To include such organizations
would defeat the purpose of setting up a flexible
activist group designed to deal with violent
and terroristic minded young anarchists.

1—100-49107   1—Each Supervisor (10)
1—Each SRA (Circulate within RA)   1—Night Supervisor
1—Squad #4 (16)

JDJ:rel
(44)

This document, which instructs Resident Agents to keep an eye
on all Philadelphia-area colleges and universities, is evidently
another response to the "Seat of Government" New Left meeting that had been held two weeks earlier. Its author, Special
Agent William Anderson, apparently took his own message
quite seriously. At about that time, the nearby field office in
Lewisburg, Pennsylvania, which kept in touch with activities
at Bucknell College, would begin to let Boyd Douglas serve as
the catalyst for discussions that, in December, 1970, would lead
J. Edgar Hoover to tell the House Appropriations Committee
there was a "plot by the Berrigan brothers" to kidnap Henry
Kissinger. At the trial of the Harrisburg 7, Anderson sat in court
each day, behind the government lawyers, taking notes on each
bit of testimony. Defendants and their lawyers were convinced
that he intended to relay all names of resisters and all details
about their relationships and operations to the "Seat of Government," as the FBI calls its headquarters in Washington. Anderson also conducted the investigation of the Camden 28; in that
case, Robert Hardy has admitted to having been encouraged by
the FBI to serve as a provocateur.

Special Agent John Morris, who was supposed to coordinate

the information about colleges and universities, also put in an appearance at the Harrisburg trial. He testified that, acting as an agent, he had made a tape recording of a defendant's press conference (an act that clearly infringes on freedom of the press. in order to have voice identifications of the people on trial.

At first glance, the document seems quite ambitious in its demands. It assigns some eighteen agents to keep an eye on sixty-nine schools with a combined enrollment of more than 140,000 students. (To save space, we have cut from the document the lists of the agents, the schools, and the size of their enrollment.) Anderson sounds as if he's responding to intense pressure when he demands that the agents produce "facts, not double talk." In the context of this memorandum and in light of the intense concern for effective domestic espionage measures that must have dominated discussions between the White House, FBI, and Justice Department at the time, it is hard to know whether his injunction that "We have a job to do and cannot get where we are going until we know where we are" is the sort of Knute Rockne talk that often comes from a gung-ho bureaucrat, or whether it refers to specific plans that arose out of meetings like the New Left Conference at the SOG.

Anderson is not asking the agents to set up a new apparatus. He is trying to find a way to make sure the established apparatus is functioning smoothly now that student agitation has become a distinct threat.

The memorandum lists seventy-six categories under which agents should file information about the schools and assigns each category its own file number. The majority of them, under the headings "Students for a Democratic Society" and "Student Agitation," bear the names of Philadelphia-area universities. Other categories, under the heading "New Left Movement," include Communist influence, publications, violence, religion, race relations, factionalism, mass media, and student disorders.

Apparently, some colleges were reluctant to cooperate with the Bureau. That is probably why Anderson not only asks for the identity of a campus figure who can provide "*advanced* information" on student agitation, but also asks for "lists of what information of Bureau interest cannot be obtained from the University or college."

TO   : SAC (100-50538)   DATE: 9/23/70
FROM   : SA WILLIAM B. ANDERSON, JR.
SUBJECT: STAG

Each Resident Agent for whom a copy of this
memo is designated has received a copy of Bureau
letter to all offices dated 8/28/70 including
the above title.

There follows a listing by Resident Agents of
colleges and universities in the area covered by
his Resident Agency with the enrollment according
to latest available figures.

[List of agents, schools, and school enroll-
ments omitted]

Each Resident Agent provide Coordinator JOHN
C. F. MORRIS of Squad #4, the following information by 10/1/70:

(1) current number of university, or college,
sources on the academic or administrative staff
including security officers broken down under
those categories.

(2) number of current student security informants or PSIs.

(3) any other current sources for information
re student agitation (by position or agency).

(4) identity (i.e., professor, police officer,
student) of any of the above who can provide you
with advanced information on student agitation.

(5) listing of what information of Bureau
interest cannot be obtained from the university
or college (not limited to STAG).

(6) brief outline of steps you propose to increase, strengthen and improve your coverage
with respect to STAG.

I want facts, not double talk. This information
is not for statistical purposes or to measure
RA accomplishments. We have a job to do and
cannot get where we are going until we know
where we are. With the data from the respective
RAs in hand, we can see where we are and go
from there.

Furnish the requested information in any legible form, informally referring to this memo and keying your answers to the above numbers. Each university or college should be listed separately.

There are some institutions of higher learning within areas covered by some RAs where there has been no student agitation and where none is to be expected. Where this is the case, so state without belaboring the six points, except for #5. This should be commented upon based on your present knowledge.

[penned in here was a note to "subscribe to each newspaper to confidential P.O. Box in Philadelphia."]

STUDENTS FOR A DEMOCRATIC SOCIETY

100-46556	SDS
100-46556-Sub A	NEWSPAPER CLIPPINGS
[list of schools deleted]	
100-46556-Sub O	FUNDS
100-46556-Sub P	PUBLICATIONS
100-46556-Sub Q	ROSEMONT
100-46556-Sub R	WEATHERMAN
100-46556-Sub S	TELEPHONE & LICENSE TAG CHECKS

NEW LEFT MOVEMENT

100-50241	NEW LEFT MOVEMENT (CONTROL)
100-50314	ORGANIZATIONS
100-50315	MEMBERSHIP
100-50316	FINANCES
100-50317	COMMUNIST INFLUENCE
100-50318	PUBLICATIONS
100-50319	VIOLENCE
100-50320	RELIGION
100-50321	RACE RELATIONS
100-50322	POLITICAL ACTIVITIES
100-50323	IDEOLOGY
100-50324	EDUCATION
100-50325	SOCIAL REFORM

```
100-50326          LABOR
100-50327          PUBLIC APPEARANCE OF LEADERS
100-50328          FACTIONALISM
100-50329          SECURITY MEASURES
100-50330          FOREIGN INFLUENCE (INTER-
                      NATIONAL RELATIONS)
100-50331          MASS MEDIA
100-50332          KEY ACTIVISTS
100-50538          STUDENT AGITATION
100-51890          MENTAL DISORDERS
[list of schools omitted]

1—100-50538
1—Each SRA (17)
WBA:ds
(18)
```

The next document shows that the national FBI wanted to
encourage college administrators to move against the "New
Left." The following routing slip was attached to a reprint from
Barrons magazine. It presented a right-wing interpretation of
events at Columbia University in the spring of 1968 and was
titled; "Campus or Battleground? Columbia is a Warning to All
American Universities." Note that the Bureau wanted the reprints mailed *anonymously* to college administrators in the
area. The article appeared in the May 20, 1968, issue of *Barrons,*
a Dow Jones publication.

```
Date ____8/9/68_____


Routing Slip
FD-4 (Rev. 4-28-69)
To:
□Director                    FILE _____100-49929_____
Att.:_____
□SA _____        Title _____
□ASAC_____         _COINTELPRO—NEW LEFT_
□Supv._____
□Agent_Tom Lewis____        _____
□SE_____         _____
□IC_____
                            RE:_____
```

☐CC_____
☐Steno_____
☐Clerk_____   ☐Rotor #:_____
ACTION DESIRED
☐Acknowledge   ☐Open Case
☐Assign___Reassign___ ☐Prepare lead cards
☐Bring file   ☐Prepare tickler
☐Call me   ☐Return assignment card
☐Correct   ☐Return file
☐Deadline_____ ☐Search and return
☐Deadline passed   ☐See me
☐Delinquent   ☐Serial #_____
☐Discontinue   ☐Post ☐Recharge ☐Return
☐Expedite   ☐Send to_____
☐File   ☐Submit new charge out
☐For information   ☐Submit report by_____
☐Handle   ☐Type
☐Initial & return
☐Leads need attention
☐Return with explanation or notation as to
   action taken.
Bureau has suggested attached reprints be fur-
nished to educators and administrators who are
established sources. It may be mailed anonymously
to college educators who have shown a reluctance
to take decisive action against the "New Left".
Positive results or comments by recipients should
be furnished to the Bureau. Let me know of
disposition, and any results.
                             SAC E. E. Sussman_____
_____See reverse side   Office_____

Tom: Can you handle Swarthmore, Haverford,
Villanova.

INDIVIDUAL INVESTIGATIONS

These documents, which are all specific case studies,
suggest some of the questions the Bureau asks as it pro-

ceeds with its investigations, some of the information it
chooses to record, and the flat, dull tone agents are trained
to write in. The documents also show the nature of the
subjects the Bureau examines and the speed with which
it sees minor left-wing activities or snatches of political
gossip as clues to potential subversive activities.

For example, a document we are summarizing rather
than including concerns the Women's International
League of Peace and Freedom (WILPF), an organization
cofounded by Jane Addams, whose membership consists
mainly of women who joined it in the 1940s and 1950s.
The report deals with an occasion on which WILPF had
invited Martin Luther King to speak at its fiftieth anniver-
sary banquet. The event took place at the Bellevue-
Stratford hotel in Philadelphia, and it was advertised
publicly. Yet the FBI relied on informer PH 27–S, who
has "furnished reliable information in the past," to tell
them that the dinner would be held. PH 27–S also obtained and passed on a copy of *Four Lights*, a WILPF
publication, which listed nominees for the organization's
national board. The Bureau included the names of the
women nominees in its report, which went to seventy
agents in thirty-eight American cities. The report also
went into the files of nine individual WILPF members,
into a file devoted to WILPF as an organization, and into
Martin Luther King's file.

We have included here the full texts of seven reports in
order to convey their flavor. As ex-agent Robert Wall's
essay in Section III suggests, the humorless, plodding
prose style is central to the FBI's technique of keeping its
employees obedient and disciplined, since it prompts
them to submerge the meaning of what they're doing in a
welter of meaningless details.

This document shows how the Bureau based a full-scale investigation of a Berkeley coed on a single allegation by a Washington,

D.C. "source" (WR 1577–S, whose code name appears at the bottom of the document, under the category "Leads") that she is "an inveterate Marxist revolutionist," "is far out," and "should be watched."

There is no indication that the Bureau evaluated WF 1577–S, whose information was eventually contradicted by every other acquaintance of the coed whom agents questioned. But there is every indication that the Bureau not only watched the coed, but also traced her from an eastern women's college to Berkeley.

Agents asked registrars at both schools about her enrollment records; they looked in the Scranton, Pennsylvania, phone book and the Berkeley phone book to establish her residence; they asked an FBI agent and two police officers if she had a criminal record. Those are usual sources. But the FBI investigation also took an unusual turn when the coed was discussed with a source on the selection committee of the Venceremos Brigade, which sent young Americans to do agricultural work in Cuba.

The Security Index, where the coed's name might have appeared if the Bureau had found anyone to corroborate WF 1577's story, is a list of the Americans whom the Bureau finds most threatening.

```
TO      : DIRECTOR, FBI
FROM    : SAC, PHILADELPHIA (100-52244) (P)
SUBJECT: JANE [——]
          SM—
```

Re Bureau Letter to San Francisco 12/9/70
Referenced letter requested Philadelphia to conduct security investigation relating to the subject.

Information developed through reliable sources indicated subject transferred from [eastern women's college] to the University of California, Berkeley, Calif. Subject's home address is listed as [address omitted] Scranton, Pa. In reference to the Scranton, Pa., area, the telephone directory noted that a JIM [same last name] resides at [same address omitted] telephone [omitted].

On 1/11/71 [name omitted] Registrar, [eastern

women's college] (protect identity by request),
advised SA JAMES E. O'CONNOR that she was unable
to locate any record pertaining to JANE as a
present or former student at the college.

Philadelphia indices are negative re subject
and JIM [same last name].

Philadelphia continuing investigation in
Scranton, Pa.

On 2/1/71, [administrative employee name
omitted], UCB, advised his files indicate JANE
[——] was admitted to the University of California at Berkeley in the month of March, 1970, and
as of the period ending December, 1970, had
completed to quarters in the College of Letters
and Science. Her chief subject of study is listed
as Greek. Due to the policy at UCB, no additional
information regarding the Subject can be released
without the written release submitted by the
Subject or the issuance of a subpoena duces
tecum.

San Francisco indices reflect Subject attended
a meeting of the Venceremos Brigade on 7/20/70,
at 23rd Avenue and 14th Street, Oakland, California. This meeting was covered by SF 2231-S
(reliable–protect) who stated Subject was one of
numerous individuals turned down on their applications to be members of the Fourth Contingent
of the Venceremos Brigade. During this meeting,
there was no discussion of violence or revolution. San Francisco source personally conversed
with Subject and received no indication that she
was anything other than the average liberal
minded student that is common in the Berkeley
area.

On 2/5/71, SF 3427-PSI, who is familiar with
radical activities in the East Bay Area, advised
Subject is completely unknown to him.

Due to lack of information and activities of
Subject, San Francisco is not submitting a
summary report at this time. Subject is not being

recommended for inclusion on the Security Index
as it is felt additional investigation is
acquired before this evaluation can be reached.
LEADS:
<u>WASHINGTON FIELD</u>
    <u>AT WASHINGTON, D.C.</u>: Will recontact WF 1577-S
and determine the precise reasons that this
source stated Subject "is an inveterate Marxist
revolutionist" . . . "is far out" . . . and
"should be watched".

2—Bureau
2—San Francisco
2—Philadelphia (100-52244)
JEC
(6)

Another alert: friends of a Boston bank robber (identified in the
FBI's code phrase "GILROB") may visit a Swarthmore professor they once knew. A college switchboard operator, the campus
police, and a postman are all questioned.

TO   : SAC (91-7264) P.   DATE: 11/13/70
FROM   : SA THOMAS F. LEWIS
SUBJECT: GILROB
           Re BS tel 11/11/70

    Referenced communication set forth information
from a Boston informant who furnished information
to the effect that MR. and MRS. DANIEL BENNETT,
[address omitted], Swarthmore, Pa. might have
some contact with the subjects.
    On 11/12/70 [name omitted], Security Officer,
Swarthmore College, Swarthmore, Pa. advised that
DANIEL BENNETT is a Professor of Phiosophy at
that School and in charge of the Philosophy
Department. He has been there about three years
having previously taught at University of Mass.
MRS. BENNETT is not employed and there are two
small children in the family ages about 8 to 12
years.
    The BENNETTs reside in a semi—detached house
located near [the security officer's] residence

although he does not have any social contact with
them. [The Security officer] has noted that there
does not appear to be anyone other than the
BENNETTs residing at their home but that numerous college students visit there frequently.
BENNETT drives a two tone blue, VW station
wagon, bearing Penna. license 5V0245. There are
no other cars in the family and no other cars
normally parked in their driveway.

[The Security officer] was funished with the
wanted flyers on the subjects and he stated he
would remain alert in his neighborhood for their
possible appearance. Also he will alert his
sources at the college for any information about
the subjects particularly any information that
subjects might be in contact with the BENNETTS.

On 11/12/70 [name omitted], Switchboard Operator, Swarthmore College, Swarthmore, Pa. (conceal
identity due to position at school) advised she
has only limited contact with BENNETT who she is
aware is in the Philosophy Department there.

She stated that BENNETT been the subject of
criticism by the school administration since he
has taken on himself without clearing with others
the responsibility of inviting controversial
speakers to the school. In early October 1970,
BENNETT invited REGGIE [——] of the BPP to talk
on campus and he did not clear this invitation
with the school administration before hand. As a
result the administration felt they received
undue adverse publicity over [Reggie's] appearance.

BENNETT also has conducted Philosophy discussion groups on the topics of political and social
Philosophy which are supposedly open to the
public and this action has not been approved by
the school administration although it is regarded
as action on his part over and beyond his authority in altering the course curriculum.

[The switchboard operator] stated BENNETT is

generally regarded as a "radical" for this and similiar type action.

[She] was shown the wanted flyers on the subjects and she stated she is certain she has not seen them around that school. She will remain alert for any information concerning them.

[She] will also confidentially furnish pertinent information regarding any long distance telephone calls made or received by BENNETT. She checked her slips for long distance calls made from the college for the past month and noted that none were listed as being made by BENNETT.

CHIEF [name omitted], Swarthmore P. D., was contacted in this matter and shown wanted flyers on the subjects. He stated that these did not look familiar and he does not recall having seen them at or around the BENNETT residence. He noted that the BENNETT's live 2 houses away from him and that his house is situated such that he can oberve the BENNETT residence from the front of his house. He said he is certain that no one other that the BENNETTs reside at this residence although a number of Swarthmore College students visit there frequently. He recalled that during the past summer the BENNETTs held a "rock festival" in their back yard attended by more than 50 college age youngsters. The Chief was required to break this up when it got too loud but this is the only occasion he has had to contact the BENNETTs in police business.

The Chief noted that the garage to the rear of the BENNETT residence has been converted into a printing shop and it houses enough equipment to publish a newspaper. He does not know that a newspaper is published there but he is keeping a close eye on the garage to ascertain what activity takes place there. He said a leaflet was printed there several months ago and that this leaflet called for support for the Black Panthers scheduled for trial in Phila. in October 1970.

The Chief is certain that no one lives in the garage but he has seen "hippie types" frequent the garage. He will remain especially alert for the appearance of the subjects and he will contact his sources and alert them concerning the subjects.

On 11/20/70 [name omitted], [post office employee], U. S. Post Office, Swarthmore, Pa. was contacted in this matter. He was furnished copies of wanted flyers on the subjects and requested to contact his carriers to alert them as to the appearance of the subjects in Swarthmore. [Post office employee] also stated that contact with the carrier who handles the BENNETT residence on South Princeton Ave. reveals that he has no recollection of mail coming to that residence addressed to other than the BENNETTs. Also this carrier is certain that no one other than the BENNETTs reside there.

[Post office employee] stated he would remain alert as to any mail to or from the BENNETT residence which might be significant in this case.

91-7264-295

TFL/tfl
(2)

A Swarthmore administrative employee helps the FBI obtain background information on a student who happens to be a congressman's daughter. (Nothing in the text suggests any reason for the investigation.)


```
TO      : DIRECTOR, FBI                    DATE: 11/19/70
FROM    : SAC, PHILADELPHIA (100-51799)
SUBJECT: JACQUELINE REUSS
          INFORMATION CONCERNING—
          SECURITY MATTER
```

Re Bureau airtels to Alexandria, Et Al, 10/23/70 and 11/12/70.

[Name omitted], [administrative employee],
Swarthmore College, Swarthmore, Pa., an established source who requests that her identity be
protected, on 11/17/70 advised the [college
files] indicate that one JACQUELINE REUSS was
born 10/15/49 at Paris, France, and is an American citizen. She listed her residence as 470
North Street, Southwest, Washington, D. C.,
20024. She listed her father as HENRY S. REUSS
and her mother as MARGARET MAGRATH REUSS, same
address as mentioned above. The records indicated
that she graduated in June 1967 from the Sidwell
Friends School, Washington, D. C., and started
at Swarthmore College as a freshman in September
1967. The records indicated that during the
spring semester of 1969 she attended the Aix-
Marseilles, Avignon, France. The following two
semesters she attended the Parix-X in Nanterre,
France. She subsequently returned to Swarthmore
College in September 1970 where she presently is
attending school. Her major is French and has
many courses in the liberal arts field. Her
residence while attending Swarthmore College is
listed as 905 South 47th Street, Philadelphia,
Pa. It was noted that in June 1969 she requested
a transcript of her credits be sent to the University of Wisconsin.

100-51799-5

2—Bureau (RM)
1—Alexandria (RM)   2—WFO (RM)
1—Milwaukee (RM)   2—Philadelphia (100-51799)

JLO:tac
(8)

A young woman is being investigated because of her membership in the Young Socialist Alliance. A local agent telephones
her parents, pretending to be a friend passing through town, and
extracts some information about her.

TO   : SAC, CINCINNATI (100-18919)   DATE:
FROM   : SAC, PHILADELPHIA (100-51777) (P)
SUBJECT: VIRGINIA [——]
          SM—YSA

Re: Cincinnati letters dated 9-25-70 and
11-18-70.

Mrs. [name and position omitted], Chester Credit
Bureau, Inc., Chester, Pa., which covers Drexel
Hill, Pa., on 11-20-70 advised the files of that
office indicated no record of the subject.

Detective WILLIAM GORDAN, Police Department,
Upper Darby, Pa., on 11-20-70 advised the files
of that office indicated no record of the subject.

A pretext telephone call (pretext of a friend
passing through Philadelphia, Pa.) was made to
the residence of of subject on 11-20-70 by SA
JAMES L. O'CONNOR. Subject's mother informed that
subject is presently working as a receptionist at
[name, address, phone, omitted]. She further
advised that captioned subject had majored in
journalism while at Ohio University and was
scheduled to graduate in June of 1970 but learned
that she was one credit short for the require-
ments for a degree.

LEADS:

Cincinnati Division
   At Athens, Ohio

Will review records at the School of Journalism
for background information regarding subject and
conduct pertinent investigation as set forth in
referenced letters.

Philadelphia Division
   At Philadelphia, Pa.

Will contact established sources and informants
for background information relative to subject.

2—Cincinnati (100-18919) (RM)
2—Philadelphia (100-51777)
JLO/
(4)

An informer reports on a meeting of the Philadelphia Labor
Committee that he attended. (The informer's identity isn't
suggested anywhere in the text.)

```
TO      :  SAC (100-46556)                      DATE: 9/24/70
FROM    :  SA JOHN T. BLAIR
SUBJECT:  PHILADELPHIA LABOR COMMITTEE
          IS—SDS
```

On 9/1/70, PH 948-S advised that on Friday
evening, 8/28/70, he had visited the residence
of JOSEPH [B.] [name abbreviated, address omitted].
He added that ANITA [——], a member of the
Philadelphia Labor Committee, had advised him
that a meeting of the Labor Committee was to be
held that evening at [place omitted]. Upon arriving, informant discovered that the meeting was
to be held on 9/1; however, he was invited to sit
and talk awhile with those present. Present was
one (FNU) BENNETT and [Mr. H.] and wife and also
DAN [——]. BENNETT, like [Mr. H.], is reportedly
an instructor or professor at Swarthmore College
and [Dan] is supposed to be a student at Swarthmore. All individuals were sitting around discussing the coming Black Panther Party Conference and smoking marijuana.

A meeting of the Women's Liberation group was
being held in another room and there appeared to
be approximately eight females participating in
this meeting including REBECCA [B.], who kept
going in and out of the meeting to attend her
small child who was in the kitchen. A number of
other rather hippie-type individuals were observed coming and going from the upper floors and
it would appear that the three-story house is
being operated as a commune.

From statements made by JOSEPH [B.], [Mr. H.],
BENNETT, etc., it would appear that they consider
themselves "intellectual revolutionaries," but

are not organizational types and not personally
activists.
ACTION: Open and Assign New 100 case on [B.]
Commune, [same address omitted].

                                              100-51883-2
9—Philadelphia   1—100-51271 [Mr. H.]
1—100-46556   1—100-51892 (Dan [——])
1—100-51492 (JOSEPH B.)   1—100-51132 (WOMEN'S
1—100-51883 (FNU BENNETT)   LIBERATION)
1—100 [B.] Commune, [same   1—100—Dead (REBECCA [B.])
      address]   1—134-1707 Sub A (PH 948-S)

JTB:btp
(9)

This document, which was written on June 7, 1968, describes
a demonstration held two months earlier protesting research
for weapons used in Vietnam. According to this portion of the
report, only 100 people attended and no incidents occurred.
Yet if you add the members of the civil disobedience team to the
number of policewomen and police officials on the scene, you
discover that the event provided an afternoon's work for twenty-
two law enforcement officers. There were seven cars on the
scene, including one communications car. And the list of names
at the bottom of the document shows that the heavy surveillance
paid off in fresh material for the dossiers of ten people and two
organizations.

TO   : SAC (100-49715)   DATE: 6/7/68
FROM   : SA WILLIAMS S. BETTS
SUBJECT: TEN DAYS OF PROTEST AND RESISTANCE,
         APRIL 21-30, 1968
         INFORMATION CONCERNING (IS)

    On May 1, 1968, Lt. GEORGE FENCL, Civil Dis-
obedience Unit, Philadelphia Police Department,
Philadelphia, PA., furnished to SA JOHN R.
WINEBERG a copy of a Civil Disobedience report
dated April 26, 1968, concerning the demonstration that date sponsored by SDS. A copy of this
item is attached for disemination to individual
files.
    Information previously reported to the Bureau
in LHM dated May 10, 1968.

Friday, April 26, 1968
34th & Market Street
(N.W. CORNER)

CIVIL DISOBEDIENCE TEAM

a.
Plcmn. J. DEVINE #2194   Plcmn. R. BAGLEY #4788
Plcmn. H. NEMETH #5052   Plcmn. R. VAUSE #4690
Plcmn. R. PAUL #6963   Plcmn. W. GRAVES #4263
Plcmn. J. GRIMES #3722   Plcmn. M. PALMER #6008
Plcmn. C. WARREN #2134   Plcmn. W. CURTIS #3696
Plcmn. P. MAGNER #2906   Plcmn. T. THOMPSON #2011
Plcmn. H. SHEPPARD #3387   Plcmn. D. LOGUE #2317
Plcmn. J. CRESSI #1813   Plcmn. L. FARRELL #1498
DET. J. CASON #717   DET. S. JEFFERSON #917
b.POLICEWOMEN: SGT. M. GRAHAM #480
                PW. S. ROBINSON #6550
c.Photographers: PHOTO'S TAKEN.
d.Police officials on the scene: Lieutenant FENCL
  #86 & SGT. GRAHAM #480
e.Cars assigned to detail: #C-7(Communications)
                            #C-4-#C-6-#C-10-
                            #C-12-#C-1-#D-27

ACTIVATED:
a. Activated, Friday April 26, 1968 1:35PM
b. Activated by Lieutenant FENCL #86 & SGT. M.
   GRAHAM #480 Civil Disobedience Unit.
c. Location of assignment: (N.W. Corner) 34th &
   Market Street
DEMONSTRATORS:

a. Name of organization: "S.D.S."
b. Reason for demonstration: Protesting research
   for weapons being used in VIETNAM
c. Demonstration leader: William DAVIDON (Coordinator)
d. There were (100) demonstrators and no spectators at the highest count taken.
e. Identification of demonstrators: WILLIAM

DAVIDON–V.F.P. (Coordinator), Stanly [——]
S.D.S., K. [——] C.N.V.A., Daniel [——]
C.N.V.A., Dr. Robert [——] "SANE", Daniel
[——] P.A.D.U., Steven [——] S.D.S. & D.L.C.

SIGNS
a. "SCIENCE IS FOR HELPING PEOPLE NOT REMOVING
   THEM IN VIETNAM OR WEST PHILADELPHIA"

INCIDENTS
a. There were no incidents during the course of
   this demonstration
b. F.B.I. notified, and also Police radio.
c. The handling of this detail was under the
   direct supervision of Lieutenant FENCL #86
   Civil Disobedience Unit.

PRESS–TV–RADIO COVERAGE
a. WCAU–TV–[name omitted]

DEACTIVATED:
a. Deactivated on Friday, April 26, 1968 4:25 PM
b. Deactivated by Lieutenant FENCL #86 CD.

FUTURE PLANS ASCERTAINED
a. On Thursday, May 2, 1968 S.D.S. will have a
   meeting at 3406 Baring Street, Time Unknown
   at this time.

13—Philadelphia
1—100-49715
1—100-48700 (PHILADELPHIA
  MOBILIZATION COMMITTEE)
1—100-46556 (SDS)
1—100-38658 (WILLIAM [——])
1—100-49158 (STEVE [——])
1—100-49938 (MIKE [——])

1—100-48980 (DAN [——])
1—100-35526 (ROBERT [——])
1—100-48755 (STEVE [——])
1—100-39330 (DAN [-,--])
1—100-Dead (STANLEY [——])
1—100-Dead (BILL [——])
1—100-Dead (CATHY [——])

WSB/hn   100-5607-1
(13)

The instruction this memorandum gives—having informants
attend a conference of War Resisters International—is echoed
on the distribution list at the bottom of the document. There,
the parentheses after the Special Agent's name—PH and then
a number—relate to specific informers whom the agent is

"handling," in the Bureau's terminology. The informer Tatman, whose name appears next to Special Agent Carter's name, appeared at last year's Princeton Conference on the FBI, where he described his work.

```
TO      : SAC (100-50737)                    DATE: 8/1/69
FROM    : SA THOMAS F. LEWIS
SUBJECT: CONFERENCE OF WAR RESISTERS,
          INTERNATIONAL, HAVERFORD COLLEGE,
          HAVERFORD, PA., 8/25-31/69
          IS—MISCELLANEOUS
```

By letter dated 7/18/69, Bureau instructed this office determine events connected with captioned conference in view of current international situation and the Paris Peace Talks.

Through established sources only make inquiry concerning this conference to determine its scope and whether or not there are any indications it will generate any anti-U.S. propaganda. <u>Be most discreet</u> in handling this matter.

Each Agent and SRA receiving this memo should discreetly contact appropriate sources and informants in line with Bureau instructions. Efforts should be made to have informants and sources attend the conference.

Submit results to #3 Supervisor by 8/22/69.

```
1—100-50737                         1—SA BREMER (PH 345-S)
1—Each SRA (14)                        (PH 506-S)
1—SA DURHAM (PH 216-S)              1—SA M.P. SMITH (PH 241-S)
    (PH 481-S) (PH 480-S)              (PH 575-S) (PH 931-S)
1—SA CARTER (PH 23-S) (TATMAN)1—SA WALSH [name omitted]
1—SA UZZELL (PH 27-S)               1—SA DOYLE (PH 398-S)
1—SA WYLAND (PH 61-S)                  (PH 431-S) (PH 1001-S)
1—SA E.A. SMITH (PH 210-S)          1—SA SNODGRASS (PH 460-S)
1—SA PIERCE (PH 55-S)               1—SA DAVENPORT (PH 469-S)
1—SA BLAIR (PH 306-S)
```

```
TFL:MS
(28)
```

Espionage

These cases show how casual contact between ordinary American citizens and Communist countries can trigger the FBI's xenophobic fears of subversion. Like some of the case studies in the third section of this book, many of those cited here may seem ludicrous at first glance. For reasons of space we have summarized several of the documents which show this, and we reprint only one in full.

In one of them, a Pennsylvania family invited a Czech folklorist to visit the United States. Once the FBI learned of this, it began to investigate the family. "PH T-L, who has furnished reliable information in the past," reports that the husband was a member of the Fair Play for Cuba Committee. The FBI also learned that the husband and wife belonged to the Society of Friends, that the husband had attended some pro-Loyalist meetings during the Spanish Civil War, and that he once wrote a letter to the Yugoslav tourist agency in New York that was handled by a man whom a defector later identified as a Yugoslav intelligence operative.

A car with a Philadelphia license plate visited the Soviet Consular office in Washington, D. C. An agent in the Philadelphia office was able to identify photos of the car's occupant, and he reported his success to the Director, Washington, D.C.

A scout leader in Moscow, Idaho, wrote a letter to the Soviet Embassy in Washington asking to be "put in touch with a Komsomol group with a similar interest to ours, and to meet Soviet youths on a person to person basis, if we possibly could." The letter was found in the Media files. Its author later told reporters that he never showed it to the Bureau. It is unclear how the FBI obtained it.

Each of these cases means an expanding file in the "Seat of Government" and years of random surveillance. At some point, having his name in a file could cost a person an important reference or even a job. But until the Media documents were examined, few people outside the Bureau understood how little material basis was needed for an investigation to begin.

Jonathan Shore, a Philadelphian, visits East Germany. The Bureau investigates, using two informants, a passenger representative for KLM, and an employee of the U.S. Army Operations and Research Detachment in Frankfurt. These documents show that PM–T–1, an army employee, routinely opened Shore's mail to obtain information.

In order to conceal such surveillance, the Bureau classified one document "Secret," and to be sure the East German and other powers remained ignorant, it added "No Foreign Dissemination." Even foreign agents with "Secret" clearance were not to be shown this one.

```
DIRECTOR, FBI (105-205033)               11/30/70
SAC, PHILADELPHIA (105-17903) -P-
NORMAN JON SHORE, aka
Jacobus Johannes Avram Norman Shore (TN)
IS—EG
(OO-PH)
```

Re letters from Legal Attache, Bonn Germany, to Bureau, dated 4/6/70, 6/5/70, 7/14/70, 8/14/70, and 10/12/70.

Enclosed herewith for Bureau are five copies of an LHM relative to captioned subject.

PH T-1 is U. S. Army Operations and Research Detachment (O&RD), Frankfurt/Main, Federal Republic of Germany, as extracted from confidential communications Intercept Service (CIS) and received by Legal Attache, Bonn.

PH T-2 is [name omitted], Passenger Service Representative, KLM Royal Dutch Airlines, JFK International Airport, New York, NY.

Two copies of LHM are being sent to Denver
Office for Investigative assistance.

Enclosed LHM is captioned SECRET—NO FOREIGN
DISSEMINATION in order to protect sensitive
source who is furnishing information of current
value as indicated in referenced letters.

Philadelphia indices indicate a case entitled
"HERBERT LANSING SHORE; SM—C", OO Denver, BUfile
100-391691, Denver file 100-9024, and PHfile
100-38072, who might be identical with father of
captioned subject. Denver letter

                                              [page missing]

2—Bureau (105-205033) (Enc. 5) (RM)
2—Denver (Enc. 2) (100-9024) (RM)
3—Philadelphia
    2—105-17903
    1—100-38072

JLO
(7)

Philadelphia, Pennsylvania
November 30, 1970

NORMAN JOHN SHORE

PH T-1, another government agency which con-
ducts intelligence investigations, advised during
March of 1970 that captioned subject, who listed
his residence as [address omitted], was during
that same month in contact with an individual
[Mr. J] at the International Division of the
"Free German Youth" (Youth organization of the
East German Communist Party) in East Berlin,
Germany. Subject related to [Mr. J] that he was
pleased to learn [Mr. J] had had an opportunity
to meet his father when subject's father visited
the G.D.R. (German Democratic Republic). Subject
informed him he was pleased to be invited again
to the camp. Subject said he learned a great deal
about socialism when he had previously attended
the camp and after his next experience at camp,

he would be able to return to the United States
and to inform the children about the camp.

Source said during May of 1970 that subject,
during that same month, was in contact with an
individual by the name of [Mr. W] at the "Free
German Youth." Subject informed [Mr. W] that he
accepted the invitation to attend the camp, and
indicated that at the next camp he would grasp
the points he could not hold on his prior visit.

Source advised during May of 1970 that subject,
during that same month, was in contact with one
[Mr. J] at the "Free German Youth," whom he
thanked for his assistance in helping the subject
to get into the camp.

SECRET—NO FOREIGN DISSEMINATION
GROUP I
Excluded from automatic
downgrading and
declassification

SECRET—NO FOREIGN DISSEMINATION

NORMAN JOHN SHORE

Source advised during June of 1970 that during
the same month an individual by the name of
MEGCHELINA SHORE [same address omitted], was in
contact with the above—mentioned [Mr. J] at the
"Free German Youth" to tell him that subject
would be arriving on flight LO256 on July 16,
1970, leaving Amsterdam, Holland, and subsequently leaving Berlin, Germany, on August 20, 1970,
on Flight 255. She told him that subject was
issued passport [——] dated June 22, 1966, which
was renewed at Dar—es—Salaam, Tanzania, East
Africa, and would be valid for five years, expir-
ing on June 22, 1971. She advised him that
subject was born April 1, 1956, in Philadelphia,

Pa., and his full name as indicated on the passport is JACOBUS JOHANNES AVRAM NORMAN SHORE. She
said he is five feet four inches tall, has brown
hair and blue eyes. She thanked him for inviting
subject to the camp and told him subject was
politically much more understanding of the problems facing all of the people throughout the
world.

Source advised during July 1970 that an
individual by the name of H. L. SHORE [same
address omitted], who presumably is subject's
father, contacted subject during July 1970 at
the International Pioneer Republic "Wilhelm
Block", Eberswalde near Altenhof, East Germany,
to tell subject of the physical and emotional
well-being of "Mom", who presumably is the subject's mother. H. L. SHORE mentioned to the
subject the war of liberation in Mozambique and
that everyone is proud of the material on
Mozambique that subject took along and of the
use he will make of it.

Source advised during September 1970 that
subject, during that same month, was in contact
with both [Mr. J] and [Mr. W], mentioned above, at
the FDJ Zeutralrat in East Berlin. Subject
thanked them for being able to attend the camp
in East Germany and said he hoped to return to
study at the camp. In his contact with [Mr. J],
subject said that the pioneer leaders were a
great help in the learning process in the camp
and that he will try to promote the

[page missing]

SAC (100-38072) (P)   1/29/71
SA CHARLES SILVERTHORN
HERBERT LANSING SHORE
SM-C
_____

Re Philadelphia letter and LHM entitled,
"Norman Jon SHORE, IS-EG."

Re communication requested Philadelphia to
contact established sources at the University of
Pennsylvania to determine if HERBERT LANSING
SHORE is identical with the father of NORMAN JON
SHORE.

The Bureau subsequently advised under the
caption, "NORMAN JON SHORE" that the case on
NORMAN JON SHORE (105-17905) should be closed
inasmuch as the individual is only 14 years old.
Also the investigation on HERBERT LANSING SHORE
should be carried out under his caption.

[Administrative employee, last name, title
omitted], University of Pennsylvania, advised
that there is an extensive file on HERBERT
LANSING SHORE inasmuch as he is now Director of
Performing Arts, Annenberg School of Communications, University of Pennsylvania. Records indicate he does have a son, NORMAN JON SHORE BORN
4/1/56.

Inasmuch as subject is identical with the
father of Norman Jon SHORE his entire record will
be reviewed at the University of Pennsylvania
and reported.

<u>LEADS</u>

PHILADELPHIA
                    <u>AT PHILADELPHIA, PA.:</u>
Will review the personnel file of Herbert
Lansing Shore, report same, and recommend appro-
priate action.

Documents like the following show that the FBI makes an in-
tensive effort to contact Americans in defense-related indus-
tries who plan to travel in Communist countries. In this memorandum, the FBI seems to be working hand-in-hand with the
Defense Intelligence Agency, the Washington Field Activities
Support Center, and industry securities officers. This document,
written at the end of November, 1970, might be another FBI

response to the pressure to cooperate with other U.S. intelligence-gathering operations, foreign and domestic. And the underlined sentence (which is in the original) suggests that, during this period at least, the FBI was tapping essentially the same professional resources as the CIA in its search for safely covered part-time operatives.


```
TO      : DIRECTOR, FBI (105-71688)          DATE: Nov 23 1970
FROM    : SAC, WFO (66-2479 Sub E)
SUBJECT: DEVELOPMENT OF SELECTED CONTACTS
          (DESECO)
          IS-R
```

ReWFOLet dated 10/4/65 and Bulet dated 10/11/65, captioned as above.

For information of offices not receiving copies of relets, according to the Office of Industrial Security Contract Administration Services, Defense Supply Agency (DSA), effective 3/22/65, all industrial security officers are required to file a report of the intention of any employee to travel to or through a Sino-Soviet-bloc country or to attend an international meeting outside the United States where Sino-Soviet-bloc personnel might be present. Copies of these reports are then furnished to the Defense Intelligence Agency (DIA) element of the Washington Field Activities Support Center (WFASC), Fort Belvoir, Virginia, where they are reviewed regularly by WFO.

The Bureau's DESECO Program provides for interviewing selected contacts, and, in this instance, alerting them to the possibility of foreign intelligence recruitment.

In accordance with Bureau instructions, receiving offices should check indices concerning individuals residing in their respective territories, and in the absence of derogatory information or other information having a bearing on the

advisability of an interview, the office concerned should contact the individuals in question
and ascertain if they had any contact with
Soviet-bloc nationals during their recent trip
abroad.

During each contact the individual should also
be alerted to the responsibilities and jurisdiction of the FBI in the internal security field.
Prior Bureau authority is necessary to conduct a
"sounding-out" interview with a DESECO candidate
who is employed in the news media, entertainment,
religious, public (local and state officials), or
educational fields, or is a labor leader or prominent person, as set forth in Section 105-K, Page
34, of the Manual of Instructions and SAC Letters
67-20 of 4/7/67 and 67-29 of 5/24/67.

If, during an interview of an individual, an
office feels such individual has potential for
possible development as an informant under the
DESECO Program, such interview should be considered as a "sounding-out" interview. Thereafter, further handling be each office should
conform with instructions contained in Section
105-K, Pages 33-35, Manual of Instructions. Particular attention is invited to Section 105-K-
6-h(3) on page 34 concerning "Contact with deseco
PSIs". Information copies to WFO are not necessary.

[List of more than thirty people, their corporate positions,
and travel plans omitted]

105-18427-1

2—Bureau
2—Boston (RM)
2—Buffalo (RM)
2—Cincinnati (RM)
2—Detroit (RM)
2—Houston (RM)
8—Los Angeles (RM)

3—New Haven (RM)
10—Philadelphia (RM)
3—Pittsburgh (RM)
2—San Diego (RM)
3—San Francisco (RM)
3—Seattle (RM)
4—WFO

CWM:kmc
(48)

Draft, AWOL

In the late 1960s and early 1970s, when most of the documents in the Media files were written, the draft was one
of the New Left's principal issues. As a response to the
war in Vietnam, the antidraft movement was growing
fast. From the tone of the memoranda that follow, it is
apparent that this phenomenon took the government by
surprise. Until then, the FBI had equated subversion
with Communism. Now they had to investigate draft
resisters, a new breed for them.

The first two memoranda show, once again, the Bureau's
inability to play by its own rules—to investigate illegal
activity, not legal dissent. In the first paragraph of the first
memorandum, for example, it's not clear whether the
Attorney General (who was then Ramsey Clark) wanted
information about people who interfered with the Selective Service Act and hence committed a crime, or whether
he also wanted a surveillance of draft counselors—people
involved in a legal, time-honored occupation. Similarly,
in the next-to-last paragraph of the same memorandum,
"demonstrations and rallies" are included in the same list
as "plans to interfere with Selective Service System activities." Is the Bureau equating the two?

The answer becomes clearer in the next memorandum,
where we learn that the Bureau is beginning extensive
investigations of leaders of the antidraft movement that
will "be directed towards developing evidence suitable
for prosecution." No hint of a crime there. The document
is talking about radicals who have found an effective issue
around which to organize. A device must be found to stop
them before they become too successful. And the same
memorandum makes the nature of that device clear:
agents are supposed to find "detailed evidence" that will
prove the existence of a conspiracy, demonstrate its scope,

suggest its ramifications, and illustrate the roles of the individuals involved.

These are some of the most interesting documents in the Media files, for they presage the Spock case, the first major conspiracy case of this era, about which Ramsey Clark, who ordered the prosecution, later expressed regret. The documents make it apparent that the roots of that important trial lay in a desire to thwart a political movement, not to punish people for crimes.

Watch everyone involved in the antidraft movement.

```
NEW YORK—8—1035PM EXR
NEWARK—4—1035PM EXR
BALTIMORE—3—1035PM EXR
PHILADELPHIA—7—1035PM EXR
DEFERRED 12-1-67 RAK
TO ALL SACS
FROM DIRECTOR 2P
```

ANTI—DRAFT ACTIVITIES, COUNSELING, AIDING AND ABETTING, SSA

YOUR ATTENTION IS CALL TO PREVIOUS INSTRUCTIONS CONCERING THE COVERAGE OF ABOVE—CAPTIONED ACTIVITIES. IN THIS REGARD THE ATTORNEY GENERAL HAS REQUESTED SPECIFIC EVIDENCE IN COMPREHENSIVE REPORTS BE SUBMITTED IN CONNECTION WITH COUNSELING, AIDING AND ABETTING UNDER THE SELECTIVE SERVICE ACT AND IN CONNECTION WITH INTERFERENCE WITH ARMED SERVICES RECRUITERS PARTICULARLY THOSE FUNCTIONING ON COLLEGE CAMPUSES.

WHERE RALLIES ARE HELD AT ARMED FORCES INDUCTION CENTERS, IT SHOULD BE DETERMINED WHETHER ACCESS TO BUILDING WAS PHYSICALLY OBSTRUCTED AND WHETHER SUCH ACTION HINDERED OR INTERFERED WITH EXAMINATIONS OF INDUCTEES OR ENLISTEES OR WITH THE PERFORMANCE BY PERSONNEL OF THE CENTER WITH THEIR NORMAL DUTIES. INTERFERENCE WITH SELECTIVE SERVICE REGISTRANTS SHOULD BE CONSIDERED UNDER

TITLE FIFTY, USC, FOUR SIX TWO AND WITH ENLISTEES
UNDER TITLE EIGHTEEN, USC, TWO THREE EIGHT EIGHT.

IF DEMONSTRATORS SUCCEED IN GAINING ACCESS TO
BUILDING INTERIOR, EVIDENCE OF THEIR ACTIONS AND
ATTENDANT RESULTS SHOULD BE OBTAINED. ANY STATE-
MENTS ORAL OR PRINTED DIRECTED TO INDUCTEES
SHOULD BE CAREFULLY NOTED AND APPROPRIATE NOTES
TAKEN AND PRESERVED FOR EVIDENCE.

IDENTITIES OF INDIVIDUALS SURRENDERING SELEC-
TIVE SERVICE CARDS AND THE IDENTITIES OF THE
INDIVIDUALS RECEIVING THEM ALONG WITH ANY STATE-
MENTS MADE SHOULD BE NOTED AND APPROPRIATE NOTES
MADE FOR EVIDENTIARY PURPOSES. CLOSE COVERAGE
SHOULD BE GIVEN TO ANY SPEECHES GIVEN AT RALLIES,
PARTICULARLY TO EXHORTATIONS OF OVERT REFUSALS TO
COMPLY WITH THE SELECTIVE SERVICE ACT.

EVIDENCE WITH RESPECT TO THE PLANNING OF
DEMONSTRATIONS AND RALLIES, PLANS TO INTERFERE
WITH SELECTIVE SERVICE SYSTEM ACTIVITIES OR IN-
DUCTION CENTER ACTIVITIES SHOULD BE OBTAINED.
SPECIAL EFFORTS SHOULD BE CONCENTRATED ON RING
LEADERS AND ORGANIZERS AND EVIDENCE OF ANY OVERT
ACTIONS SHOULD BE OBTAINED.

THESE INVESTIGATIONS SHOULD BE IMMEDIATELY
THOROUGHLY INVESTIGATED AND REPORTS SUBMITTED TO
THE BUREAU AT THE EARLIEST POSSIBLE DATE FOLLOW-
ING RALLIES AND DEMONSTRATIONS WITH THREE COPIES
TO THE BUREAU.
END

Develop evidence suitable for prosecution.

Air tel

To: SACs,	Boston	Milwaukee	Pittsburgh
	Buffalo	Minneapolis	Portland
	Chicago	Newark	Sacramento
	Cincinnati	New Haven	St. Louis
	Cleveland	New Orleans	San Francisco

Denver	New York	Springfield
Detroit	Philadelphia	Washington Field
Los Angeles	Phoenix	

From: Director, FBI
ANTIDRAFT ACTIVITIES
COUNSELLING, AIDING AND ABETTING
SELECTIVE SERVICE ACT, 1948

Reference Bureau teletype to all SACs 12/1/67.
Offices receiving this communication will immediately review files to insure in all instances
individual cases are being opened regarding
leaders of antidraft organizations and individuals not connected with such organizations but
who are actively engaged in counselling, aiding
and abetting in the antidraft movement. Reports
are being furnished the Department of Justice.
Investigations concerning these individuals must
be probative, penetrative, and conducted with a
view towards prosecution. It is not sufficient to
report the policy and purpose of antidraft activities useful for intelligence information but you
must bear in mind that investigations must be
directed towards developing evidence suitable for
prosecution. Detailed evidence is needed to prove
not only the existence of a conspiracy but its
scope and ramifications and the roles of the
individuals involved.
Reports must include a complete physical description and background information. Books,
leaflets, and pamphlets pertaining to the antidraft movement in which it is evident the individual has taken part in preparing or otherwise
involved must be included as enclosures to your
reports. Oral statements made by the individual
must be completely and accurately reported. News
media is a valuable source of information concerning photographs and statements made by the
individual and your reports should refer to

identity of the news media and what they obtain.
If it is ascertained that the news media has
obtained items of an evidentiary nature such as
photographs or statements, the news media must
be contacted promptly in order that the evidence
may be securely maintained for possible future
use. Local police reports and/or interviews with
police officers who were at the scene may be
extremely valuable in developing prosecutable
cases.

It is recognized that reports regarding some
individuals who are considered leaders of the
antidraft movement have been previously furnished
to the Bureau, therefore, by airtel to reach
Bureau by 1/17/68 you are directed to advise the
names of the leaders presently under investigation and the names of the individuals of the
investigations being instituted by your office.
If reports have been furnished to the Bureau
concerning leaders, you are to advise Bureau the
name of the dictating Agent and date of report.

It is to be noted the Department of Justice has
established a so-called "task force" to handle,
coordinate, and prepare for prosecution of conspiracy, counselling, and interference-type
cases in regard to Selective Service Act and
Sedition matters. Bureau cannot stress the need,
too strongly, for prompt, expeditious handling
of these cases.

Agents handling these investigations should be
alert to the possibility of harassment during
each interview and cautioned to conduct the investigations in a most businesslike manner.

Initial reports concerning leaders of the antidraft movement which are being opened in your
office must reach the Bureau by 1/29/68.

In submitting reports, submit two copies of
pending reports and three copies of closing reports to the Bureau. Submit reports by cover

routing slip marked Attention: "Special Investigative Division."

```
1—25-39622                 1—SA HANNIGAN
1—SA BASS                  1—SA METCALF
1—SA CULLEN                1—SA P. MORRIS
```

This 1970 investigation of a philosophy professor who was
sympathetic to draft resistance suggests the lengths to which
the Bureau went to carry out the instructions in the previous
two memoranda. Here are nine separate entries, containing
1,200 words, including interviews with FBI agents, former
employers, undercover informants, and casual acquaintances
of a man who has never done anything more than attend a few
meetings, give a few speeches, sign a few petitions.

The file shows that the FBI's vigilance extends to the surveillance of people who distributed leaflets one afternoon at
Haverford high school. It suggests that there are 1,126 entries
in the Philadelphia FBI Bureau's file on the Committee for a
Sane Nuclear Policy (SANE). (The first number in the code
above the entry on SANE is 100, which means left wing. The
second is 43508, which seems to be SANE's code. The third,
1126, is the number of the entry.)

Finally, this document, like that of the Berkeley coed who
was called an "inveterate Marxist," shows that chance remarks
by a casual acquaintance (in this case "queer fish," "smarty-
pants," "oddball") can stay in a person's record to help justify
future investigations. When H. R. Haldeman requested FBI
files on White House "enemies" like CBS correspondent Daniel
Schorr, it was more than likely that what he got were documents
composed of just such random episodes and impressions.

```
TO      :  SAC (25–42675)
FROM    :  [name omitted]
DATE    :  11/18/70
SUBJECT:  ROBERT [——]
           SSN 31-18-46-37
           SSA
```

Re Philadelphia letter to Charlotte captioned
as above dated 11/12/70. The files of the Phila-

delphia office reflect the following information possibly identical with [Robert].

31753*

Master file concerning Robert [——] born 2/——/35 in Philadelphia, Pa. [Robert] registered with LDB 59, Upper Darby, Pa., classified 1-A on 3/13/58. Registrant executed a special form for CO on 4/26/56, by reason of his religious training and belief, he is opposed to participation in noncombatant training and service in the Armed Forces. On 3/24/58, his appeal was forwarded to the Appeal Board.

Synopsis of reports in file reflect that Robert [——] attended [illegible] UNIVERSITY, Middletown, Connecticut, 9/52 to 6/10/56, at which time he graduated and received a B.A. Degree. Registrant graduated with honors in general scholarship, and on 6/7/56, was elected to Phi Beta Kappa Fraternity. Registrant was member of John Wesley Club and resided there during junior and senior years. References described Registrant as reliable and of very high character. Members of John Wesley Club described Registrant as trustworthy and of good character. Registrant was arrested by Middletown, Connecticut, Police Department, 5/10/54, on a charge of breach of the peace resulting from an incident at the Loyalty Day Parade in Middletown, Connecticut, on 5/2/54. He was fined $5.00 on 5/11/54.

In 1958 Robert [——] resided Apt. 4A, 230 E. 30 St., NYC. Employed since 9/3/57, Receptionist-Interviewer, NYU-Bellevue Medical Center NYC. Volunteered for experiment involving "massive blood interchange" between himself and insane person, to establish whether blood carries substance causing schizophrenia. At employment, regarded as of good character, sincere. Reported to have planned to become a minister, but disillusioned, now plans to study for doctorate in

theology and teach subject. Currently studying
philosophy at [illegible] for Master's degree,
has creditable record there.

Psychiatrist with whom blood experiment planned
considers registrant altruistic, sincere, be-
liever in God but not in conventional religion.
Two acquaintances stated registrant told them
he did not believe in God, but they consider him
sincere in conscientious objection to violence.
Registrant described as "queer fish," "screw-
ball," "smarty-pants".

Birth of Robert [——] born 2/——/35, Philadelphia, verified Registrant graduated from Haverford High School, 1952. Registrant's yearbook
reflected desired to become a Lutheran minister.
Registrant advised [name omitted], former employer, he attended a communist-type organization
meeting in Chicago "as a lark." Registrant advised former employer he intended to do humani-
tarian work overseas without salary.

Registrant was associated with American Friends
Service Committee.

Philadelphia LHM 3/8/68 captioned LEAFLET
DISTRIBUTION AGAINST THE WAR IN VIETNAM AND THE
DRAFT, OUTSIDE HAVERFORD SENIOR HIGH SCHOOL,
HAVERTOWN, PA., JANUARY 29, 1968 reflects that on
1/29/68 Detective Sergeant JOHN SCANLIN (NA),
Haverford Township Police Department, Havertown,
Pa., advised that the individuals who appeared
in the vicinity of Haverford High School on the
afternoon of January 29,1968 and distributed
leaflets to students included [names omitted].

Master file concerning Robert [——], professor
of [field omitted], Temple University. This file
contains newsclippings from various papers indicating that Robert [——] was a member of the
Faculty Draft Counseling Board, Temple University.

These clippings also set out information con-

cerning the distribution of leaflets at Haverford
High School which was set out above.

25-38672-2
  Philadelphia LHM 5/17/67 captioned FACULTY
DRAFT COUNSELING BOARD TEMPLE UNIVERSITY, PHILA-
DELPHIA, PENNSYLVANIA reflects that the "Temple
University News," Philadelphia, Pa., student
newspaper of Temple University, 2/16/67, carried
an article captioned, "Faculty Offers Draft
Advice to Conscientious Objectors."
  Listed as a member of this organization was
Robert [——], Assistant professor of [field
omitted].

25-39533-2
  "The Evening Bulletin" newsclipping 11/16/67
captioned COLLEGE TEACHERS HOLD ANTIDRAFT MEET-
ING AT PENN reflects that a number of college
teachers held a conference at the University of
Pennsylvania today to report what they are doing
to resist the war in Vietnam and the draft.
  The speakers were signers of a statement
titled, "A Call to Resist Illegitimate Authority"
calling the war in Vietnam "unconstitutional and
illegal."
  The speakers included Robert [——], Temple
University.

    25-39823-2
          -3
          -4
  These serials contain information previously
set out in this memo.
  25-40219-3 n. 11

On 7/10/68 Col. [name omitted], Field Supervisor,
Pennsylvania State Selective Service System,
Philadelphia, Pa., made available to Local Board
139, 3207 Kensington Avenue, Philadelphia, Pa.,

the Selective Service file of Robert [——], who registered with Local Board 139 on 11/23/60. Included in this file was the following letter: To be submitted to the file of registrant Robert [——]

Today in Boston, four men, Dr. BENJAMIN SPOCK, REV. WILLIAM SLOANE COFFIN, MITCHELL GOODMAN and MICHAEL FERBER, are being sentenced for the "crime" of "conspiring to aid and abet" young men who protest the draft. We have come as Philadelphia area residents who are equally guilty of this "crime". We carry with us a list of some 450 more Philadelphians pledged to support draft resisters.

The trial and sentencing of the four in Boston is a blatant example of growing repression in our country. Their crime was the exercising of free speech: talking to young men about the war and the Selective Service System and supporting those men who, as an act of conscience, decide to resist the draft. SPOCK, COFFIN, GOODMAN, FERBER, and all of us maintain that the war and draft systems themselves are illegal and immoral, and therefore we have not only a right, but a duty, to oppose them.

We are here also to support the stand of [name omitted] who was chosen to non-cooperate with the Selective Service System. We are submitting this letter and list of names to his file in order to show that he does not take the position alone, but that we have counselled and aided him in his stand. If he is guilty for opposing the Selective Service System, so are we all.

Among the signers of this letter was Prof. Robert [——] Temple Univ. Phila., Pa. 19122.

100-0-41865

Letter from 109th Counter Intelligence Corps Groups, Philadelphia, Pa., forwarding a copy of

a Sworn Statement executed by [name omitted],
along with an Agent Report indicating results of
an interview with [name omitted], concerning the
details of his qualification of his DD Form 98,
Loyalty Certificate for Personnel of the Armed
Forces.

This statement explains his attendance at a
meeting sponsored by the Proletarian Party of
America in 1955.

100-43508-1126

Letterhead of Greater Philadelphia Council
Committee for a Sane Nuclear Policy (SANE) includes the name Prof. Robert [——] is a member
of the Executive Board.

This letterhead was furnished by PH 27-S on
2/3/69.

100-46423-17

"Daily Collegian" campus newspaper of the
Pennsylvania State University 11/16/62 captioned
Robert [——] DISCUSSES DRAFT FROM ETHICAL VIEW-
POINT. This clipping sets forth the speech
Robert [——] gave at a meeting of SENSE, Students
for Peace.

100-46423-18

"Daily Collegian" 11/14/62 ad reads as follows:
"Thinking about the Draft? Hear Robert [——] of
the [——] Dept. speak about the draft tonight,
109 Osmond, 8 p.m. Sponsored by S.E.N.S.E."

The files of the Philadelphia Office fail to
reflect any references concerning Robert [——]
however the following information was located
under Mrs. [name omitted].

62-0-20504

This serial is a letter addressed to FBI Head-

quarters, Washington, D.C., with return address
of Mrs. [name and address omitted], Pennsylvania
postmarked December 6,1965, states as follows:
"To Whom It May Concern,

   Dear sirs, some months ago an F.B.I. agent
came to my house asking for information. The
information which I gave him was inconsequential
and of a trivial matter. When he left he asked
me to keep the information confidential. This I
didn't do because at the time I thought my higher
obligation was not to be an anonymous informant.
Now I realize that the breaking of my word to one
of you agents (however casually that word was
given) was wrong. I wish you to know that in the
future there is at least one citizen you can
count on to (1) tell you the truth (2) respect
the law and (3) keep their word.

                                   Sincerely,
                           Mrs. [name omitted]
May God grant to us all the wisdom to know what
is right and the power to act on that knowledge."
INDICES HAVE BEEN CONSOLIDATED WITH THIS MEMO.

                                   25-42675-4
(2)
1—25-42675
1—25-31753

Right-Wing Groups

Of the 800 pages of material in the Media documents,
only four—two reports—concerned right-wing groups.
Here they are.

An interview with a Ku Klux Klan informant.

```
· TO    : SAC, (157-1646)          DATE PREPARED 12/1/70
  FROM  : SA DONALD G. COX
  SUBJECT: UKA, PA.
           IS-KLAN
```

DATE RECEIVED   11/20/70
RECEIVED FROM (name or symbol number)
  PH 811-R (RELIABLE)
RECEIVED BY   SA DONALD G. COX
METHOD OF DELIVERY (check appropriate blocks)
  ☒ in person ☐ by telephone ☐ by mail
  ☐ orally ☐ recording device
  ☒ written by Informant

If orally furnished and reduced to writing by
Agent:
  <u>DATE</u>
DICTATED.....to............
TRANSCRIBED................
AUTHENTICATED BY INFORMANT.................

DATE OF REPORT   11/17/70
DATE(S) OF ACTIVITY   11/15/70
BRIEF DESCRIPTION OF ACTIVITY OR MATERIAL
  Visit with GEORGE [——] at [George's] home.

FILE WHERE ORIGINAL IS LOCATED IF NOT ATTACHED
  170-33-SUB A-33

*INDIVIDUALS DESIGNATED BY AN ASTERISK (*) ONLY
ATTENDED A MEETING AND DID NOT ACTIVELY
PARTICIPATE. VIOLENCE OR REVOLUTIONARY
ACTIVITIES WERE NOT DISCUSSED.

  Information recorded on a card index by........
on date........

ACTION: NONE

```
1-157-1646     (UKA, PA.)       INDEX
1-157-1844     (AL) [——]
1-157-1798     (GEORGE) [——]   OTIS (LNU)
1-157-2192     (BARRY) [——]    VIRGINIA [——]
```

```
1-157-NEW       (NANCY) [——]
1-157-NEW       (RICH) [——]
1-157-1790      (ALAN) [——]
1-157-2133      (AL) [——]
1-157-1898      (CLAUD) [——]
1-157-4347      (ROBERT) [——]
1-170-33-SUB A (PH 811-R)
```

DGC:rel

(11)

157-5710-1

PHILADELPHIA, PA.
NOVEMBER 17, 1970

Date: November 15, 1970
Time: 10 A.M.-1 P.M.
Place: [name omitted] Farm, Upper Chichester Township

People whom I know: ALAN [——]
                      GEORGE [——]
                      BOB [——]
                      OTIS (LNU)
                      VIRGINIA [——]
                      NANCY (LNU)

[Alan] arrived at [George's] farm at approximately 10:00 p.m. [George] told [Alan] there would be a klavern meeting of Klavern [designation omitted] on Thursday, November 19, 1970, at Keystone Hall, Upper Darby, Pa. [George] told [Alan] he would show the new klan movie he bought in New York City for $300 in which it shows a "nigger with KKK carved in his chest and another nigger who was castrated by the klan."

Alan asked OTIS if he ever heard from his friend CLAUDE [——]. OTIS said he had received a letter from CLAUDE in Weaverville, S.C., where OTIS lives.

CLAUDE was living in Winchester, Va., on [street omitted] as recently as September 1970.

Also present at [George's] farm was a young
woman called NANCY (LNU) whose husband is called
RICH (LNU) and is a new member of the klan.
NANCY was operating a yellow Pontiac convertible
approximately 1964 with Pennsylvania Registration
[registration number omitted]. NANCY (LNU) is a
member of the women's unit in O. [city abbrevi-
ated] Pa.

[George] asked [Alan] to call AL [——] and find
out BARRY [——]'s phone number and call BARRY and
tell him that he was welcome to start attending
klavern meetings in Upper Darby. [George] further
explained to [Alan] that [Barry] and AL [——] of
the T. [city abbreviated], Pa., unit had been
fighting and that [Barry] would no longer attend
meetings where [Al] was.

This concludes this report.

This report on the Jewish Defense League shows that the FBI
uses a member of the Anti-Defamation League as a regular,
protected informant. It also shows that the Bureau considered
two JDL members, as it considered the Berkeley coed, for inclusion on the Security Index.

```
TO       :  SAC, 105-18173                    DATE: 10/21/70
FROM     :  SA EDWARD A. SMITH
SUBJECT:    JEWISH DEFENSE LEAGUE (JDL)
            IS—NATIONALISTIC TENDENCY—JDL
            BUDED 10/28/70
```

Attached hereto is one copy of Bureau airtel to
Philadelphia dated 10/20/70, captioned as above.

Agents having individuals listed as members of
JDL are requested to immediately conduct credit,
criminal and public sources for additional identifying data on JDL members. This information
must be submitted by memorandum no later than
10/26/70, in order that BUDED be met.

On 10/21/70, SOI SAMUEL LEWIS GABER, ADL (Protect), advised SA EDWARD A. SMITH that RUSSELL

[——], a teacher at [location omitted] High
School, has been active in JDL affairs. He further advised that BENJAMIN [——], also active in
JDL is an attorney with office and residence in
[location omitted]. In addition, he indicated
that one IRVING [——] has been active in JDL
matters and resides in [location omitted]. In
view of Bureau instructions, new cases are being
opened on [Russell] and [Irving] in order to obtain details of background and activities for
evaluation as to need for interview and/or inclusion on SI.

100-52260-4

2—105-18173	1—105-18315 (GERALD [——])
1—105-18318 (RABBI [name omitted])	1—105-18319 (BENJAMIN [——])
	1—105-18314 (NEIL [——])
1—105-18312 (BEVERLY [——])	1—105-18310 (ED [——])
1—105-18317 (HERSCHEL [——])	1—105-18311 (BERNARD [——])
1—105-18316 (LEONARD [——])	2—105-NEW (RUSSELL [——])
1—105-18313 (PHIL [——])	2—105-NEW (IRVING [——])

EAS/mlb
(16)

Black Groups

The remaining documents concern the FBI's investigations of black communities, black students, and black
militant organizations. When reading them, it is crucial
to remember that standardized, obedient, highly disciplined—and mostly white—FBI agents are making vital
judgments about communities and cultures about which
they have limited understanding.

These documents seem to be filled with a much higher
expectation of violence than were the ones pertaining to
white people. Read, for example, this sentence about the
importance of recruiting racial informants in the ghetto:

"The purpose of these informants is to be aware of the potential for violence in each ghetto area." Or this sentence on Black Student Unions: "Increased campus disorders involving black students pose a definite threat to the Nation's stability and security and indicate need for increase in both quality and quantity of intelligence information on Black Student Unions and similar groups which are targets for influence and control by violence-prone black Panther Party and other extremists."

GHETTOS

Anyone in the ghetto might be dangerous.

```
TO      :  ALL RESIDENT AGENTS              DATE: 3/29/68
FROM    :  SAC (170-6)
SUBJECT:  RACIAL INFORMANTS—GHETTO
```

Attached is a memo to all headquarters agents concerning development of racial informants—ghetto.

Each resident agent is to develop these informants in ghetto areas of his territory. The purpose of these informants is to be aware of the potential for violence in each ghetto area.

If an individual RA covers only a county which does not encompass any municipality containing a ghetto, so specify by memorandum for 170-6 with a copy for the RA's error folder, so that he will not be charged with failure to perform.

```
1—each resident agent (37)     1—170-00
1—170-6                        1—66-244
1—170-93

JDJ:ec
(41)
```

The Bureau tries to set up a wide network of sources to provide advance word about racial disturbances.

TO   : ALL HEADQUARTERS AGENTS   DATE: 2/26/68
FROM   : SAC (170-6)
SUBJECT: RACIAL INFORMANTS

It is essential that this office develop a
large number of additional racial informants at
this time and that we continue to add and develop racial informants and exploit their potential during the months ahead. In the inspection
just passed, the Inspector pointed out, as we
all know, that this is a problem of the entire
office in which every Agent and every squad
shares responsibility. There is no question but
what, if a riot does occur, especially in Philadelphia, all Agents will be working on riot problems. It is a major part of our responsibility to
learn in advance, if this is humanly possible, if
a riot is planned or is expected to occur. In
this way it may be possible to actually forestall
a riot or at least to be better prepared if it
does happen. Whether or not a riot does occur,
the Bureau holds us responsible to keep the
Bureau, the Department and the White House advised in advance of each demonstration. The
Bureau expects this coverage to come through
informant sources primarily. In addition, we
must advise the Bureau at least every two weeks
of existing tensions and conditions which may
trigger a riot. This type of information can
only come from a widespread grass-roots network
of sources coupled with active informant coverage by individuals who are members of subversive
and revolutionary organizations.

The Bureau has set up three types of racial informants using classification "170" for all
three: 1) Persons who are members of and give
information regarding white hate groups; 2) Persons who are members of or give information regarding black nationalist and black revolutionary
groups; 3) racial informants (ghetto). The last

are individuals, white and black, who live and/or
work in ghetto type areas and are in a position
to advise of activities, rumors, tensions, etc.
in those ghettos. More specifically, they may
be able to advise of the activities of individual
trouble makers and rabble rousers. (Details regarding the creation and handling of racial informants (ghetto) will appear below).

This office must expand its coverage in all
three categories, but especially 2 and 3. Racial
informants and racial informants (probationary)
in the first two categories will normally be
handled by Agents on the No. 3 squad and by resident Agents where pertinent.

The Agents of other squads who develop such
informants will, of course, be given full credit.

Each Agent is required to obtain at least one
racial informant (ghetto).

Sources of ghetto informants:

Preferably these should be people known to you
as PCIs former PCIs or neighborhood sources who
you believe will cooperate if requested and
given appropriate instructions.

We are exploring other sources which may produce large numbers of prospects such as men
honorably discharged from the armed services,
members of veterans organizations and the like.
Any additional ideas along these lines will be
appreciated and should be brought to SA EDWARD
COLE.

The Bureau suggests that employees may have
friends, relatives or acquaintances who can be
of help in gathering racial intelligence. These
would include people now residing in other field
divisions who could be called to the attention
of pertinent offices. Other sources which should
be kept in mind are employees and owners of busi-
nesses in ghetto areas which might include tav-

erns, liquor stores, drugstores, pawn shops, gun shops, barber shops, janitors of apartment buildings, etc. The Bureau also suggests contacts with persons who frequent ghetto areas on a regular basis such as taxi drivers, salesmen and distributors of newspapers, food and beverages. Installment collectors might also be considered in this regard.

Supervision and Coordination:
   As the "170" files are opened they will be assigned to Agents throughout the office preferably to those Agents who are already acquainted with the individuals and suggested them as prospects. Supervision will be by the No. 3 desk. Coordination will be handled by SA EDWARD COLE.

Administrative and investigative procedures:
   Each prospect will be the subject of a new 170 case. Pertinent information regarding administrative handling appears in the handbook part I, pages 19i, 19j, 20, 20a and 20b. Notification to the Bureau appears on 19i. The background investigation necessary appears on page 20 as does information regarding 4 month progress letters and payment. Contact must be made at least every 2 weeks. An FD 209 must be submitted at the end of each month. Each contact should be recorded thereon with information as to whether it was positive or negative. All information should be recorded by memo or in the FD 209, with copies for the files on any individuals or organizations mentioned. Information pertinent to the general racial situation should be designated for Philadelphia file 157-1214.
   Pertinent information must be submitted at once so that any necessary teletypes can be furnished to the Bureau immediately and information disseminated to the PD and intelligence agencies.

Regular contact should also be made with existing criminal and security informants and potential informants who live and/or work in ghetto
areas or have access to pertinent information.
Some of these should undoubtedly be converted to
racial informants or racial informant (ghetto).
There is no reason why such a person cannot also
be given criminal or security assignments. The
Bureau has, in fact, already instructed this
office to convert several such persons to racial
informants.

For your information, all of these sources,
regardless of their designations, will be set up
in an area breakdown index of 3 x 5 cards which
will be maintained in the office of the No. 3
supervisor. Accordingly, as each is developed
and agrees to assist, pertinent information regarding his coverage should be recorded in the
file and furnished to SA COLE. The area breakdown will be as follows:

1. South Philadelphia
   A. South Street
   B. Other areas
2. West Philadelphia
   A. Lancaster Ave.
   B. 52nd St.
   C. 60th St.
   D. Mantua
   E. Powelton Village
   F. Other areas
3. North Philadelphia
   A. Columbia Ave.
   B. Susquehanna Ave.
   C. Germantown Ave. east of Broad
   D. Germantown
   E. Strawberry Mansion
   F. Other areas*

*Ridge Ave. being a diagonal street, will be

broken down to the areas nearest the major cross
streets such as Columbia Ave., Susquehanna Ave.,
Strawberry Mansion, etc.

```
1—each Agent (144)          1—170-00
1—170-6                     1—66-244
1—170-93

JDJ:ec
(148)
```

More suggestions about surveillance.

```
TO      :  ALL AGENTS                    DATE: 8/12/68
FROM    :  SAC (170-6)
SUBJECT:  RACIAL INFORMANTS
          RM
```

By letter dated 7/24/68 the Bureau instructed
that all offices must now give serious and penetrative thought to methods for obtaining maximum
productivity from the ghetto informants developed
by each individual office. The instructions from
the Bureau set forth a number of assignments
which the Bureau feels should be given to each
such informant in order to insure such productivity.

1. Attend and report on open meetings of known
or suspected black extremist organizations.

In the Philadelphia area the following places
can be considered logical meeting areas where
ghetto informants might be sent in order to
gather information for this office:

Black House (157-2446)
738 West Columbia Avenue
(This establishment is open nightly and
has classes in Negro history on Wednesday
nights and on Thursday Swahili is taught.)

CORE (157-2827)
2229 North Broad Street

SCLC (100-47194)
2511 Girard
Second Floor (over state
liquor store)

The Black Coalition (157-2678)
5918 Chestnut Street

The Ghetto Training Center
1441 South Street

Church of the Advocate
18th and Diamond
(Rev. PAUL WASHINGTON)
(This location is the site
of the Third National Black Power
Conference (157-2808) to be held
in Philadelphia 8/29-9/1/68
2. Identify criminal individuals and gangs
operating in the ghetto areas and analyze the
effect they have on creating or aggravating
situation of violence.
3. Determine if efforts are being made by black
extremists to take over such criminal activities
as narcotics traffic and the operation of numbers rackets.
In this regard it should be noted that any information received from racial informants concerning gambling activities in the Philadelphia
area should be directed to Philadelphia File
92-1570 Sub B so that this office might receive
credit for any handle from such a gambling operation.
4. Visit Afro-American type bookstores for the
purpose of determining if militant extremist
literature is available therein and, if so to
identify the owners, operators, and clientele of
such stores.

The following are known bookstores in the
Philadelphia area which have been described in
the past as distributing extremist literature

    The New World Book Fair
    113 South 40th Street

    [name omitted]
    [name illegible] Book Store
    200 Block of South 60th Street

    Community Book Mart
    10-12 North 52nd Street

5. Furnish copies of black militant literature
being circulated in the ghetto areas.
6. Travel to and furnish running telephonic
reports on areas where situations of violence are
rumored.
7. Identify black extremist militants who attempt to influence the Negro community and report on the effect of such efforts.

In order to assist the agents in Philadelphia
handling ghetto informants the following individuals are to be brought to the attention of ghetto
informants as being active in the Negro militant
movement:

WALTER [——] 157-2459
  Black House
DAVID [——] 157-2399
  Black House
ARTHUR [——] 157-2547
  Teaches African history at Black House
WILLIAM [——] 157-1933
  CORE
GEORGE [——] 157-2849
  The Black Coalition
GEORGE [——] 157-1975
  The Black Coalition
L. [——] 157-2387
  The Black Coalition

S. [——] 100-47093
  The Black Coalition
JAMES [——] 100-49161
  Ghetto Training Center
WALTER [——] 100-48776
  Was leader of Phila. Black Peoples Unity
  Movement (No known office address)
M. [——] 105-8999
  RAM [address omitted]
WILLIAM [——] 100-43189
  [address omitted] [name omitted] is the pub-
  lisher of a bi-monthly newsletter [name
  omitted]
8. Report on changes in the attitude of the
Negro community towards the white community which
may lead to racial violence.
9. Report on all indications of efforts by
foreign powers to take over the Negro militant
movement. In those cases where you have an exceptionally intelligent and knowledgable informant, such an informant may be given the assignment of reporting on the general mood of the
Negro community concerning susceptibility to
foreign influence whether this be from African
nations in the form of Pan-Africanism, from the
Soviet or Chinese communist bloc nations, or from
other nations.
In addition to the above designated places and
persons in which Philadelphia has interest, the
below listed establishments have been furnished
by the Philadelphia Police Department as being
places where militant Negroes have been known
to congregate.

North Philadelphia
  [the names of four lunch rooms omitted]

West Philadelphia
  [the names of two bars, one theater, and one
  cafe omitted]

<u>South Philadelphia</u>
[name of settlement house omitted]

The bars and luncheonettes located on South
Street from 13th to 16th Streets

The Bureau has also instructed that we immediately ascertain among all Negro informants,
including ghetto informants, which informants
are planning to enter college this fall and
would be in a position to infiltrate black power
groups on campuses. Bureau desires that we furnish them with the identities of these informants and the colleges they plan to attend. Any
agent who has a Negro informant who is contemplating college attendance should immediately
report such to SA TERENCE D. DINAN.

1—170-6   1—66-3910
1—170-419   1—Each Agent

JDJ:FSM
(147)

BLACK STUDENTS

The Director of the FBI orders Special Agents in Charge to
watch all Black Student Unions.

AIRTEL

TO   : SAC, Albany   DATE: November 4, 1970
FROM   : Director, FBI   PERSONAL ATTENTION
BLACK STUDENT GROUPS ON
COLLEGE CAMPUSES
RACIAL MATTERS
BUDED: 12/4/70

Increased campus disorders involving black students pose a definite threat to the Nation's
stability and security and indicate need for increase in both quality and quantity of intelligence information on Black Student Unions (BSU)
and similar groups which are targets for influ-

ence and control by violence-prone Black Panther
Party (BPP) and other extremists. The distribution of the BPP newspaper on college campuses
and speakers of the BPP and other black extremist
groups on campuses clearly indicate that campuses
are targets of extremists. Advance information
on disorders and violence is of prime importance.
We must target informants and sources to develop
information regarding these groups on a continuing basis to fulfill our responsibilities and to
develop such coverage where none exists.

Effective immediately, all BSUs and similar
organizations organized to project the demands
of black students, which are not presently under
investigation, are to be subjects of discreet,
preliminary inquiries, limited to established
sources and carefully conducted to avoid criticism, to determine the size, aims, purposes,
activities, leadership, key activists, and extremist interest or influence in these groups.
Open individual cases on officers and key activists in each group to determine background and
if their activities warrant active investigation.
Submit results of preliminary inquiries in form
suitable for dissemination with recommendations
regarding active investigations of organization,
its leaders, and key activists. These investigations to be conducted in accordance with instructions in Section 87D of the Manual of Instructions regarding investigations of organizations
connected with institutions of learning.

Each office submit by airtel to reach Bureau by
12/4/70, a list of BSUs and similar groups by
name and school which are or will be subjects of
preliminary inquiries. This program will include
junior colleges and two-year colleges as well as
four-year colleges. In connection with this program, there is a need for increased source coverage and we must develop network of discreet

quality sources in a position to furnish required
information. Bear in mind that absence of information regarding these groups in any area might
be the fault of inadequate source coverage and
efforts should be undertaken immediately to improve this coverage.

A prior inquiry or investigation of a group or
individual is no bar to current inquiries and
inquiries should not be postponed until submission of airtel due 12/4/70. Initiate inquiries
immediately.

I cannot overemphasize the importance of expeditious, thorough, and discreet handling of
these cases. The violence, destruction, confron-
tations, and disruptions on campuses make it
mandatory that we utilize to its capacity our
intelligence-gathering capabilities.

Above instructions supersede instructions in
Bureau letter to all offices 1/31/69, same caption.

2—All Offices   157-3550-3

Special Agents in Charge tell the Director that they are watching all Black Student Unions.

```
Via AIRTEL
TO      :  DIRECTOR, FBI              DATE: 12/2/70
FROM    :  SAC, PHILADELPHIA (157-3562) (C)
SUBJECT:  BLACK STUDENT GROUPS ON
           COLLEGE CAMPUSES
           RM
           BUDED: 12/4/70
```

Re Bureau airtel to Albany 11/4/70 and captioned as above.

In accordance with instructions set forth in
referenced Bureau airtel, established sources of
four-year colleges, junior colleges and two-year
colleges located within Philadelphia Division

were contacted regarding any Black Student Union
(BSU) or similar organization on the respective
campuses which is organized to project the demands of Black Students.

As a result of the inquiries, investigations
are being opened or reopened on the following
black student organizations to determine the
size, aims, purposes, activities, leadership, key
activists, and extremist interest or influence
in these groups. This list includes the Black
Student Union of Pennsylvania State University
and the Students For An Afro-American Society at
the University of Pennsylvania, organizations
which are currently under investigation within
Philadelphia Division:

Black Student Union (BSU, PMC)
Pennsylvania Military College, Chester, Pa.

Black Student Union (BSU, WCSC)
West Chester State College, West Chester, Pa.

Black Student League (BSL, MCCC)
Montgomery County Community College, Consho-
   hocken, Pa.

Black Student Union (BSU, DIT)
Drexel Institute of Technology, Philadelphia, Pa.

Association of Blacks for Progress (ABP, BU)
Bucknell University, Lewisburg, Pa.

Black Student League (BSL, TU)
Temple University, Philadelphia, Pa.

Black Student Union of (BSU, PSU)
Pennsylvania State University, University Park,
   Pa.

Afro-American Society (AAS, FMC)
Franklin and Marshall College, Lancaster, Pa.

Swarthmore Afro-American Students Society
   (SAASS, SC)
Swarthmore College, Swarthmore, Pa.

Afro–American Society (AAS, DC)
Dickenson College, Carlisle, Pa.

Black Student League (BSL, VU)
Villanova University, Villanova, Pennsylvania

Black Student League (BSL, OC)
Ogontz Campus
Pennsylvania State University, Abington, Pa.

Students for an Afro–American Society
  (SAAS, UP)
University of Pennsylvania, Philadelphia, Pa.

Results of preliminary inquiries at above institutions will be submitted to the Bureau in
form suitable for dissemination at a later date
along with recommendations regarding active investigations of each organization, its leaders,
and key activists.

2—Bureau	1—157-2587 (BSL, TU)
14—Philadelphia	1—157-2664 (BSU, PSU)
1—157-3562	1—157-2674 (AAS, FMC)
1—157- (BSU, PMC)	1—157-3403 (SAASS, SC)
1—157- (BSU, WCSC)	1—157-3471 (AAS, DC)
1—157- (BSL, MCCC)	1—157-3575 (BSL, VU)
1—157- (BSU, DIT)	1—157-4796 (BSL, OC)
1—157- (ADP, BU)	1—157-4804 (SAAS, UP)

JIH/AED   157-5663-1
(16)

Special Agents watch the National Association of Black Students.

TO   : ALL AGENTS   DATE: 6/17/70
FROM   : SA KENNETH K. SMYTHE
SUBJECT : NATIONAL ASSOCIATION OF BLACK
          STUDENTS CONVENTION
          WAYNE STATE UNIVERSITY
          DETROIT, MICHIGAN, 6/26-7/5/70
          RM

The National Association of Black Students
(NABS) is headquartered in Washington, D.C. It
was formed in August, 1969, when Black Students

split from the National Students Association. The
National Coordinator for NABS is on the AI.

NABS has announced its first convention scheduled for June 26-July 5, 1970, at Wayne State
University, Detroit, Michigan.

The Bureau has requested that each Field Division canvass logical informants to locate NABS
chapters and representatives.

The Bureau is also desirous of having informants, in a logical position to do so, attend
the convention.

Any information about NABS activity, the scheduled convention, or an informant in a position
to attend the convention, should be brought to
the attention of the #9 squad supervisor.

1—157-4250   1—Each Agent (185)

KKS/vrh
(186)

In this document, a high administration official at Lincoln University becomes part of the information-gathering apparatus
the FBI is setting up.

PENNSYLVANIA STATE POLICE   CODE 421
INTELLIGENCE REPORT
Troop "J"/Station Lancaster

NAME
    LINCOLN UNIVERSITY
ADDRESS
    LINCOLN UNIVERSITY, CHESTER COUNTY, PENNA.
CATEGORY
    SECURITY
(a)-Report submitted on subject, dated 12 Oct.
    67.
(b)-[name omitted] [an administration official]

    Lincoln University, interviewed at his office
    on 17 Oct. 67.

Stated that he has only been in his position
since September 1967 and during this period he
has attempted to determine what student organizations are formed at the University. Related
that some of the students have been in contact
with him to discuss his views on the Black Power
Movement.
Stated that he has learned that the organization,
BLACK STUDENT CONGRESS, with approximately 60
to 90 students attend the meetings on campus.
The leader Anthony [last name omitted], Negro,
[illegible] and Michael [——], Negro, Student,
registered at the University [name omitted] and
is a brother of Anthony H. [——], a Negro extremist and member of the [name omitted] organization who was arrested in Philadelphia recently.
Related that most of the meetings held by the
students related to the new Civil Rights Laws of
interest to the students. No indications of violence or civil disturbances proposed by the
students.
[The administration official] related that he
will be in contact with the members of the BLACK
STUDENT CONGRESS and their activities which will
be supplied to the undersigned in the event of
any violence on or off campus.

Less consciously, perhaps, two officials of Swarthmore College
help the FBI keep tabs on black students. They tell the local
police their worries about a disruptive incident. Probably without their knowledge, their opinions and a list of the school's
black students winds up in an FBI file.

INIATIAL REPORT RE: STUDENT PROTEST AT SWARTHMORE
COLLEGE
On Friday January 3, 1969, Mr. Edward Cratsley,
Vice President of Swarthmore College and William
Stanton, Superintendent of Swarthmore College
appeared at Swarthmore Police Headquarters for

a meeting with me. This meeting was prearranged
a day or two before. Purpose of this meeting was
to inform me that the College had been served a
set of demands by a group of their students known
as the Swarthmore Afro Students Society. They
number approximately twenty although this figure
seems to fluctuate somewhat. The demands which
were made were non-negotiable according to this
group and that they fully intend to take whatever steps they feel necessary to obtain these
non-negotiable demands. This is what their
spokesman announced.

Mr. Cratsley and Mr. Stanton inquired as
to what action I would take if the College called
for assistance due to student violence. I informed them that in this case I would ask for
State Police assistance and they agreed this
would be the best procedure. Their only request
at this time was for the Police not to be involved until asked as they wanted an opportunity
to play their hand. They felt the College could
handle this problem as long as outsiders did not
appear on the scene.

Late this same afternoon Sgt. John Peacock of
the Penna. State Police appeared at headquarters
to check a report of problems at Swarthmore College. I told him what had just taken place with
Mr. Cratsley and Mr. Stanton. I added that when
it becomes necessary I would be asking for State
Police help and he informed me that this was
available at my request. Certain things would
have to be arranged in advance. This would include routes to and from target area, a building
to house men and equipment etc. This was all
arranged on January 4, 1969 when Sgt. Peacock
returned to our headquarters with Sgt. Hankenson
of Media Barracks and Trooper Prokopchuk and
Trooper Priscilla.

Surveillance of Swarthmore College Campus was

maintained continually. Sgt. Peacock would check
by phone or stop in at close intervals. His two
men were here daily observing and obtaining all
printed literature from College available. Jim
Haebel and Jim O'Connor
[text continuing not available, list of students omitted]

A highest-level administration official of the University of Maryland becomes part of the FBI apparatus and reports on a campus militant.

```
AIRTEL           REGISTERED MAIL
TO      :  DIRECTOR, FBI                  DATE: 2/17/71
FROM    :  SAC, BALTIMORE (157-5119) P
SUBJECT:  [name omitted]
           RM BLACK NATIONALIST
           00: BALTIMORE
```

  Re: Bureau letter to Baltimore, 11/12/70 and
airtel 1/28/71.
  On 12/22/70 [name omitted], [high administration
official], University of Maryland, Eastern Shore
Campus, Princess Anne, Maryland advised that subject is presently a senior at that branch of the
University of Maryland (U of M), and is an exceptionally bright young man who comes from a
well-to-do family. [Name omitted] has been a constant source of agitation at the University for
the past few years and in April, 1970, was one
of the leaders in a student demonstration on
campus which resulted in one hundred eighty-one
arrests by Maryland State Police for trespassing
and disorderly conduct. [Name omitted] is the
President of the Student Government Association
at the University and has constantly attempted
to raise issues with the University Administrator
with no success. [The administration official]
recently confronted [name omitted] with the rumor
that he was a member of the Black Panther Party,
but [name omitted] denied this. [Name omitted] did

state, however that he had worked for the Black
Panther Party in New York City during the summer
of 1969. [Name omitted]'s Report of Extra Cur-
ricular Activity Record dated 9/30/70 reflected
that he was an "Amigo de parte," New York Branch
of the Black Panther Party. [Name omitted] [the
administration official] advised that

                    [Remainder of document not available]

2—Bureau (REGISTERED MAIL)   2—Denver (REGISTERED MAIL)
2—Philadelphia (REGISTERED   2—New York (REGISTERED MAIL)
   MAIL)   3—Baltimore
2—Alexandria (REGISTERED MAIL)
                                            157–5127–5
RFM:sah
(13)

Here, three sources report on a Black Student Union at Pennsylvania Military College. Though the organization is a legitimate student group, not militant, and rather disorganized, the
FBI plans to keep in touch with the sources about it. The Bureau
opens cases on two people simply because they assumed important positions in the organization.

                                        February 26, 1971
              BLACK STUDENT UNION:
              PENNSYLVANIA MILITARY COLLEGE,
              CHESTER, PA.
              ─────────────────────────────────

    A confidential source, who has furnished re-
liable information in the past and is in a position to know of activities among students at
Pennsylvania Military College (PMC), Chester,
Pa., advised during November and December, 1970,
the following information:
    During October, 1970, a Black Festival Week was
held at PMC. This was organized by about ten of
the 35 Negro students who are currently enrolled
as students at PMC. The arrangements and activity
were not well-organized, and did not receive
recognition or publicity outside the college
community.

The purpose of the festival was to invite persons to view the works of art and products developed out of neighborhood arts and crafts programs which were displayed at the school. Those
items had been created reportedly by the black
students at PMC and the black high school and
grade school students in the predominately black
neighborhoods adjacent to the urban campus of
PMC.

This source stated that out of this activity,
and as a result of the planning that went into
the activity, there was formed on campus, a Black
Student Union (BSU).

The BSU, at the outset, reportedly comprised
all of the black students at PMC who had stated
that the purpose of this organization was to en-
kindle a "spirit of black awareness" among the
whole student body, and encourage a larger number of black high school students to seek enrollment at PMC.

This source stated that BSU at PMC is a legitimate organization in that it is recognized by the
school administration as a proper school activity; however, the organization is not funded
through the student council nor does it have
representation on the student council. There does
not appear to be any connection between this organization and others on campus, insofar as control or influence on the activities of BSU. Also,
there has been no indication that the BSU is
influenced or controlled by any black militant
individuals or organizations outside the campus.

The source stated the BSU has not engaged in
any militant-type activity on campus, and have
not advocated or supported any such activity
elsewhere.

On February 24, 1971, this same source advised
that he had learned that the BSU does not have
designated officers or leaders with specific

titles as do so many of the other campus student
groups. He noted, however, that the leaders of
the BSU are:
   HERBERT [——], a student who resides on campus.
   DENISE [——], a commuting student, residing at
      [address omitted].
   This first source, as well as a second and
third confidential source, who are in a position
to know of black militant activity in the Chester, Pa., area, and have furnished reliable information in the past, advised the BSU at PMC
have been basically dormant as an organization
on campus and in the city of Chester. The group
has not taken an active role in any local black
militant activity and has not advocated or taken
part in any disruptive action on campus.
   These sources described the BSU as a somewhat
disorganized group of students, possibly having
a membership and/or following of no more than
30 students and possibly a few as a half dozen,
who have not displayed radical or militant ideas,
and do not appear to be aligned with any radical
or black militant groups.
   This document contains neither recommendations nor conclusions of the FBI. It is the
property of the FBI and is loaned to your
agency; it and its contents are not to be
distributed outside your agency.

                                         157-5904-1

BLACK STUDENT UNION;
PENNSYLVANIA MILITARY COLLEGE,
CHESTER, PA.
   Re Philadelphia airtel, 2/22/70, captioned,
"Black Student Groups on College Campuses; RM."
   Enclosed herewith for the Bureau are eight
copies of an LHM on captioned student groups.
   In view of the information developed concerning
this group, specifically, that the group has not

been involved in advocating or sponsoring black
militant activity, it is a legitimate student
activity and does not appear to be linked with
any black militant group on or off the campus.
Philadelphia is suggesting that no further action
be taken on this organization. The activities of
this organization will be followed through regular contacts with our sources in the racial field
in Chester, and should any information come to
our attention to indicate the organization is
engaged in militant activity, the Bureau will be
promptly advised.

Philadelphia will, however, open cases on the
two individuals listed as the leaders of the BSU
and information will be developed on these individuals so that this office is aware of their
identity and background.

The first source listed is [name omitted], Security Officer, PMC, the second source is [name
of white reporter on local paper omitted], Ghetto
Racial Source, and the third source is Sergeant
JOHN F. PEACOCK, Pennsylvania State Police, Community Relations Officer.

Indices of the Philadelphia Office contain no
information identifiable with HERBERT [——], and
DENISE [——].

2—Bureau (RM) (Encl. 8)   1—157–New
3—Philadelphia   1—157–New
1—157–5663

TFL:eg
(5)

BLACK LEFT

The report of a day's tapping of the Black Panther Party
phone (page 133) should be read in connection with this
section, too, since it shows the extent to which the FBI is

willing to intrude upon the privacy of everyone it considers a black militant.

The order to get information on the Black Panther Revolutionary People's Constitutional Convention.

```
TO      : ALL AGENTS                        DATE: 10/12/70
FROM    : SAC JOE D. JAMIESON
SUBJECT: REVOLUTIONARY PEOPLES CONSTITUTIONAL CONVENTION
          ORGANIZED BY THE BLACK PANTHER PARTY
```

For the information of all receiving agents, the Black Panther Party (BPP) sponsored a planning session for the above convention which was held here in Philadelphia 9/4-7/70.

At the conclusion of the above convention, the BPP held a press conference and stated that the actual convention would be held in Washington, D.C., on 11/4/70.

On 10/7/70 the Bureau advised that the dates of the above had been changed to 11/6-9/70 and that about 15,000 are expected to attend; this group will comprise of white as well as black extremists.

The Bureau has issued instructions that all offices must report the following information on a weekly basis:

1. various organizations planning to participate.
2. mode of travel and identities of persons planning to attend
3. identities of organizers and persons who are to head work shops
4. identities of the leading speakers at the convention
5. agenda of the convention
6. plans for violence or disruptive demonstrations
7. plans to carry weapons or explosive devices

8. convention security precautions to be observed
9. literature regarding the convention
10. details concerning available housing

In view of the above, all agents are requested
to contact logical informants regularly to obtain current data as per Bureau instructions. All
such information should be reported to SA PHILIP
E. BROWN.

1—157-4854   1—EACH AGENT (191)
1—157-2004

(194)

Here is the way that order was carried out for one person who
may have attended the convention.

```
TO      : SAC, PHILADELPHIA            DATE: 2/22/71
FROM    : SAC, NEWARK (157-5183) (P)
SUBJECT: CHANGED
          DENISE [——]
```

Re Portland letter to Bureau, 1/8/71, captioned, "REVOLUTIONARY PEOPLES CONSTITUTIONAL
CONVENTION ORGANIZED BY THE BLACK PANTHER PARTY".
   Relet, a copy of which was designated for Philadelphia, contained the name of the subject and
identified him as being from Livingston College,
LPO 11373, New Brunswick, New Jersey.
   On 2/4/71, [name omitted], Assistant Chief,
Rutgers Campus Patrol, an established and reliable source (Protect), advised that there is no
indication that the above-listed organization is
active on either the Rutgers or Livingston College campuses. [The Ass't. Chief] advised
Livingston College is a division of Rutgers University. He advised, however, that a DENISE
[——], a resident of House 27, Livingston Post
Office 11373, is a permanent resident of [address

omitted] Drexel Hill, Pa. She is a freshman at
Livingston College. [The Ass't. Chief] advised he
would attempt to obtain additional background
data on [Denise].
LEADS:
   PHILADELPHIA
At Drexel Hill, Pennsylvania: Will obtain background data on subject from high school records
and contact with sources.
   2. Will conduct credit and identification
checks for subject.
   3. Will determine from sources whether subject
is known to be associated with BPP or similar
New Left activities.
   NEWARK
At New Brunswick, New Jersey: Will maintain
contact with Assistant Chief [name omitted] for
information on [Denise].

2—Philadelphia (RM)   157-4954-639
3—Newark
   (1—157-4866)

DRS/md
(5)

Here the FBI uses an informer to obtain information on the
Black Panther Party, the Black United Liberation Front (BULF)
and a couple of bank robbers.

                                        DATE: 1/27/71
TO   : SAC (170-708)   ☐ CI   ☐ SI   ☐ R (Prob)
FROM   : SA RICHARD E. LOGAN ☐ PCI   ☐ PSI   ☒ R GHETTO
SUBJECT : MARGARET [——]   ☐

DATES OF CONTACT   1/22, 26 and 27/71

FILE #S ON WHICH CONTACTED (Use Titles when File
#s not available or CI positive info.)

157-5420 Black United Liberation Front (BULF)
91-7684 BR SUSPECTS
88-7433 James [——]
157-5789 George [——]
62-3910 Dissemination

PURPOSE AND RESULTS OF CONTACT
☐NEGATIVE
☒POSITIVE
☐STATISTIC

157-5420

Informant advised, on 1/22/71, that the BULF
is not going to buy a type setting machine. They
are buying an electric typewriter and are supposed to have the use of a type setter the location of which she does not yet know. She said
the members are fighting and drinking more than
ever. On 1/26 she advised that HAWK had left the
BULF but [Reggie] thinks he will be back. She
also said the WES [——] is no longer around the
BULF and [Reggie] is becomming very discouraged.
On 1/27/71, informant said that there are only
four persons staying at the BULF Headquarters
now, [Reggie], RONNIE, CURTIS and PHIL. ROBIN
[——] stays there from 9A.M. until closing time
but no longer sleeps there. She said [Reggie] is
"fed up" and seems to be "blowing his stack." He
is even talking about getting a job. It is the
informant's opinion that the BULF is on the verge
of breaking up.

91-7684

On 1/22/71, informant said that HAROLD [——]
usually wears an army style raincoat, dyed blue,
and an apple hat which is old, beat up and dirty,
when engaging in holdup activities. The hat is
black in color.

This information was furnished to Inspector
Bernard Bartley, Major Crimes Ph PD who said that
the above clothing fits the description furnished
by some of the witnesses. BARTLEY had previously
advised that the witnesses failed to identify the
photo of WILLIAM [——] as one of the robbers even
though, in BARTLEY'S opinion, his Police photo
is identical to the photo taken of one of the

unsubs by bank camera. BARTLEY said [William]
would be picked up for a lineup.

<u>88-7433</u>

Informant said on 1/22/71 that the photo of
[James] looks familiar but she is not certain she
ever met him. She recommended that GLADYS [——],
wife of [R.H.], present leader of the Black
Panther Party in Phila., be contacted. She said
GLADYS is very angry at [R.H.] now and may be
receptive. [Gladys] lives at [address omitted].

<u>157-5789</u>

Informant said she does not recall a GEORGE
[——]. She did know WILLIE LEE [——] and one [N.]
She had given [N.] her home phone number before
the convention in Wash. D.C. (BPP). She said she
was talking to him on the phone when she did
this. She assumes either [Willie Lee] or [N.] gave
her phone number to [George].

She knows [Willie Lee] and [N.] went south and
were not able to come back but she didn't know
why.

xxInformant certified that he has furnished all
    information obtained by him since last
    contact.

COVERAGE   Same

PERSONAL DATA   Informant now resides at [address
omitted] Phila.

1—(170-708)
REL

The **National Black Economic Development Corporation** is a
militant black organization. The first two reports about it show
that the FBI infiltrated the organization with a shrewd informant who is able to provide cogent information about discussions within the group. The third report shows two middle-level
executives at a Chester County bank becoming cogs in the FBI's
information-gathering apparatus by furnishing information
about the NBEDC and its leader, Muhammad Kenyatta.

```
TO      : SAC, PHILADELPHIA (157-3852)
FROM    : SA JAMES I. HALTERMAN
DATE    : 2/4/71
SUBJECT : NATIONAL BLACK ECONOMIC DEVELOPMENT
          CONFERENCE
          RM-NBEDC
RECOMMENDATION: INDEX JOANNE [——]
```

On 1/26/71, PH 307-R, a source who has furnished reliable information in the past, advised
that NBEDC met from 8:00 P.M. to 10:30 P.M.,
1/25/71, at the Institute of Black Ministries,
Girard and Broad streets, Philadelphia, Pa. The
following people attended the meeting:
    MUHAMMED KENYATTA
    MARY [——]
    WALTER [——]
    JOANE [——]
        [title omitted]
    GEORGE [——]
    J.C. [——]
    ADRIANNE [——]
    O. [——]
    MOHAMMOUD [——]
    Three or four unidentified people

```
1—157-3852                      1—157-4915 (ADRIANNE [——])
1—157-1567 (KENYATTA)           1—157-5047 (WALTER [——])
1—157-3038 ([J.C. ——])          1—157-5768 (MOHAMMOUD [——])
1—157-3913 ([——])               1—170-437 Sub A 489
1—157-4584 (MARY [——])            (PH 307-R)
```

```
TO      : SAC, 157-3852                         DATE: 2/9/71
FROM    : SA EDWARD M. COLE
SUBJECT : BLACK ECONOMIC DEVELOPMENT CONFERENCE
          RM—BEDC
```

The following information was furnished to the
writer by PH 897-R on 1/29/71:

A meeting is to take place on 1/30/71 between
[J.C.], WALTER [——] and MUHAMMAD KENYATTA to set

up the Executive Board and now organization for
BEDC in Philadelphia. According to source KEN-
YATTA is trying to form a new stronger organization which will bring in other black groups in
the city of Philadelphia. The organization will
be set up with an executive committee which will
be composed of the chairmen of ten regular committees. The executive committee will meet whenever necessary. In addition to the executive committee a black senate will be formed which will
be composed of chairman of each committee and
representatives or officers of other organizations, church groups or community groups which
will join with them. The ten committees to be
formed are Women, Church Relationships, Finance,
Ways and Means, Tactical (reperation and confrontation), Managership, Communications, Defense
(self-defense or legal defense), anti-war and
draft and Education.

The following individuals are being considered
for Chairmen of the various committees. When
Chairmen are named and the Chairmen accept these
committees, a memo will be submitted to the individuals' files:

Rev. [name omitted] will be Chairman of the
Tactical Committee as this will be the best way
to have his name before the public.

EDNA [——]—Ways and Means
ROXANNE [——]—Women

                                              157-1567-357

1—157-3852
1—157-   ([J.C.])
1—157-1567 (KENYATTA)
1—157-5047 ([Walter ——])
1—170-53   (PH 897-R)

EMC:kpb
(5)

On 5/20/70, [name omitted], Cashier, Southeast
National Bank (formerly Delaware County National
Bank), 4th and Market Streets, Chester, Pa.,
advised that as of 1/1/70 the Delaware County
National Bank merged with several Chester County
banks to form the Southeast National Bank.

Subsequent to this merger, this bank instituted
a new computer system for checking accounts.
Under this system all checks drawn on active
checking accounts are recorded on microfilm and
available for review at the Computer Center of
this bank at 24th and Edgmont Avenue, Chester,
Pa.

[Same name omitted] stated there is a current,
regular checking account at that bank in the
name National Black Economic Development Conference, Pennsylvania Office, 217 Concord Avenue,
Chester, Pa. There are two persons authorized
to sign checks on this account and they are
MUHAMMAD KENYATTA and MARY [——]. As of 5/20/70,
the balance in this account was $44.32.

On 5/20/70, [name of administrative employee
omitted], Computer Center, Southeast National
Bank, 24th and Edgmont Avenue, Chester, made
available for review copies of the statement for
checking account #550-723-1, which is in the
name National Black Economic Development Conference, Pennsylvania Office. These statements
dated 3/16, 4/15, and 5/15/70 reflect activity
on this account during the 30—day period prior
to the date of this statement. A review of the
statements reveals the balance in this account
has ranged from a high of $1,948.56 on 4/9/70 to
a low of $38.19 on 5/14/70.

[Same administrator's name omitted] stated it is not possible under their computer system to identify the nature and source of deposits and credits to this account. He would, however, make available for review the microfilms containing checks drawn on this account during the periods covered by the above statements.

A review of these checks reflects almost all are signed by MUHAMMAD KENYATTA and made payable to cash. All of these checks have a space on the face of the check after the word "for" in which is written the purpose of the check. On the vast majority of these checks the notation in this space contains such language as "operating expenses," "clothing allowance," "maintenance expenses."

An average of 15 to 20 checks were drawn on this account for each of the three months reviewed. Among these checks the following are noted:

  Check dated 3/9/70 in the amount of $300, payable to Thomas Jefferson Hospital for hospitalization of JUANITA [——];

  Check dated 1/5/70 in the amount of $100, payable to ED [——], care of Young Afro American Willow Games for supplies;

  Check dated 3/5/70 in the amount of $100, payable to ED [——] for grant to Nat Turner Community Center;

  Check dated 5/8/70 in the amount of $144.95, payable to Bell Telephone Company for phone #s [two local telephone numbers omitted];

  Check dated 5/13/70 in the amount of $50.00 made payable to THOMAS [——] for emergency grant;

  Check dated 5/14/70 in the amount of $1,000 made payable to cash for clothing allowance.

  <u>LEADS</u>

PHILADELPHIA:

__AT PHILADELPHIA, PA.__

Will ascertain through Bell Telephone Company identity of subscribers to [same two phone numbers omitted].

__AT CHESTER, PA.__

Will continue to monitor bank account of National Black Economic Development Conference at Southeast National Bank.

157-3852-216

2—157-3852
TFL:rel
(2)

III
AGENTS OF FEAR

Since informers are the most dreaded cogs in the machinery of fear, the truth that they are frequently bumbling and unstable is not an easy one to accept. The case studies in this section ought to make that hard truth more acceptable. To judge from the profiles that follow, Boyd Douglas, the informer in the Harrisburg-Berrigan trial, would never be picked for an assignment on "Mission Impossible." Robert Hardy's actions in the Camden Draft Board case exclude him too from such an assignment—in fact, put him outside the range of skills and background that common speculation attributes to police informers. And Barbara Herbert's portrait of informer Jack Weatherford adds depth to the picture that unfolds—one of people driven by strange ambivalences to take on a policeman's role without training, without patriotism, without political commitment.

These people, to be sure, are not the only kinds of informers. Police agents who infiltrated the Panther 21 and the Chicago 7 did act with some of the professionalism generally attributed to their calling. Yet those agents are the exceptions. More typical is the amateurish performance of mercenary FBI informers like Hardy, Weatherford, and Douglas.

Robert Wall, the only professional enforcement officer included in this section, was never an informer. He was a regular FBI Special Agent whose job it was to conduct investigations, for which one of his recourses was to use informers. His recollections hint at just what it is in the *modus operandi* of an investigatory agency that dictates the kind of undercover agents it chooses.

Robert Hardy, an Affidavit

Robert Hardy, thirty-five, is a construction worker in Camden, New Jersey, an ex-marine, a recent convert to the Catholic church, a defeated candidate for Camden's City Council. He ran a Robert Kennedy–style campaign in 1970, directing his appeal to the city's black and Puerto Rican voters.

In June, 1971, Hardy learned that some antiwar activists, including some friends of his, hoped to invade Camden's Federal Building, where they intended to destroy draft records. He passed on the information to the FBI and volunteered to serve as an informer. Because of him, the group of activists, who became known as the Camden 28, were arrested inside the Federal Building on August 23, 1971.

Five months later, Hardy made an about-face. He submitted to the defendants a statement in which he said that he had been more than an informer. Perhaps without ever intending to, he had become a provocateur. This statement, which he reiterated as a defense witness during the Camden 28 trial, was a principal reason for their acquittal in May, 1973. Hardy's defection from the prosecution is as difficult to explain as his first change of heart in turning informer on his friends. His sworn statement follows.

AFFIDAVIT

Robert Hardy, being duly sworn according to law, deposes and says, to the best of his knowledge, information and belief, that:

I am making this affidavit on my role in the Camden 28 case because it is important that the truth come out at the trial. No one has coerced or forced me or given or offered me any reward. I am not apologizing to anyone or condemning anyone; I am only setting down exactly what happened, the truth. This affidavit is the result of a private meeting in Woodbury, New Jersey, with myself, Mike Doyle, and Mike's lawyer, David Kairys. Mr. Kairys took notes, quoting me as much as possible, and prepared this affidavit from what he had written down, as I agreed he should do. I, Robert W. Hardy, have carefully read every word of it before signing it. It is almost all written in my words.

My involvement began on a Thursday, I believe it was June 24, 1971. Mike Giocondo, a long-time friend, came to our house before dinner time. He was really upset. He told me about a civil disobedience action against the Vietnam war that had apparently been discovered by the FBI and fallen through. It concerned a plan to enter the Camden Draft Board, in the Post Office Building in Camden, and destroy draft files. The FBI had just broken up the group at its meeting place, in one of their houses. Also, one of them had been confronted by an FBI agent outside of the Post Office while doing surveillance on the building in preparation for the action, and the practicalities of breaking into the building seemed insurmountable. Mike asked for my help; he seemed to want advice and, most of all, encouragement. I told him the action seemed to me to be a senseless thing to do. Mike and some of the others were good friends of mine, and some of the best people I've ever known, and I didn't want them to get hurt.

The next day, at about 4:00 P.M., I went to the FBI office in Philadelphia. I knew some of the agents, as I had given them tips before (but I was not a regular agent). I told them what my friends had considered, and may consider again, and asked them for advice. I told them that I did not want my friends to go to jail. They just told me to keep them posted on developments.

Later that night, I met John Grady and some of the others. From then on I was an integral part of the group, and one of its leaders.

It's difficult for me to determine whether they had completely given up the action when I joined them. I was new, and I brought with me practical experience with mechanical things, and a kind of leadership and spirit I bring to any project I join. Certainly the ones who knew me were reinvigorated. And I know all of them were demoralized and it was a great lift to have someone who could do things. I could see they minimized any pessimistic talk around me so as not to discourage me. However, Cookie Ridolfi did say she thought it was impossible to pull off, and Mel Madden said it should be forgotten. I was also aware that they knew they had just been discovered by the FBI, at their meeting place and outside the Post Office, and that, at least to them, the practicalities were insurmountable. It is quite possible that they had totally given up on this project, but since I was not in on prior discussions, I can't be sure. It was also apparent that many, if not all, of them gave up on it later when we found out the guard at the Post Office was carrying a gun, until we put together a plan, which I played a large role in formulating and having accepted, that allowed them to keep away from the guard.

In regard to guns or other weapons, they were wholly opposed to the use of any force or any action that chanced someone getting hurt. At one point I tested Keith Forsyth by offering him the u_e of my gun, and he flatly rejected it.

I had a leadership role from the first night I was in it. Many of them knew me and my abilities. It was difficult for me, because of my nature, not to assume leadership. After a short time, I was in command or at least equal to John Grady (we competed for leadership of the group), and this is a matter of record with the FBI. I told the FBI many times that it couldn't have happened if I wasn't there. After a while, any time a problem came up, they would ask, "How would you do it, Bob?" Throughout I actually wanted just to stop the action, but I think I became, unknowingly, a provocateur.

Besides the leadership role and the spirit uplift, I provided indispensable physical and informational needs. It's really impossible to exaggerate how inept, undisciplined, and generally unable to pull off this action they were. They wouldn't keep to schedules, and they'd make simple matters complicated. I never doubted their moral conviction, sincerity, and honesty. They are the finest group of Christian people I have ever been associated with. They are not even capable of hurting anyone. They were willing to give up everything they had for what they believed, and at no time did they show any un-Christian behavior. For me, it was the best cooperative effort I've ever experienced; it was a community of people bound together by love and dedication. I will never forget them. But as far as mechanical skills and abilities, they were totally inept. I would not hire any of them to work with me on a construction job. They possess incredible moral strength and intelligence, but they are baffled and incompetent about practicalities. It definitely wouldn't have happened without me.

I provided 90 percent of the tools necessary for the action. They couldn't afford them, so I paid and the FBI reimbursed me. It included hammers, ropes, drills, bits, etc. They couldn't use some of the tools without hurting themselves, so I taught them. My van was used on a daily basis (the FBI paid the gas). I rented trucks for the dry runs and provided about twenty dollars to forty dollars worth of groceries per week for the people living at Dr. Anderson's. This, and all my expenses, were paid for by the FBI.

When I first came in, they had discussed a number of very vague plans, but none of them were concrete or agreed upon. The main problem was they couldn't figure out how to get into the building and up to the fifth floor to the Draft Board. There was a fire escape they had considered using, but they didn't even notice the alarm on it. After looking over the building, I told them how they could get up the fire escape without tripping the alarm by putting a tripod under the bottom part, so it would not lower, and climbing up to it with ladders (which I provided and taught them how to use at my house). The solution of this problem was most important to reinstigation of the project, as it had been a big stumbling block. This plan was later modified; the ladders were to be placed at another point and the fire escape mounted from a ledge on the building, again to avoid the alarm. Then I told them how to break into a window on the fifth floor by taping it, drilling holes in a semicircle near the lock, punching out the glass, and reaching in to unlock it. I provided a portable drill and special bits for use on glass. I also suggested and provided special pry bars for opening the files that contained the draft records.

During the first week I was involved, I volunteered to enter the Board and draw a schematic diagram of it. They had ob-

served the guards and knew their schedules, but they didn't
have a floor plan of the Board. When I returned with the schematic, which was complete with dimensions, it was an incredible
morale boost; they cheered, and we celebrated. Later, I did a
diagram of the whole building and took one of them with me
who needed a boost in courage. He was really turned on by
doing this with me. I also provided necessary information on
alarms, which cars in the area were unmarked police cars, and
the traffic light pattern.

During the whole period, I reported daily to my FBI contacts.
Usually I met them in the morning in diners or parking lots.
Each day I collected my thoughts on everything that had happened and had been said, and then dictated it into my contact's
tape recorder. It was transcribed daily by two stenographers at
the FBI. Also, a radio was installed in my van so whenever the
ignition was on, the conversations would be directly broadcast
to the FBI. The FBI recorded these conversations and had them
transcribed. I saw to it that many conversations took place in
my van, and I used it sometimes to give the FBI information.

I was paid on an hourly basis at a rate equivalent to what I
normally made, sixty dollars per day, plus all expenses. Every
Wednesday I told my contact how many hours I had spent and
what my expenses were. I was also given a small cash amount
after the arrests, which I did not expect.

It is important to emphasize that I was promised by the FBI
many times that they would stop our activities before the action
actually happened. I never thought that the information and
materials I provided would be used or that anyone would ever
get into the building. I was told my friends would be prosecuted
for, at most, a conspiracy, and that they would not go to jail. As
things progressed, I was specifically told that the arrest would
come when we did a dry run scheduled for August 18, 1971, at
11:45 P.M. The dry run proceeded, and the FBI had about
eighty agents in the building ready to make the arrest. I was in
my van watching, but nothing happened. I waited and watched
until 2:00 A.M. on August 19, and still nothing. I was really disturbed. I contacted the FBI, and I was told that, against the
wishes of some of the local FBI people, the higher ups, "someone at the little White House in California," they said (which I

took to mean someone high in the FBI or Justice Department then in California), wanted it to actually happen.

ROBERT HARDY

Sworn to and subscribed
before me this 28th day of
February, 1972.

[signature]
_____

NOTARY PUBLIC
My commission expires: 10/23/72

Jack Weatherford
by Barbara Herbert

When Jack Weatherford came to court in July, 1970, he was probably the best liked and most trusted person in the movement in South Carolina. He testified that his job for the previous year had been to infiltrate and report on radical political activities in the state. At the time of his testimony, he had just been accepted as a special applicant to the Venceremos Brigade. He had applied late (probably for the FBI) and had passed special screening by people in Atlanta and New York.

For me it was an extraordinary betrayal, mingling personal with political treachery. Jack had been one of my closest friends for a year. He had first played country music for me, taught me about southern foods, even pretended I was his wife so that we could both visit his brother in jail.

His testimony in that trial resulted in a conviction and an eighteen-month sentence. His investigations may have helped convict three coffeehouse operators as "public nuisances"; they are appealing six-year sentences. At least ten more of us face possible maximum sentences of fifteen years each, arising from a university incident he helped provoke.

Columbia, South Carolina, could be Anytown, Amerika. It has about 100,000 inhabitants. The black poor live in pockets sprinkled throughout the city, many on dirt roads without any municipal services like sewage or trash collection. The white poor tend to cluster near the mills, which are nonunion and horribly oppressive. The mill owners and moneyed people manipulate the racism of the whites for their own ends. There are vestiges of the Klan, and violence is always near the surface. There is no liberal tradition.

Columbia sees itself as a cosmopolitan center in a country of rednecks—people so oppressed that they can't comprehend their oppression. Columbia is the state capital. Besides the state legislature, it harbors the state university and Fort Jackson, a major military installation and an economic pillar of the town.

Columbia, and places like it all over the country, supply the bodies to execute the Man's imperialism. Men volunteer to go into the army (though not as much as before the Indochinese war) out of duty and boredom and lack of other possibilities, and their women, wives and mothers, proudly display gaudy, sentimental silk kerchiefs embroidered "MOM" and "When I die I'm sure to go to Heaven 'cause I served my time in Vietnam."

Those kinds of rednecks make up Jack's people. Because he's gone to college, he's a step above them, and he knows it. He is also more sophisticated. He is opposed to the war, and (now) describes himself politically as a liberal. He had relatives among the people who overturned the schoolbuses in Lamar, South Carolina, last spring as a protest against integration.

Weatherford is the oldest of a poor white South Carolina army family. He worked his way through college in three years, always fearing his dad would be killed in Vietnam and the burden of supporting the other kids would be on him. He was the first in his family to get a B.A. After college he served six months in the National Guard, married, made a downpayment on a house, went to work for the State Department of Mental Health.

In January, 1969, Jack went to the Nixon counterinaugural, apparently at the height of his dissatisfaction with electoral politics. Shortly thereafter, he split with his wife, began several relationships with men, and got very involved with dope. Then his brother David was arrested with another boy for attempted robbery. The other boy's parents had money; he was released with a suspended sentence. David was held 180 days in pretrial confinement because he could not raise bail, then given one to eight years. Jack claimed that injustice completed his radicalization. I found it all quite convincing.

We later discovered that sometime during David's arrest and trial, Jack became friendly with Columbia's SuperNarc, and they began a relationship.

Early in the summer of 1969, Weatherford was busted for selling acid. The bust became the critical lever in the making of the pig. It is standard procedure to offer a deal —no prosecution in exchange for informing. But Jack got a special offer. The State Law Enforcement Division would hire him to be an undercover agent; they would not prosecute him or the friend he was busted with; they would pay his tuition so that he could build his grade-point average for graduate school. They might have used David, already in prison and so completely under their control, as additional pressure. They could have threatened to move David to a less desirable prison, to take away his privileges, or to put him in solitary confinement. They might not have needed any threats.

Weatherford was bored with his old job; he desperately wanted the security of a Ph.D. Too, his field was sociology and this seemed an interesting way to really learn the objective truth about political radicals, he later told me.

Weatherford had perfect qualifications for his new role. Because he was covertly homosexual, he had had much practice hiding an important part of his life. He was from the area; people trusted him; his background story was believable. Under other circumstances he might easily have become a radical.

The pigs played on his chauvinism. He could exercise a kind of fatherly responsibility over the lives of innocent and vulnerable people, they told him. His main assignment was to "get Bursey," a local movement brother who had had the audacity to burn the Confederate flag in public as a protest against racism some months before. In addition, he could help bust the pushers who were ruining people's lives with dope, and perhaps counter the growing radical movement on campus. They promised never to make him testify against or participate in the arrest of a person he knew.

In some ways, Jack represents to me what it would mean to be crazy. His life seems a study in disintegration, categorized into little boxes that do not go together. Being an agent was just one particularly destructive box. My understanding of his pigdom now is that it was an expression of his confused self-hatred—the kind of self-hatred that can come from internalizing oppressor's values. One of his techniques of survival was to develop a very "together" facade, to repress all the contradictions in his life that might hurt him.

The fundamental contradiction was of course political. In one box he kept all that he knew about the "problems" of Amerika; his family's poverty, the injustice done to David, rampant racism, the war. In another, he kept his belief that with enough school degrees and property he could make a good life for himself.

Similarly with his sexuality. He kept his involvements with men secret and separate from his more acceptable relationships with women.

His participation in dope culture is an even better example. Although he was engaged in a moral crusade against dope, he was very much a part of the dope world, sometimes tripping four or five times a week. At one point a close friend and fellow doper worried that Jack would completely flip out, he was so heavily into drugs. Around me, however, Jack talked about how destructive drugs like acid and mescaline were and feared they could destroy a person's spirit.

I was opposed to drugs for political reasons—I thought they provided an excuse for political busts. Weatherford agreed with that position and may have saved me from a set-up bust. It is ironic, to say the least, that Jack may well have saved me from a dope bust out of friendship and set me up (by provocation) on political charges out of duty.

Sometimes the contradiction verged on simple hypocrisy, however, as when the city narcs were having a race with the county narcs about making the most dope busts, and Weatherford helped set up several grass busts for his lover in the county division.

If we had known about the contradictions, we might have been alert to the more serious tip-offs that he was an agent. I feel that during many of the first months he was infiltrating us, he was moved by much of our analysis. But he was not involved in any sort of consciousness raising; in that time he never made the vital connections between "abstract" politics and his life.

I remember a conversation we had immediately after Christmas last year, when Jack talked about how useless political effort was, how we should all give up. I was struck at the time by a particular desperation in his voice. I remember the conversation well because it was the last of a series of good conversations we had had through the fall. Although we spent some time together through the winter and spring, we were never again so close. Then, I attributed it to increased pressure from external political events. Now, I wonder if that conversation (he disappeared to the beach for several days after) marked a turning point. If he had come almost to believe in our radical politics, and had become almost too fond of us to continue being dishonest, he must have had to move our box farther away from his feelings to continue his job.

It is tantalizing to think how close we might have come to converting Weatherford. I tend to believe that if he had been a woman attending consciousness-raising all fall, we would have won him over. The idea is not far-fetched; four men who had originally gone to the UFO coffeehouse as agents for Military Intelligence came forward to testify for the defense. On a main street where merchants went out of their way to bilk soldiers, the coffeehouse had been remarkably nonexploitative, and the concern and commitment of the coffeehouse folks had won them over.

After his bust in July, Weatherford did discreet dope busts all summer. He registered at the university in the fall and then became cochairman of the local Southern Students Organizing Committee–SDS group. He seemed really tied into the spirit of the group; he wasn't interested in running things or being a star; he was always around doing shitwork and talking to people. People respected him; he (accidentally?) recruited some really good people to the movement. He also played on the doubts of the alienated. He helped convince one guy to drop out of school, politics, and our commune.

In January, city, county, and state pigs (probably with federal encouragement) busted the coffeehouse. They arrested the operators and padlocked the door. It was such clear repression that all fairminded people in Columbia were outraged. For the next few months, most political

energy went into defense and efforts to reopen a shop.
Jack wasn't much involved with that, although he became
very fond of some folks from Boston who came down to
help in the emergency. He even asked one woman to stay
and live with him.

At the end of "End the Draft Week," Weatherford took
part in a Draft Board trashing. Four guys threw a brick
and a can of paint through the Draft Board window. The
following day, Jack was arrested with Bursey, the brother
he'd been sent to get, at the university. The pigs clearly
knew exactly what had happened within hours after the
action. It was scary, and we were all somewhat shaken.
We decided another of the foursome (who wasn't arrested)
was an agent (he may well be).

Immediately after Jack's arrest for the Draft Board
action, David was thrown into solitary confinement. It
was just at the time he should have been coming eligible
for parole. Fifteen days later, he was moved to a different
prison and released (as it turned out) on special orders
direct from the governor. David did not go through the
ordinary prerelease procedures.

By the beginning of May, the campus was tense. Students had seen John Doe warrants with names to be filled
in after dope busts; state legislators were pressing the
school to keep GIs and longhairs out of the student union;
the coffeehouse trial had just ended with six-year sentences and $5000 fines. Nixon's Cambodian invasion was
a last straw. There was an explosive rally and a sit-in. The
National Guard was called on campus. Finally, during a
rally before university disciplinary hearings, people
occupied the administration building and trashed the
treasurer's office. Weatherford was a major voice urging
people to take the building and trash the IBM cards.
Damage was not very extensive. The university replaced
the cards within a few days.

A film picked up by national TV showed Jack and Walker

(the woman he lived with) climbing out a window of the administration building. There followed a series of almost random arrests. I was picked up; Jack wasn't.

After the university explosion, I saw little of them. Jack seemed somewhat edgy around me. His talk now was constantly that we needed to change people, not systems. Whenever we talked about my upcoming trial he advised me to split. "They" were sure to get people this time, he said, and we both knew how bad the prisons were from David's experience.

He applied to go to Cuba and was accepted but at Walker's request, didn't go. Then in mid-July he was called out of class unexpectedly and put on the stand to convict one of the other participants in the Draft Board trashing. There is some evidence that he was called to testify as a kind of petty recrimination because he had refused an assignment to do an investigation of a "homosexual ring" at the university.

When we first learned of Jack's double role, he took on an aura of SuperPig. There had been few discrepancies in his background, none in his finances. His discovery was largely a fluke. If he had been in Cuba, he might have returned with excellent movement credentials and done more damage.

After he surfaced, some of us went to talk with him. We took a lawyer with us because we were apprehensive about talking to the Man—even if he had been our friend. Most of what Jack said was standard liberal talk. He saw himself as being responsible for saving the country from the violence of a few wild-eyed crazies and the destruction and chaos they could create. He knew I was sincere, he told me, but so were the fanatics on the other end of the political spectrum. When I said to him, "Jack, you may send me to jail for several years," he responded that perhaps jail would do me good.

He believes the country has problems and we need change. But it mustn't come so fast as to challenge the

existing order, at least not before there is an alternative
system that is just as workable as the old one. After all, he
said, we do have the best, most stable and most equitable
system of government the world has ever seen.

Too, he said, being an undercover agent is a disagree-
able task, but in times like these, when the orderly fabric
of Our Nation is threatened, someone must do it. Better
to have a liberal than a fascist pig. Liberals have enough
integrity not to plant dope on us (but not enough to miss
the excitement of being a provocateur).

The shock of his discovery brought our community
closer together. We consciously fought the inevitable
paranoia that came with the shock. We knew suspicion
is the Man's game, that if we let ourselves be divided by
Jack's discovery, we would be letting him do yet more
destruction to our community. We came together to talk
about Jack; we talked in pairs and groups.

As we talked, we found chinks in his story. Perhaps the
most serious was that he had been busted on a serious
charge (selling acid) and not brought to trial (a sure give-
away that he was an informer, at least). His cover had been
that he was coming up next session of court. After several
sessions we should have been curious. Also, although Jack
had served six months' active duty in the National Guard,
he never attended weekend reserve meetings after his
bust. He claimed his drug arrest made him unfit for service, but as he had never been convicted, that was clearly
not the truth. Too, David was released from prison without going through the ordinary prerelease procedure. Our
ignorance of the workings of the prison system hurt us.

Many of the people who had boarded at Weatherford's
house recalled his going off into his room and typing for
hours. As we all talked, we discovered too that he had
disappeared for weekends (usually to the beach, ostensibly
to "straighten out" his head) at fairly regular monthly intervals.

When we talked about his politics, several of us spoke

of being confused about how he integrated his objective,
social scientist, school thinking (which included belief in
people's natural competitiveness, avarice, and aggressive-
ness) with his radical political commitment. One woman
had accused him of being a spy for the Young Americans
for Freedom, but she had never mentioned that to anyone else.

Weatherford had once admitted, while tripping with a
man he loved, that he had to do a number of dope busts
to "pay off" his own. The other man, out of loyalty to
Jack, had never told anyone, and when Weatherford
told him he was no longer obligated, the other man
believed him.

How might we have caught him? Probably only by tail-
ing him to a weekend meeting or an evening report. But
we would only have done that if we had had reason to distrust him, which would only have come through greater
responsibility to each other and our common beliefs than
to our friend.

Boyd Douglas

by Paul Cowan

Boyd F. Douglas, an ex-convict-turned-informer, was the
government's star witness at the trial of the Harrisburg 7,
who were indicted for conspiring to kidnap Henry Kissinger, to bomb federal heating systems, and to destroy Selective Service records. The government's case consisted
of some speculative passages in an extensive correspondence between Sister Elizabeth McAlister and Father
Philip Berrigan—especially two passages in which the

priest and nun discuss the possibility of kidnapping
"somebody like Henry Kissinger"—and Douglas's testimony about conversations he'd had with six of the seven
defendants. Most jurors distrusted the informer's assertion that he'd been in on an extensive bombing-kidnapping
plot. The vote was ten to two for acquittal on conspiracy.
(Sister McAlister and Father Berrigan, though, were
convicted of smuggling letters in and out of the Lewisburg
penitentiary. McAlister's conviction has since been overturned on appeal.)

Nevertheless, during the summer of 1970, Douglas
had won the trust of some active members of the Catholic
left and of some students and faculty members at Bucknell University, which he attended on a study-release
program while he was still a prisoner. And for a while it
seemed as if he'd manipulated those relationships into a
bonanza for himself, a windfall for the FBI. Here is a portrait of his activities at Bucknell, based on his testimony
in court and on interviews with some of the people he
knew best there.

Boyd Douglas first met Philip Berrigan in May, 1970, a
few days after Berrigan had been sent to the Lewisburg
prison for destroying draft records at Catonsville, Maryland. Though an inmate, he was attending Bucknell on a
study-release program. Until then, he had never struck
most of his Bucknell acquaintances as being a very political person, though he had made contact with Richard
Drinnon, a history professor who was a friend of Berrigan's, and had offered to smuggle documents from jail.
Since Douglas had entered Bucknell in January, 1970, he
had spent most of his spare time at a fraternity house on
campus, although he didn't make many friends there.

The day after Berrigan arrived in jail, Douglas sent him
an urgent message requesting a meeting. They held their
first conversation that Sunday, after mass. During that

chat, Douglas told the priest that he had been a demoli-
tions expert in Vietnam—a remark that seems to have
provoked the rambling discussions of explosives that
Douglas later sought to describe as a plot. He also volunteered to smuggle letters between Berrigan and Sister
Elizabeth in and out of jail.

It's not clear whether Douglas was an FBI informer at
the time. During the trial both he and his handling agent,
Delmar Mayfield, testified that his relationship with the
Bureau began in early June, after a prison guard had
searched Berrigan's cell and found a letter that Douglas
was supposed to have smuggled. The pact was sealed the
next day, during a meeting between Douglas and several
agents. Terry Lenzner, a defense attorney who had spent
a year investigating the case, said that another prisoner
had told him Douglas originally planned to hoard the
letters between the priest and nun and use them to black-
mail the Catholic left.

Schemes were not new to Douglas. He'd spent much
of his adult life in jail for various frauds. At eighteen, he
had left the small Texas town where his father laid pipe-
line for an oil company. Since then, he had often been on
the run, heading toward the hustle centers of the world
—Acapulco, Reno, Miami, Las Vegas, even Hong Kong.
His exploits were often daring. For example, by forging
checks he made $50,000 in a single year, and the itinerary
of his swindles sounds like a page from John Dos Passos:
Rochester, Baltimore, Milwaukee, Denver. Once, he de-
frauded a bank in Las Vegas to pay for a hunting trip in
Wyoming.

He must have learned to size up every friendship, every
situation he found himself in, for the most promising
hustle it offered. He had to do that with the banks. He did
that in jail. And he did it at Bucknell. He must have seen
his fortuitous relationship with Philip Berrigan as a wild
card in a game he was just learning. And as he met Berrigan's friends on the Catholic left and liberal students on
campus, he raised the stakes with each small personal

transaction. The pot was the reward his information would bring from the FBI.

As Berrigan's "Minister with Portfolio" (a phrase the jailed priest frequently used in his letters), Douglas was able to get close to Sister Elizabeth McAlister, Father Joseph Wenderoth, and Father Neil McLaughlin, all of whom became defendants in the Harrisburg trial. He encouraged them to spend time in Lewisburg, introduced them to people at Bucknell, and telephoned their homes to exchange information. He pressed them to talk about the fantasy of disrupting federal heating systems in Washington, D.C., and once gave Father Wenderoth an ROTC manual on explosives that agent Delmar Mayfield had given him to help him polish his cover. (The government used that exchange as an important bit of evidence at the trial.)

He used those prestigious relationships to win a special role for himself in Bucknell's movement community. In May he asked Tom Love, a nonstudent in his early twenties who'd been a leading Lewisburg radical for years, if he could share Love's apartment. Soon he began to meet Love's friends. Throughout the summer he paid most of the rent on the apartment. (A year earlier he had obtained a $15,000 settlement from the Bureau of Prisons because he'd suffered severe radiation burns after volunteering for a prison medical experiment.) He could have gotten into very serious trouble if prison authorities had discovered he was using an apartment.

He began a complex, intense relationship with Jane Hoover, a Bucknell student, who was living in the apartment above Love's during summer school. Jane, the daughter of an employee of the Penn Central Railroad, was raised in Sunbury, Pennsylvania. In high school she'd always been reserved and very straight; as a senior she won a DAR award for good citizenship. At college she became part of the new culture, but she'd never been very political until she met Douglas.

There was constant political and cultural tension between them. (He was thirty-four and had spent most of his adult life in the army or in jail; she was twenty-one.) Once, for example, she was reading *Women in Love* and Douglas told her sarcastically that she should be reading Bobby Seale. He often complained that she and her friends were too involved with dope, music, and a kind of collective humor he couldn't share, that they'd never make good revolutionaries. He was always pushing her to make more contacts in the Catholic left and to become more active herself.

He had her act as his mail drop since, as a convict, he was forbidden to receive mail outside jail. He convinced her to copy letters from Sister Elizabeth to Father Berrigan into the notebooks in which he smuggled them into jail. (He said that the guards, who'd already found one letter in Berrigan's cell, were less likely to look in notebooks than to discover new letters. He got Jane into the act by telling her that his handwriting was illegible. Of course, his explanation was a lie since prison authorities knew Douglas was bringing the letters in and out.) In July, he tried to persuade her to attend the Baltimore wedding of Tony and Mary Scoblick, an event that was disrupted by FBI agents who searched the church for Daniel Berrigan.

He urged her to get involved in one of the Draft Board raids the Catholic left was organizing that summer. He encouraged her to visit Sister Elizabeth in New York (Sister Elizabeth would inspire her to a deeper commitment, Douglas said) and offered to pay her plane fare. Jane went, but in a friend's car, and spent most of her visit asking advice on how to respond to Douglas's efforts to push her further than she wanted to go. Sister Elizabeth told her to heed her own conscience, Jane recalls.

Shortly after she returned to Bucknell, Douglas proposed to her. When she refused him, he cried for hours.

She still believes he was genuinely upset, but it is also possible that her refusal frustrated a long-range plan that may have flickered through his mind. A wife who'd participated in an illegal Draft Board action, who was trusted friends with people like Sister Elizabeth and the Scoblicks, would be in a position to learn a good deal about the movement, information she'd almost certainly pass along in casual conversation. Such a wife would also strengthen Douglas's own position in the Catholic left.

If he was upset by Jane's refusal, he certainly wasn't paralyzed by it. In late July he arranged for a group of students—not including Jane—to meet with some people who were planning the action that would become the Flower City Conspiracy in Rochester. When one of the students seemed interested in joining the action, Douglas paid his way to Rochester. Though he finally decided not to become involved in the conspiracy, he learned a great deal about the plans. The unwitting student shared what he knew with Douglas. The participants were caught in the midst of their deed. At the trial Delmar Mayfield, the FBI agent who handled Douglas the previous summer, testified that the informer received $2000 for supplying information that led to the arrest.

Later that summer he tried to persuade at least two other people to become involved in Draft Board raids, promising to introduce them to the appropriate intermediaries as soon as they were ready to make their commitment.

Douglas seems to have been involved in a scheme to catch even bigger game. By early August the FBI was very frustrated by its failure to capture Dan Berrigan. One day during that period, Douglas made a special appointment with an undergraduate friend and confided that he planned to go underground soon—to leave Lewisburg one day instead of returning to jail. By doing so, he claimed, he'd enrage the FBI still more. It seems likely that he—

and whatever agents were advising him—toyed with the idea that he might enter the "Berrigan underground" in the hope that it would lead him directly to the fugitive priest. After Father Dan was arrested, Douglas never mentioned the possibility of going underground to his undergraduate friend or to anyone else I interviewed. (But he did provide the information that allowed the FBI to make the arrest by intercepting a letter in which Sister McAlister disclosed the fugitive priest's whereabouts. The FBI gave him $500 for that catch.)

Douglas's aborted relationship with Jane Hoover seems to have convinced him (or his advisers) that he had to find a way of overcoming the generational distance that separated him from most Bucknell undergraduates. Throughout August he pushed his friends on the Catholic left to send a younger organizer to Bucknell—assuring them, one friend recalls, "that there's a lot of potential here." Most likely, the organizer would have accepted his suggestions and confided in him. None was ever sent, but Douglas always made a point of introducing younger members of the movement who were passing through town to undergraduates he hoped to recruit.

Early in the fall he began a new intense relationship with Betsy Sandel, another Bucknell undergraduate. Betsy had been Jane Hoover's roommate during summer school. Like Jane, she came from a small town in middle Pennsylvania, had received awards in high school (she was grand champion in an essay contest sponsored by the Americans for Competitive Enterprise), was into the new culture but relatively apolitical when she and Douglas met. But Douglas was more cautious with her than he'd been with Jane. For example, he didn't criticize her cultural tastes as much. He always bought the records she suggested. (Douglas always had plenty of money and always spent it freely on his undergraduate friends.) Though his musical instincts ran to Burt Bacharach and

Dionne Warwick, he soon got into James Taylor and began to play "Fire and Rain" all the time.

Instead of pushing Betsy to take bold political actions, he urged her to write an honors thesis on the Catholic left, which she began to prepare during the fall. But he remained willing to use his (or the FBI's) money as a sort of travel fund for unwitting students who might furnish him valuable information. When Betsy expressed interest in attending a conference on "Liberation Movements in Theological Perspective" that would be held at the Chicago Theological Seminary over Thanksgiving, Douglas offered to pay half her plane fare and she accepted. He suggested that Betsy look up Eqbal Ahmad, a Pakistani scholar who was teaching at the Adlai Stevenson Institute in Chicago and later became a defendant in the Harrisburg case. Ahmad was the only defendant Douglas had never met. He was thwarted that weekend, too, since Betsy could never get in touch with Ahmad. Douglas must have had an informer's hungry response to the phrase "liberation movements," Betsy thinks now, but the conference was actually quite academic and tame.

Douglas was scheduled to be released from prison in mid-December. During the fall he enrolled at Bucknell for a second term and paid a deposit on the apartment where he planned to live. Each January Bucknell has a program called "the Jan plan," in which students work off campus all month. Douglas planned to use that period to visit penal institutions around the country. The faculty gave him permission to take several undergraduates with him. "They'll make me look more innocent," he told one friend. To another, he boasted that he really planned to use his "Jan plan" project to build up movement contacts around the country. In fact, he and the FBI had another scheme. He would use the "Jan plan" to meet radicals, particularly members of the Catholic left, and inform on them to the Bureau. At the trial, Douglas and agent Mayfield testified that he was slated to receive $1000 a month for his services.

Meanwhile, his activities still restricted to Lewisburg, he tried to attract as many movement activists as possible to the Bucknell campus. Here, too, he seems to have been as much provocateur as informant. He suggested that Sister Elizabeth McAlister and William Stringfellow (at whose house Daniel Berrigan was caught) be invited to Bucknell's Colloquy weekend—Sister Elizabeth accepted, Stringfellow did not. Her visit was one of the "overt acts" in the Justice Department indictment. Douglas arranged for Father Neil McLaughlin and Father Joseph Wenderoth to stay at the house of Zoia Horn, a Bucknell librarian. That was another "overt act."

Other visits he hoped to arrange were aborted. He urged a friend on the Catholic left to invite Eqbal Ahmad to Bucknell, but the invitation was never passed along and the visit never occurred. He asked William Kunstler to give a speech on the campus at a fund-raising event for the resisters who had been caught in Rochester. Though Kunstler had never met Douglas he agreed to come, but sent Father William Cunningham in his place at the last minute. Some people speculate that if Kunstler had come Douglas might have involved him in a conversation that could have led to his inclusion in the indictment.

In late October Douglas began to plan the party he'd throw December 18, when he was scheduled to be released from prison. He hand-printed an invitation that included the peace symbol and a motto, "Persevere for Peace," and sent it to his friends at Bucknell and to most of the people who would be named as defendants and co-conspirators in the alleged kidnapping and bombing plot. But by then J. Edgar Hoover had already alleged that the Berrigans were involved in a bombing-kidnapping plot, and word had spread throughout the Catholic left that Douglas might be an FBI informer. No one from outside the Bucknell community came to his party. (During the previous two weeks, Douglas had been meeting extensively with the FBI about the discussions he'd had with Father Berrigan and Sister McAlister. Hoover's statement had triggered a full-scale after-the-charge investigation, and Douglas was the key). He got very drunk at his party and had to be carried to his car and driven home.

After that, Douglas's relations with movement activists disintegrated and his confidence apparently began to dissolve. On December 19 he took Betsy Sandel to the Justice Department in Washington to attend a demonstration that had been organized to protest Hoover's statement. Betsy recalls that he was in a desperate hurry to get to the demonstration, but once he arrived he was afraid to be seen. He told her that he didn't want the FBI to take his picture. At a party that night he seemed very depressed because many of the radicals there seemed to distrust him. He was excluded from a meeting that took place afterwards. A few days later, in New York, some friends from the movement told him frankly that they thought he was an informer.

Back at Bucknell, Betsy Sandel decided to break up with him. Like Jane Hoover, she became convinced that his swaggering, frightened personality was too much for her to bear. He cried for hours, she says, just as he had done with Jane. But the next morning, completely cool, he stopped by her room, suggesting by his manner that he didn't need her anyway. Three days later he testified before the grand jury.

Some friends of Jane's and Betsy's live in their old apartment now, and one night we sat up until 2:00 A.M. discussing the events of the summer of 1970. They were the kind of bright, sensitive people one might have met in the civil rights movement or the McCarthy campaign. All of them, especially Betsy and Jane, still wonder why they never let themselves suspect Douglas. They were particularly dismayed by the fact that they'd accepted his claim that he was a political prisoner, a Vietnam vet who'd been jailed for conspiring to blow up a napalm truck. (In fact, he was in prison for forgery.) As they talked it became clear that they'd all indulged Douglas because he was a convict, a member of an oppressed class. They'd each wondered about things he said and did, but they felt too guilty about their own privilege to trust their doubts. For his part, they guessed, Douglas may have felt an increasing contempt for the students and faculty members who failed to see through his cover.

Still, it doesn't seem likely that he got what he wanted out of his effort to become a movement super-spy. He must have hoped to trade his ability to produce information about the Catholic left for a long-term hustle. But the FBI betrayed that hope. Several people I talked to recall that he was depressed in August, 1970, when the government sent both Berrigans to the Danbury prison. Did that decision suggest that their confidence in him was waning? And most people who knew him say that he was stunned and enraged in November when J. Edgar Hoover alleged the existence of a bombing and kidnapping plot. Did he realize that the FBI director's statement would soon blow his cover? He never did get to go on the Jan plan. And after the Harrisburg trial—for which he'd once requested a $50,000 payment—he was no use at all to the FBI.

The FBI wants its informers to be people it can control completely. Douglas must have seemed too erratic to the people who were evaluating him. He spent money too freely—that always causes suspicion. Jane Hoover recalls that he destroyed the originals of several letters she copied—a good agent never destroys evidence. He let his anger or grief show too often—agents are supposed to be cool. Perhaps he was too much of a self-starter, initiated too many little schemes, (like writing letters recruiting people he'd never met to join the conspiracy he kept describing to the FBI); broke the bureaucratic routine, and risked unnecessary suspicion.

No one I met at Bucknell displays much rancor toward Douglas. Both Jane and Betsy are still convinced that during their relationships with him they sometimes glimpsed a human being who was struggling to find himself. That was the part of him, Betsy thinks, that responded to "Fire and Rain." And Zoia Horn, the librarian who went to jail rather than testify at the trial and who was one of the gentlest members of the gentle community whose lives Douglas disrupted, warned against focusing much anger on him. "He's another Calley," she said. "I suppose he victimized us, but he was misused, too. Sometimes I think of him as another victim."

Five Years
As a Special Agent
by Robert Wall

The fact that surveillance by a police agency has taken place is often mentioned and discussed in newspapers and on television. But few people really have any idea of what a surveillance involves. In the past, the word evoked a picture of a trench-coated figure furtively glancing over the top of a rumpled newspaper. Today, the same word calls forth a picture of a minute marvel of electronic gadgetry capable of projecting a whisper to the eager ears of unseen listeners miles distant.

We often read that the police placed a suspect under surveillance and after an undisclosed period were able to apprehend him with the evidence of his foul deed. But what of those who watched, bleary-eyed, bone weary, and

cramped, until the fateful moment when they could catch
the subject in an unguarded incriminating action? Who
they were we never learn. What sustained their enthusiasm through untold hours of fatigue-filled watching is
covered by the cloak of their anonymity.

Since I was a Special Agent of the FBI for five years and
since a large portion of my time with the Bureau was
spent in what may loosely be called surveillance, I will
try to recall what I thought and did during those seemingly
interminable periods when my job was to sit silently and
watch or listen.

My baptism into the art of surveillance took place in
Miami, Florida, during the fall of 1965. An informant had
reported that a local thug had purchased $10,000 worth of
stolen bank traveller's checks at the very reasonable price
of $1,500. It was apparently his intention to cash as many
of them as he could before they became too "hot." The
agent to whom the case was assigned proposed that we
follow the suspect around and attempt to catch him in the
act of cashing one of the checks. Being young, eager, and
inexperienced, I quickly volunteered to assist in the
operation.

The individual we were to watch and apprehend was
reputed to be the strong-arm man in a local extortion
racket. He had harassed, brutalized, and maimed innocent
victims of the racket and somehow avoided justice. Here,
I thought, was an assignment that offered a challenge and
perhaps some of the excitement I had envisioned as part
of the job. I had sought an appointment as Special Agent
of the FBI much as a knight of old must have sought a
place at the Round Table of King Arthur's Court. Now I
had an opportunity to protect the innocent by removing
this evil from society. It was in these terms that I had
described my idealistic notion of "helping to make society
better" during the endless round of interviews that were
a part of the FBI screening process.

Armed both conventionally and with a thermos of coffee,

I set out with two other agents to stake out the home of the suspect. After a quick check to determine that his car was still in the garage, we took position about half a block away from his house on a quiet palm-shaded street in one of Miami's many little suburbs. I used the next two hours to question my more experienced associates searchingly on the art and lore of surveillance, all the while keeping my unblinking eyes locked on the offender's closed garage door.

"Discreet" seemed to be the keyword of our conversation. We had to be discreet or we would blow the operation. With my eyes locked on the target area, it was easy to ignore the parade of neighborhood children who passed through my peripheral vision enjoying the cool evening air after the heat of the day. But behind my eyeballs, my mind was trying to accommodate the conflicting thoughts raised by the word "discreet," on the one hand, and the knowledge, on the other, that our stakeout was readily apparent to anyone who cared to glance in our direction.

Some three hours after taking up our position, as we were discussing the propriety of taking a break to relieve our burdened bladders, the suspect exited the house, opened the garage door, entered his car, and drove off into the darkening night. With thoughts of internal discomfort momentarily supplanted, we took up the trail. Being discreet, we allowed a two-block gap to develop. This gap, plus the presence of other traffic, necessitated that we disregard, where safety permitted, some of the usual traffic control devices. Just past the second red light we had run, we became the quarry of a local police officer. The brief moment it took to identify ourselves and account for our behavior was sufficient to lose our suspect for the night.

The lessons of the night remained, however. When the call for volunteers went out the next day, I remained "discreetly" silent.

The air of adventure that made my first contact with the

practice of surveillance somewhat bearable was already
a thing of the past. The romantic notion of the super-sleuth
secretly stalking his prey quickly dissolved in the realiza-
tion that the actual tracking was but a momentary inter-
lude. The endless hours filled with physical discomfort
and mental ennui were the depressing reality.

When it was decided to establish a physical surveillance,
the choice of a base of operations was not determined by
the comfort of the watchers but rather by the practical
necessity of having a place from which to watch that was
not itself open to observation.

Shortly after I was assigned to work in the field of internal security in Washington, D.C., I received for investigation a case on a budding left-wing group. The agent
previously assigned to the case turned over a file containing a few reports that said in essence that the group was
not active in Washington. Tucked away in one of the reports was the notation that the organization had recently
opened a regional office in northwest Washington. I reasoned that a regional office was the most likely place to
look for activity, so I set out to determine who used the
office, when, and for what purpose.

The office was actually a three-story row house on a
quiet residential street. The fact that the street was one
way and was used for parking by commuters from the
suburbs made a surveillance from a car or panel truck
difficult. So I decided to find an apartment or room in the
neighborhood where I could observe anyone entering or
leaving, discreetly photograph them, and record the
licenses of any cars utilized by the occupants of the office.
I concocted the story that I was a student recently arrived
in town who had been told that some of the homeowners
on the street had rooms available for students. In this way,
if I were fortunate, I could get a room without having to
tell the real reason that I wanted it. If the person didn't
rent rooms, the story provided an opportunity to engage

the person in conversation and thereby assess whether he or she might cooperate by making a room available.

With my story rehearsed, I approached the house directly across from the office of the radical group. There was no sign on the house indicating rooms for rent, so I was somewhat surprised to learn from the woman who answered the door and listened to my story that she did indeed rent rooms. She explained, however, that she had a contract with the welfare department to rent the rooms to persons recently released from St. Elizabeth's mental hospital. It was a halfway house of sorts for mental outpatients. She was quite considerate and suggested other areas of the city where I might find space available.

With the knowledge that I obtained from this interview, I returned to the office, where I did a quick check of the woman and her story. Her story proved accurate, so I decided to approach her again without a cover story and attempt to elicit her cooperation. On my second visit, when I explained to her in vague, general terms the reason that I needed the room, she readily agreed to provide one free of charge.

Though I had mentioned no specifics, she quickly guessed that I was interested in "those beatniks" across the street. She expressed relief that someone would be keeping an eye on them because she was certain they would cause trouble in the neighborhood with their drugs and free love. When I questioned her further about the occupants of the office, she admitted candidly, with no hint of embarrassment, that she really didn't know who lived there or what, if anything, went on there. But she was anxious to help in any way she could because she had a "responsibility to her roomers."

The room provided was almost perfect. It was clean, comfortable, and warm, with large screened windows directly facing the front of the office building across the street.

My plan at this point was a simple one-man spot check operation. I intended to occupy the room at different hours of the day and night for about two weeks to get a general idea of when the office was utilized and how many persons used it. Because there was no way to secure the room in my absence, my equipment was modest, limited to what I could conveniently carry in and out with me. I had a 35mm camera, a collapsible tripod, binoculars, a supply of regular film for daylight use, and some special film for night photography.

The only drawback to the room was that the occupants of the other rooms, unaware of my secret mission, presumed that I, like them, had recently been released from St. Elizabeth's. Shortly after I had installed myself in position at one of the windows and was setting up my photographic equipment, a delegation, anxious to welcome the new arrival, knocked at my door. It was customary, I later learned, for the residents of the house to greet new arrivals and attempt to ease their transition from the institutional life of St. Elizabeth's to the more relaxed atmosphere of the halfway house. They interpreted my repeated refusals to join them as an indication, perhaps, of my embarrassment at having been in a mental hospital and doubled their efforts to have me join them. Finally, I was forced to hide my equipment and greet my new friends. After about an hour of handshaking, name swapping, and storytelling, I pleaded fatigue and was allowed to return to my room.

After enduring all this to get established, the real blow to my fledgling operation came when I put on paper a formal request to Bureau headquarters for permission to do what I had already done. The answer was a flat no. The reasons given for the rejection were logical in a bureaucratic sense but I suspected that the underlying reason was an unwillingness to allow an agent to spend so much time out of contact with the office in a quiet room with a nice comfortable bed.

As my time in the Bureau lengthened, I became more involved in investigations of antiwar and civil rights organizations. When I first began doing investigations and surveillances, I occupied my mind with the nuts and bolts problems of the actual operation of a surveillance, such as where to set up, how to avoid detection, how to utilize the physical layout, and how to prepare for any attempt to detect the surveillance.

In the internal security field, these preparations were really more for the sake of drill than a practical necessity. Surveillance of an antiwar or civil rights group consisted mainly in watching picketers outfitted with signs and banners ambling around the entrance of some federal office building. Initially I might discreetly jot down the license numbers of cars bringing the demonstrators, note a representative selection of the signs they carried, approximate the number, age, race, and sex of the picketers, and pick up any literature they were handing out. After reporting this vital information to a paper-man (an agent in the office writing the report on the day's activities), I would retire to a position where I could watch the remainder of the action as unobtrusively as possible.

Later, when the routine became somewhat familiar, the focus of my attention became the why of the surveillance. Why were we investigating certain groups? Why not others? Why this particular individual? Those questions, directed as they were to the motivation behind an investigation, were not the type that could be discussed with Bureau supervisors. We were trained to do what we were told, to do it quickly, precisely, and professionally. We were not encouraged to question the reasons for an investigation, nor could we decline to do one if we disagreed with the reasons behind it.

Underlying and prodding my questions of motivation was the fact that I had begun to realize that any investigation by the FBI could have serious consequences for the one investigated. Even in those instances in which the organization was blameless and innocent, the investigator could, just by asking questions, harm the reputation of that group or its members. Knowing this, and knowing that the Bureau had no solid legal justification for most of its intelligence-gathering investigations, I spent a great deal of my time debating with myself the propriety of the investigations and surveillances I was conducting.

In September, 1967, an organization called SANE (Committee for a Sane Nuclear Policy) held a conference in Washington, D.C., in preparation for the October, 1967, march on the Pentagon sponsored by a coalition of peace groups. Since I was relatively unknown in Washington at the time, I was recruited to attend the conference and report on the plans of the organization for the march. SANE was a nonviolent political pressure group that had previously been very active in lobbying for the nuclear nonproliferation treaty. Members espoused no violent tactics, made no threats against government officials or institutions, and yet, there I was sitting in on their conference to report their plans. Of even more note is the fact that they had mimeographed and distributed a pile of information bulletins detailing their plans. My own report, based on the notes taken at the conference, did not vary significantly from their own prepublished information and was understandably less detailed.

When the march on the Pentagon took place in October, the FBI was there en masse, watching, listening, photographing, and recording the events of the day. The mounds of intelligence and photographs were then used to open hundreds of new investigations on individuals who had taken part in the march. Whoever could be identified from the throng might come under investigation either as an activist, for participating in the march, or as a potential informant. The identities of the participants were ascertained from informants, from bus and railroad company officials, or from the local police intelligence units that photographed the boarding of buses for the march.

The names of persons arrested at the Pentagon were obtained and forwarded to the FBI offices covering the cities from which those arrested had come. At the local level, the number of investigations actually opened on these individuals who were identified depended primarily on the number of agents available for the task. The investigation of the individual himself might be extensive or cursory, depending on his status in the movement and the enthusiasm and interest of the agent assigned. But the point is that for the "crime" of expressing dissent against the war in Vietnam, hundreds of citizens became the objects of FBI surveillance and investigation. And when, in the course of those investigations, relatives, friends, employers, and associates were contacted, no one protested that the person contacted might himself be deterred from expressing dissent in the future by the chilling effect of such an investigation.

Most of the FBI agents involved did not seem to question the official Bureau explanation for those investigations. They accepted J. Edgar Hoover's vision of a worldwide Communist conspiracy organizing and subsidizing the antiwar movement to subvert the nation. Participants in activities such as the march on the Pentagon were seen as actual or potential fifth columnists who needed careful watching if the nation were to be prepared to defend itself.

Nor was it surprising that those agents did not question Hoover's dicta, because few people in the country doubted the validity of his pontifical pronouncements. Moreover, the elaborate screening process for future agents was designed by Hoover to provide a corps of men whose hallmark was fidelity: fidelity to home, fidelity to church, fidelity to country, and above all, fidelity to Hoover. Those who showed independence or initiative, those who expressed dissent, those who questioned the way things were and sought their own answers were rejected. Those few agents who retained enough independence of spirit to question the FBI's incursion into the antiwar movement did so privately and with an air of resignation to the inevitable, for they were well aware of the fact that Hoover did not appreciate dissent and was willing and able to purge dissenters from the ranks. Nor was I different. Long after I began to question the Bureau's right to utilize this shotgun approach to investigations of the antiwar movement, I docilely continued to do as I was told.

But the boredom of the actual operation of a surveillance made some agents look for something else to occupy their time. Some became expert at the daily crossword puzzle. Others memorized the stock reports. Still others chose to conduct their surveillances from the comfort of local movie theaters.

My personal diversion was to seek out those whom I was watching, identify myself, and attempt to engage them in conversation. This was both an intelligence-gathering operation and an educational experience. Admittedly, this destroyed my anonymity, but it elicited much more useful information about a person than merely watching at a distance could have provided. It was also an ego trip for me because I enjoyed debating and arguing the history of the Vietnam war and U.S. foreign policy. And while I was almost always able to convince those with whom I talked that I was simply doing the job I was ordered to do and was actually sympathetic to the antiwar movement, I was often put in the position of defending the FBI's investigations of antiwar groups. In fact, I was sympathetic to an extent, but the years of red scare propaganda I received in school, in the navy, and in the Bureau made it hard for me to divest myself of the lurking suspicion that there might be some secret conspiracy behind the movement. I kept looking and listening for some hint, some innuendo, some clue to the conspiracy. Needless to say, I didn't find any. I found, instead, sincere individuals who had thoughtfully analyzed the war, had concluded that the U.S. involvement in it was unjustifiable, and had taken steps to bring about the end of our involvement.

Shortly before I left the Bureau, I became involved with an older agent in a discussion of the practice of surveillance of political dissidents. It was my conviction that the Bureau's elaborate investigations and surveillances of persons involved in the antiwar movement were a form of political repression. He, citing his long experience, said that investigations of the antiwar groups were no different from the investigations of members and suspected members of the Communist party in the forties and fifties. His advice to me in parting was that I should be careful not to get involved with the persons I was investigating, not to pay much attention to what they said, because such involvement would interfere with my ability to do my job. And he was right.

IV
"HOW STUPID DO THOSE PEOPLE IN WASHINGTON THINK WE ARE?"

Beating the Machine

NAT HENTOFF

A twenty-two-year-old New York woman is fighting a Civil Service Commission order that she be fired from her job as a substitute postal clerk. The commission has learned from FBI files that in 1969, this woman, exercising her First Amendment rights, took part in a campus demonstration at Northwestern University. According to the FBI, she was also at that time a member of Students for a Democratic Society, a legally constituted organization.

Says a staff member of the Senate Subcommittee on Constitutional Rights about her case: "This demolishes the Justice Department's assertion that the only reason for surveillance of political bodies is to protect against civil disturbances. The effect is to penalize citizens who participate in various dissent activities."

In Philadelphia, former mayors James Tate and Richardson Dilworth charge that the present mayor, former police chief Frank Rizzo, is tapping their telephones. Rizzo denies it. Yet Kent Pollock, an investigative reporter for the *Philadelphia Inquirer,* claims that following publication of a story he wrote on police corruption, his private life has been investigated. Greg Walter, on the staff of the same paper, has also been critical of Rizzo and of the police department. As a result, Walter charges, "persons who are close to me or who are contacts of mine in the city of Philadelphia have been questioned extensively about my life, my drinking habits, and God knows what else. And this information is all filed away."

Pamela Haynes, city editor of the *Philadelphia Tribune,* observes that several reporters in that city have now censored themselves by not writing articles critical of Mayor Rizzo because they fear the consequences.

In Cleveland, an article in *Point of View,* an investigatory local publication, quotes a police officer who was sympathetic to the administration of Carl Stokes when the latter was mayor of Cleveland. According to the officer, Stokes's staff knew that the mayor's private office was bugged and that its phones were tapped by the Cleveland police (many of whom were quite hostile to that city's first black mayor). But the mayor's staff felt, the maverick cop explained, "that if they brought the Cleveland police intelligence unit in to remove the bugs, they would have removed five and put in ten." The staff also decided that hiring a private firm to do the bug-clearing and wiretap-removing job was not worth the cost, since the cost would be persistently recurring.

I checked out the story with a source who was very high in Carl Stokes's administration. He confirmed the story. "I will authorize you to say," my source added, "but without revealing my name, that while Carl Stokes was mayor of Cleveland, he never held any really important meetings in his private office. He always used rooms in different hotels, and he would call those hotels at a moment's notice, just prior to the time the room was needed for the meeting. That way the Cleveland police did not have time to bug that particular room or put taps on its phones."

A letter from an ordinary, apolitical citizen appears in the letters column of the July 1, 1971, *Milwaukee Journal:*

"I never used to look at our country from the political

aspect for I have always felt secure. But now I do, and I am confused. . . .

"I personally have been involved in a situation which tends to make me raise grave doubts. Recently, a friend and I were walking down Brady St. around midnight. While stopping for a 'don't walk' sign, we heard a series of clicks. Looking around, we saw an unmarked police car with one officer inside. He had his camera aimed at us and was taking pictures.

"I rather believed in the law, but this action caused me to wonder. Why was it done? Does someone have an answer?"

The New York Times, in a lead editorial in October, 1972, tried to provide part of the answer. It described the chilling ambience created by the Nixon Administration and noted that its effect has been felt not only on the federal level but also, in terms of the encouragement its practices give, on the state and local levels. This, mind you, was before the revelations connected with Watergate. "The President and his men," the *Times* pointed out, "have injected into national life a new and unwelcome element—fear of Government repression, a fear reminiscent of that bred by the McCarthyism of twenty years ago. The freedom of the press including the electronic media, the right to privacy, the right to petition and dissent, the right of law-abiding citizens to be free of surveillance, investigation and harrassment—these and other liberties of the individual are visibly less secure in America today than they were four years ago."

One explanation for the indifference of the majority of the electorate to the danger that we are approaching what former Congressman Cornelius Gallagher has called "postconstitutional America" is that many Americans have come to *accept* such ominous phenomena as the precipitous rise in dossier-collecting and spying by secret police (local, state and federal). The majority has surely not welcomed the prevalence of secret surveillance, but the practice is accepted as a normative fact of late twentieth-century existence in the United States.

On May 27, 1971, *The New York Times* quoted Inspector Anthony V. Bouza, then commander of the city police department's planning commission, as being worried that "with the unrestricted collection of information now possible, we might be a great deal closer to 1984 than the thirteen years on the calendar." The inspector noted that even in the *precomputer* era, the New York City police department had in its files more than a million cards on individual citizens and organizations.

The story died instantly, even though the source of alarm was a highly regarded police officer—not a radical or a civil liberties lawyer. There was not the slightest discernible public reaction. No politician seized on the issue. Nor did the *Times* bother to get more details from the inspector.

In view of the lack of intense public interest in the rise of secret surveillance, along with the rapidly increasing sophistication of the technology of surveillance, Justice Brandeis's 1928 dissent in *Olmstead* v. *United States*— the first time the Supreme Court declared judicially authorized wiretapping to be constitutional—is in retrospect all the more poignant and powerful.

"The makers of our Constitution," Justice Brandeis wrote, "conferred, as against the Government, the right to be let alone—the most comprehensive of rights and the right most valued by civilized men."

The extent to which our right to be left alone has been eroded is appallingly clear in recent research done by the Senate Subcommittee on Constitutional Rights, the Lawyers' Committee for Civil Rights Under Law, the American Civil Liberties Union, and the staff of the University of Missouri School of Journalism's Freedom of Information Center. In addition to my own research, I have consulted their work and the valuable digging of Michael Sorkin, an investigative reporter for the *Des Moines Register.*

In a detailed account of America-the-watched-society that appeared in the September, 1972, *Washington Monthly,* Sorkin reveals that the FBI is well into the process of compiling "the largest single depository of information ever gathered about U.S. citizens by their government. The FBI's data bank is fed by a computerized network designed to receive and store information from all fifty states through 40,000 federal, state, and local agencies. The raw material is coming in with increasing speed, and by 1975, some 95 percent of the nation's law enforcement agencies will be hooked into the mammoth privacy-shedding machine.

The central depository of files, including the names of millions of Americans, many of them never convicted of a crime, is the National Crime Information Center in Washington.

To begin with, anyone ever arrested is likely to be in the national data bank. Until Congress passed an amendment to the Law Enforcement Assistance Act in August, 1973, the master computer was not required to show if an arrest led to an indictment or trial, let alone conviction. Now states operating data banks with federal Law Enforcement Assistance Administration funds are required to show the dispositions of cases fed into the computers. Nonetheless, even if the disposition is acquittal, an arrest record has been routinely filed. A man may have been found innocent in the courts, but police and potential employers throughout the country will know that he has been arrested.

The harm of having arrest records centrally available for checking by government and private employers is incalculable. As a 1971 study by the President's Commission on Federal Statistics has emphasized, "An applicant [for a job] who lists a previous arrest faces at best a 'second trial' in which, without procedural safeguards, he must prove his innocence; at worst the listing of the arrest disqualifies him *per se*."

One recent study of employment agencies in the New York area, for example, revealed that 75 percent would not accept an applicant with an arrest record even though the arrest had not led to a conviction.

Consider, too, that an estimated 50 million Americans now have arrest records of one sort or another. And since the probability of a black urban male being arrested at least once before he dies is estimated to be as high as 90 percent, the national data bank is going to be exceptionally well integrated.

In this respect, it is essential to realize that in 20 to 30 percent of arrests, the police do not go on to bring charges. They drop cases for a diversity of reasons, such as lack of evidence and mistaken identification. Furthermore, according to the 1969 FBI Uniform Crime Reports, of 7.5 million people *arrested* that year for all kinds of criminal acts, excluding traffic offenses, more than 1.3 million were never prosecuted or charged, and 2.2 million were acquitted or had charges against them dismissed.

Yet, in those millions of cases in which an arrest does not lead to conviction, only eight states have statutes providing for expungement of those arrest records. And of those eight, only one provides for the expungement of arrest records (without conviction) for a person with a previous conviction.

But much more than arrest records are in the national data bank and in the burgeoning files of state and local police. First of all, because of a decision made by the late J. Edgar Hoover and John Mitchell when the latter was Attorney General, there is no requirement that *any* of the raw materials in the electronic surveillance network have to be evaluated for accuracy. This means that even if you have not been arrested, derogatory information about you can be supplied to the data bank with no check as to its reliability.

For instance, a 1971 study by the Law Enforcement Assistance Administration (LEAA), which provides federal funds for the FBI data bank, noted that half of the 108 computer projects already in existence at that time were collecting data on *potential* troublemakers. (The Justice Department alone keeps copious records on persons who are "violence prone" and on other "persons of interest" for national security reasons.) The LEAA study recommended legislation to restrict and monitor the use of such information, but not a single copy of that LEAA study was given to Congress.

As the FBI's computer network now operates, each state decides what kind of information it will put into the network, and many states are alarmingly permissive as to what they permit individual cities to supply to the state data banks, which then go to the National Crime Information Center.

As *Washington Monthly* points out:

Kansas City is feeding its computer the names of area dignitaries such as councilmen, judges, and other municipal leaders; parolees; adults and juveniles with arrest records; people with a history of mental disturbance (would Thomas Eagleton have been listed?) or who have confronted or opposed law enforcement personnel in the performance of their duties; college students known to have participated in disturbances; suspects in shoplifting cases; and people with outstanding parking ticket warrants. . . .

Maryland's computer network will link police department dossiers with records kept by state health and education agencies and "other interested departments and agencies." The District of Columbia computer already is programmed to include a "Prisoner Control System" for information taken at "mass field arrests and civil disturbances."

Welcome to Washington, all ye who would exercise your First Amendment right "to petition the government for a redress of grievances." (During the first week of May, 1971, nearly 13,000 people, protesting the continuation of American involvement in Southeast Asia, were swept up in dragnet arrests by Washington police with the enthusiastic support—and direction—of the Nixon Justice Department. It was the largest illegal mass bust in American history, a judgment substantiated by the fact that only 128 of those arrested were found guilty after trial. Nonetheless, administration officials have said such mass arrests will take place again under similar circumstances; and in that event, the arrest records of all those caught in the net will be included in the national data bank.)

On the state level, some states say they may limit access to their computer files—and to what they obtain, on request, from the national data bank—to law officers only. Other states may decide, as Iowa is contemplating, to make the information available to anyone willing to pay a fee. It must be emphasized, moreover, that unless legislation is enacted to the contrary, each state can determine whether its raw files will include data going beyond criminal matters.

New York State's Identification and Intelligence System (NYSIIS) has files on more than 6 million people — many of whom do not have criminal records. Among the latter are applicants for civil service jobs, with resultant reports by state investigators on their job histories and private lives; people who have attended various political demonstrations considered "suspect" by state and local secret police; and other "persons of interest" for reasons known only to state law enforcement officers.

Iowa, according to *Washington Monthly*, "is proceeding with plans to house criminal intelligence files in the state's main computers—the same computers also hold tax return forms.... Iowa's system will also connect with the state's Revenue Department, the Highway Commission, county treasurers and county recorders (notorious for being highly active in local politics), the Commerce Commission, the Department of Public Instruction, the Conservation Commission, the Department of Social Services (which keeps welfare records), and others."

Let us suppose, however, that somehow you don't end up in the FBI's computerized central files—with circuits to and from state data banks. You're not safe yet. There are many other data banks that are in the process of interfacing—exchanging information with each other. As of this writing, federal investigators already have access to 264 million police records, 323 million medical histories, 279 million psychiatric reports, and 100 million credit files. Among their sources are the files of the Secret Service; the Civil Service Commission; the Federal Communications Commission; the Department of Health, Education, and Welfare (hospitals are required to forward to HEW the private, confidential records of patients receiving Medicare and Medicaid benefits); the Department of Housing and Urban Development; the Census Bureau, whose detailed forms you have to fill out every ten years; and the Internal Revenue Service.

If you have been under the illusion that your federal tax returns are held in strict confidence, you may be disquieted to learn that your returns are available to state tax officials, to any select committee of the House or the Senate, and to anyone authorized by executive order. The University of Missouri's Freedom of Information Center reports that "between 1953 and 1970, fifty-three of those orders were issued, two of the chief beneficiaries being the old House Un-American Activities Committee and the Senate Committee on Internal Security."

A statement of dissent, even by a prominent American, can lead to his harassment through release of his income tax returns to investigatory agencies. A distinguished professor of government, long a critic of the Vietnam war, was puzzled and quite disturbed when, over a period of years, his income tax returns were intensively gone over by Internal Revenue agents while evidence accumulated that other agencies of the government were privy to those returns. Finally, a former White House assistant whose conscience had been bothering him about the dogging of the professor admitted to the victim that it had all come about on direct order from Lyndon Johnson, who had been especially exasperated by some of the professor's comments concerning Johnson's military involvement in Vietnam.

Nor, by any means, are dossiers and data banks a creation only of the government. In a 1971 report for the American Civil Liberties Union, Ralph Nader focused on how very private information about you can be collected even if you're not a dissenter or a "freak" of one kind or another and even if you escape the various federal data banks.

By way of illustration, Nader wrote:

When you try to buy life insurance, a file of . . . intimate information about you is compiled by the "inspection agency." The insurance company not only finds out about your health, it also learns about your drinking habits (how often, how much, with others or alone, and even what beverage), your net worth, salary, debts, domestic troubles, reputation, associates, manner of living, and standing in your community. The investigator is also asked to inquire of your neighbors and associates whether there is "any criticism of character or morals."

The "inspection agency" that obtains this information puts it back into a dossier and saves it. The agency may later make another investigation for an insurance company, or for an employer, a prospective creditor or a landlord. In fact, the agency will probably make this personal information available to anyone who has $5.00 and calls himself a "prospective employer."

Private credit bureaus have similar masses of data on individuals, and they, as well as insurance companies, will open their files to agents of the federal government. In January, 1972, Edward Brennan, Jr., vice-president of TWR Credit (a completely computerized national credit reporting company), admitted on an ABC-TV special, "Assault on Privacy," that the Fair Credit Reporting Act "now makes it mandatory that we supply information to people like police departments and any governmental agency that has a legitimate reason for accessing." TWR Credit has information on more than 30 million individuals. All told, the more than 2,500 credit reporting companies in the country have files on at least 110 million Americans. Some files are limited only to credit information; others contain more about your personal habits, finances, medical history, and life style than your closest friends may know.

With all these private and government computers exchanging information about millions of Americans, probably including you, we may be close to that time when, as Ramsey Clark has warned, "a person can hardly speak his mind to any other person without being afraid that the police or someone else will hear what he thinks. Because of our numbers and the denseness of our urban society, it will be difficult enough in the future for us to secure some little sense of privacy and individual integrity. We can trap ourselves, we can become the victims of our technology, and we can change the meaning of man as an individual."

How have we come this close to trapping ourselves by allowing our privacy to be so increasingly violated? Why do we acquiesce as the rapidly growing information being fed to and distributed by the FBI national data bank threatens to become what Senator Charles Mathias, a liberal Republican from Maryland, calls "the raw materials of tyranny"?

Part of the answer is fear—a national fear, accelerating in the late 1960s, of disorder created by demonstrating and sometimes rioting blacks and students. There is also the precipitously rising fear of crime. The national desire, an almost desperate desire, is for order. In this climate, the majority of the people are much more concerned with their safety than with civil liberties—their own or those of others.

A seminal congressional reaction to the fears of the populace was the Omnibus Crime Control and Safe Streets Act of May, 1968. The bill, with only four senators and seventeen representatives voting against it, sharply limited the rights of criminal defendants and, with regard to privacy, greatly broadened the permissible use of bugging and wiretapping by the government. During the debate on the measure, then Senator Ralph Yarborough, who was not one of the four opposing the bill later, declared that "the Senate has opened a Pandora's box of inquisitorial power such as we have never seen in this country." Senator Hiram Fong, who *did* vote against the bill (along with Philip Hart, Lee Metcalf, and John Sherman Cooper) added, "I am fearful that if these wiretapping and eavesdropping practices are allowed to continue on a widespread scale, we will soon become a nation in fear—a police state."

Two years later, in an amendment to the Omnibus Crime Act of 1970, Congress authorized the FBI to keep centralized criminal records, thereby leading to the establishment of the FBI's national data bank. During that same year, Congress passed a drug bill permitting police to break into any place, without warning, if they had a court order and believed that a preliminary knock on the door might result in the destruction of evidence. Commenting on this "no-knock" bill in *The New York Times*, Tom Wicker asked: "How long will it be before agents come bursting without warning into the houses of political dissidents, contending under this law that any other procedure would have resulted in the destruction of pamphlets, documents, and the like, needed by society to convict?"

As Congress yielded to the fear of its constituents, the Supreme Court, the ultimate protector of our privacy, became markedly less sensitive to the need for safeguarding the Bill of Rights. As Richard Nixon became able to appoint new justices—there are now four Nixon selections on the Court—the egalitarian spirit of the Warren Court began to be reversed.

A significant though little-noted decision by what can now be called the Burger Court was handed down in December, 1970. By a 5–4 majority, the Court ruled that state courts can now use, in criminal proceedings, hearsay evidence that would not be admissible in federal courts. As *The New Yorker* made clear, "The Sixth Amendment to the Constitution gives defendants in criminal cases the right to confront witnesses against them, and, by extension, this (with a few exceptions) rules out hearsay evidence, since the person who makes the accusation, not the person who heard it second-hand, is the one to be confronted." This Burger Court ruling narrows every citizen's liberties, particularly since, as *The New Yorker* emphasized, "93 percent of all criminal cases are tried in state courts.... The decision places 93 percent of all defendants, guilty and innocent alike, at a severe disadvantage."

Whenever fear of dissenters intensifies, state criminal charges of "conspiracy" can, under this ruling, be brought against political defendants on the basis of second-hand testimony from secret police agents who do not want their identities publicly revealed.

During its 1971–72 term, the Supreme Court handed down a particularly dangerous decision maintaining that it was no longer necessary in state criminal trials to have a unanimous jury verdict. As Melvin Wulf, legal director of the American Civil Liberties Union, has pointed out:

The decision wipes out two crucial ingredients of the jury trial. It effectively abolishes the need for a jury to agree that the prosecution has proven guilt beyond a reasonable doubt. . . . Second, the decision effectively nullifies earlier Supreme Court decisions which require that juries consist of a fair cross-section of the entire community. Now, even though blacks may sit frequently on juries in the South (or Chicanos in the Southwest or Puerto Ricans in New York City), and though they may vote to acquit a black defendant because they will not automatically accept the testimony of white witnesses as true, they can be outvoted by their fellow jurors.

Again, consider the potential effect of this ruling on state and local "conspiracy" cases against dissenters, particularly contentious members of minority groups. In such cases—as in various trials of Black Panther Party members—the base of the state's case is usually testimony by informers and secret police infiltrators. Moreover, now that "hearsay" evidence is allowed, part of that testimony can be secondhand. Since, therefore, a unanimous jury verdict is no longer constitutionally mandated, the state's chances to convict have been appreciably improved.

Another Burger Court decision that is disheartening to civil libertarians allows police to stop and frisk people on the street under circumstances that, as Melvin Wulf of the ACLU points out, "come nowhere near satisfying the Fourth Amendment's 'probable cause' standard for arrest." It is now, therefore, much easier for the police to intimidate dissenters and possible dissenters by literally putting them up against the nearest wall.

Still another ominous ruling by the Burger Court has made further inroads on the right to refuse to testify before a grand jury or a trial jury on the Fifth Amendment ground of possible self-incrimination. This right has been steadily eroded in recent years as witnesses have been compelled to accept immunity from prosecution and thereby testify or be held in contempt of court. Under the Burger Court decision, that kind of pressure from the government has been considerably strengthened. The forced witness used to be given *transactional* immunity, which meant that the government could not prosecute him for anything connected with his compelled testimony. Now a witness can be forced to testify in return for only *use* immunity, which means that he still can be prosecuted but the government cannot use his own testimony or any leads from it to build its case against him. But how will it be possible to prove that a subsequent lead that the government does indeed use against a witness was not developed, however obliquely, from something the witness said under forced testimony?

In addition, if the government is less interested in a particular witness than it is in certain people he knows, then forcing him to take immunity, whether *transactional* or *use*, can compel him to testify about others —or face contempt charges against himself. The government, in sum, is free to engage in "fishing expeditions."

It used to be that dissenters, whether under grand jury pressure or not, had recourse to the press to reveal information they believed to be in the public interest or give their side of a case in which the government was prosecuting them or associates of theirs. In such cases, the dissenting source often did not want to be identified, for fear of government retaliation, and he would talk only to a reporter whom he trusted not to reveal his identity.

This avenue for dissenters and others to get information to the public has been seriously limited by another Burger Court decision. In the case of *New York Times* reporter Earl Caldwell, the Court declared—with all four of the Nixon appointees in the majority—that a reporter does not have a constitutional right to protect his sources.

The effect of the Caldwell decision became evident soon after the Supreme Court ruling. In Caldwell's own case he burned the tapes and notes he had collected for a book he was preparing on the Black Panther Party. This material, which had not appeared in the *Times,* had been obtained by a pledge of confidentiality, and Caldwell did not want to take the chance that, under repeated threats of being jailed unless he handed over both the material and the names of his sources, he might finally break that pledge. The burning of Caldwell's tapes and notes is a loss to history and to the public's First Amendment right to information about public issues.

In another instance, following the Caldwell decision by the Supreme Court, a journalist who had written a justifiedly well-received book about militant political activists was about to start a new book on the same theme. This time, however, he consulted a lawyer before he began his research. He was told that since the book could not be written without his using confidential sources, he faced a considerable risk of eventually being forced to reveal those sources or go to jail. It is now unlikely that he will write that book.

An especially chilling illustration of the increasing willingness of government to subvert the Bill of Rights has been the pressure against Beacon Press and its parent church organization, the Unitarian Universalist Association. On October 22, 1971, Beacon Press published the Senator Gravel edition of the Pentagon Papers. These were public documents that Senator Gravel had inserted into the records of a Senate subcommittee he was heading. Seven days after publication date, FBI agents, acting for the Justice Department's Internal Security Division, appeared at the bank in which the Unitarian Universalist Association had its accounts. The agents had a federal grand jury subpoena calling for the delivery of all the *church*'s records—not just those of Beacon Press—including copies of each check written and each check deposited by the church group between June 1 and October 15, 1971.

Every member of the church, throughout the country,

who sent a check to the Unitarian Universalist Association during that period of time is now in the FBI files. As Robert Nelson West, president of the UUA, reasonably puts it, "This kind of treatment is a way of striking at a denomination with respect to its present and potential membership and with respect to the contributors on which a denomination depends for its very existence."

Predictably, donations to the church declined following the news of the FBI's collection of its bank records. And Mr. West reported other ominous effects of this government action. The church had a vacancy for a secretary in its headquarters and placed an ad in a Boston newspaper. "We put the phone number, working conditions, the salary," West says, "but we did not put the name of the organization. The day after the ad was run, six people called and wanted that job. When they were told the name of our organization, five of the six said, 'I don't want anything to do with that organization.'"

Furthermore, West adds, "Everywhere I have spoken about this to Unitarian Universalist groups, except one, the question has been asked by somebody, 'If I buy a copy of the Pentagon Papers, am I subject to investigation? Will a file be opened on me?' Clear evidence that this kind of apprehension and fear is being instilled, even perhaps subliminally, by this kind of treatment."

The experience of this church group indicates that we may be coming closer to a state in which, as Justice William O. Douglas has warned, "Our citizens will be afraid to utter any but the safest and most orthodox thoughts; afraid to associate with any but the most acceptable people. Freedom as the Constitution envisages [it] will have vanished."

Meanwhile, the technology to make this a pervasively watched society continues to advance.

The 40,000 law enforcement agencies in the country are spending almost $700 million annually (much of it provided through federal Law Enforcement Assistance Administration funds) on equipment. Included in that equipment are continually evolving devices for electronic surveillance of all of us.

There are the inviting possibilities, for instance, of closed-circuit TV. In 1972 the Committee on Telecommunications of the National Academy of Engineering prepared a study that you might not have been informed of on television or in your local paper. The study, paid for by the Justice Department, recommended twenty-four-hour television surveillance on city streets.

It's already happening. Among the cities that now have or soon will have twenty-four-hour uninterrupted surveillance of a downtown area are Hoboken, New Jersey; Mt. Vernon, New York; Saginaw, Michigan; and San Jose, California. Any city, if it has the money, can do it, because so far, there are no laws against electronic surveillance of large public areas.

The all-seeing-eye operation underway in Mt. Vernon has been described by Frost & Sullivan, a New York market research and management consultant firm, in its publication "The Public Law Enforcement Market":

The city of Mt. Vernon, New York, was awarded a $32,000 LEAA grant to install a police-operated, low-light-level television system. This system is being used to provide around the clock remote surveillance of the downtown shopping district. The system consists of two all-weather cameras which are mounted on poles. These cameras can be rotated 360 degrees in azimuth and tilted vertically to angles of 90 degrees. The monitoring police officer can zoom and focus the lens to follow the movements of any suspicious persons. The camera is automatically protected from bright light and has an automatic control which adjusts the camera to maintain a clear picture. The camera has been recently developed for use in closed-circuit television and has the capability of detecting and recording a man one-half mile away in extreme darkness. The camera is sensitive to light levels that are below the threshold for normal human vision.

The immediate purpose of keeping watch on the citizenry in public places is to cut down street crime. But among other consequences of having the police department's unblinking eye on certain parts of a city is that demonstrators converging in those areas can be photographed and their identities filed for future use—all from the comfort of police headquarters.

The psychological effects—and the danger to the Bill of Rights—of unceasing police surveillance of public areas have been analyzed in a probing and most disturbing article, "Police Use of Remote Camera Systems for Surveillance of Public Streets," in the Winter, 1972, issue of *Columbia Human Rights Law Review*, published by students at the Columbia University Law School.

The article quotes privacy expert Professor Alan Westin of Columbia on the impact of such surveillance on human behavior: "When a person knows his conduct is visible he must either bring his conduct within accepted social norms in the particular situation involved or decide to violate those norms and accept the risk of reprisals."

Certainly, criminals who violate social norms should suffer reprisals, but the effect of an all-seeing police eye on a public place will reach many other kinds of people besides muggers.

Says the *Columbia Human Rights Law Review*:

'To begin with, police can use a Mt. Vernon–type surveillance system to read a pedestrian's lips or to read documents in his possession. More generally, police can direct the cameras to observe and magnify people in their apartments, cars, or on the street in situations where one anticipates freedom from surveillance or at least freedom for the close scrutiny that the cameras are capable of.... One might reasonably fear that police abuse of the system would lead to increased dossier-building. In a way not presently practicable, the police could use widespread surveillance systems to track associational ties and mark the day-to-day habits of revolutionaries, activists, homosexuals, and other people of police interest.

Even if one were to discount the possibility of police abuse, the deployment throughout our urban areas of electronic surveillance units introduces very real questions concerning the psychological and social well-being of our society. . . . Within a surveillance area, we may alter or entirely suspend certain associations or activities. Eventually, these associations and activities may be deterred even outside the surveillance area. . . . To the extent that America adopts the ethic of a watched society, we inevitably lose the sense of participatory democracy and trust that privacy nourishes.

Among other coming surveillance attractions in the watched society is spying-by-helicopter. New York City recently completed a two-year test of this avant-garde way of bypassing the Bill of Rights. The cost was $409,000. Frost & Sullivan describes the marvels of having an unwavering, nonsectarian eye up above:

The system comprises a TV camera, zoom lens, image stabilizer and microwave transmitting equipment installed in a helicopter. The signal is received at the Empire State Building via antennas. The signal is then relayed via microwave television relay links to Police Headquarters. The signal can be distributed to various offices throughout the building including the Command and Control Center, where the information can be evaluated and manpower and equipment be assigned to cope with the problem. This installation is equipped with recording equipment so that a permanent record can be made of the transmitted audio and video signals. Live TV images can also be projected on a 6-foot by 8-foot screen for close observation. Receiving antennas on the Empire State Building provide 360 degrees of coverage to enable the helicopter to fly in any direction and still transmit back to the Empire State Building. The helicopter's omni-directional antenna provides complete flight flexibility as well.

The wonders of surveillance-by-helicopter are not limited to the police departments of such big cities as New York. Kettering, Ohio, a suburb of Dayton, has a population of 150,000; and those citizens, if they look up, can occasionally see two police helicopters equipped with siren, public-address system, searchlights, radio—and a portable video-tape camera.

With the market for police equipment zooming, manufacturers are zestfully promoting their spying wares. The March, 1972, issue of *The Progressive* tells of firms setting up "elaborate displays of equipment at police conventions. . . . Helicopter companies park their craft outside some law enforcement convention halls and give free rides to prospective customers. In convention hospitality suites, salesmen . . . circulate among police officials and tout the latest developments from computers to night-vision scopes to cigars rigged with radio transmitters."

In a characteristic sales pitch, Eugene G. Fubini, former vice-president for research at IBM and now a private consultant, tells those attending a National Law Enforcement Symposium: "Wouldn't you like to be able to frisk every citizen without him knowing he is being frisked? . . . Just to take an example, you can put multi-dimensional magnometers in turnstiles and movie theaters, and lots of other places. Let me try another one: You could put on all bridges and parkways a device which reads license plates and automatically matches them against a list."

We are well into what the Lawyers' Committee on Civil Rights Under Law calls a "police industrial complex" that will serve "to increase an already extensive, easily abused police capability for surveillance, harassment and interference with noncriminal activities."

And what the police see and record will be filed and then hooked into local, state, and federal data banks.

In September, 1972, conservative columnist James J.

Kilpatrick wrote: "For many years, politically active Americans have been wondering: Were they suffering a kind of paranoia, or was Big Brother really watching them? Answer: He is watching."

Now, every year, he watches and puts into dossiers more and more of what we're doing and saying. A grimly reasonable case can be made that University of Michigan Law School Professor Arthur Miller is being prescient rather than fanciful when he speculates in his book, *The Assault on Privacy* (1971): "An identification number given to us at birth might become a leash around our necks and make us the object of constant monitoring through a womb-to-tomb computer dossier."

Most of us already have such an identification number. It's on our Social Security card. As Senator Sam Ervin has noted, although the Social Security card states on its face that it is not to be used for identification purposes (except for Social Security and income tax needs), citizens now have to submit their Social Security numbers on job applications, voter registration affidavits, credit applications, telephone records, arrest records, military records, driver's licenses, and many other forms.

Such widespread use of a single number of identification, Senator Ervin adds, can lead to the government maintaining extensive computerized data banks of information on all of us. The one Social Security number, he points out, could be the single, common key required "to link computers, enabling them to talk among themselves, promiscuously combining accurate, inaccurate, and incomplete information about nearly all Americans." And, as far back as 1967, the senator emphasized that this correlating process among computers can "make possible a massive invasion of the privacy of millions.... Decisions affecting a person's job, retirement benefits, security clearance, credit rating, or many other rights may be made without benefit of a hearing or confrontation of the evidence."

Yet there is a move in Congress to fulfill Professor Arthur Miller's prophecy of an identification number for each American at birth.

The New York Times, March 3, 1972: "The Senate Finance Committee voted today to require that every child be issued a Social Security card upon entering the first grade."

The New York Times, March 21, 1972: "Representative Martha W. Griffiths, Democrat of Michigan, proposed today that every American baby be assigned a Social Security number at birth."

Once the numbered leash is in place and the computerized data banks busily exchange all kinds of information being fed into them by private and government invaders of our privacy, some of us may remember why in 1972 Justice William O. Douglas, in one of his dissenting opinions against another abuse of privacy, included this statement made to an American reporter by Russian novelist Alexander I. Solzhenitsyn:

"And if you consider that they listen around the clock to telephone conversations, and conversations in my home; they analyze recording tapes and all correspondence, and then collect and compare all these data in some vast premises . . . you cannot but be amazed that so many idlers in the prime of life and strength, who could be better occupied with productive work for the benefit of the fatherland, are busy with my friends and me, and keep inventing enemies."

Yet it would be foolish and foolhardy simply to allow postconstitutional America to come into being without fighting to keep and to regenerate *this* Constitution. There *are* ways to do more than privately bemoan the drifting-away of the Bill of Rights.

One way is through the courts. With regard to political surveillance by secret police, for example, as of 1973 at least thirty suits have been brought by the American Civil Liberties Union that challenge spying on political activities by the FBI, the National Guard, state antisubversive agencies, and state and local police departments. And more suits will surely be filed by the ACLU and other civil liberties organizations in the months and years ahead. Considering the composition of the Burger Court and its probably chilling effect on Bill of Rights sensitivities of some judges in the lower courts, this is likely to be a long journey, with many reverses, some of which have already occurred. But there have also been some victories.

The main thrust in most of these court actions against the secret police is to force disclosure of how dossiers on individuals and organizations are opened and nurtured, on whom they are kept, and to whom their contents are distributed. A corollary request for relief is that the secret police be forbidden from then on to gather information for political dossiers and that they be instructed to destroy those they already have.

A characteristic suit of this nature has been brought by the Civil Liberties Union of Southern California against the Los Angeles police department. The CLU charges in its complaint that the police are keeping files on a variety of organizations—church, political, educational—and individuals associated with these groups, even though neither the police department nor any police officer *"has any information that such group or person has committed, will commit, or intends to commit any criminal offense."* (Emphasis added.)

That case and others like it are still in the courts. There has been one significant triumph in this area, along with one seeming victory that turned into a defeat because of what Richard Nixon has done to the Supreme Court.

The defeat, which is not terminal (other suits can still

be brought despite this particular Supreme Court decision), concerns a case brought against Melvin Laird, then
Secretary of Defense, by Arlo Tatum, a Quaker, and other
plaintiffs, who charged that the United States Army had
been secretly keeping track of their lawful civilian political activities. Mr. Tatum and his associates in the suit had
long publicly opposed the war in Vietnam, and that made
them fodder for those army spies who, according to Senator Sam Ervin, had kept tabs until at least 1969 on more
than 100,000 civilians and organizations.

In April, 1971, a U.S. Court of Appeals sent the case
(*Laird* v. *Tatum*) back to the lower federal district court
that had denied relief to Arlo Tatum and his associates.
The Court of Appeals disagreed with the lower court's
findings, declaring that the plaintiffs did have a case and
it ought to be heard. The Court of Appeals, moreover,
stressed the danger to the country of army political surveillance of civilians and went on to order that the following facts be determined:

"The nature of the Army domestic intelligence system ... specifically the extent of the system, the methods
of gathering the information, its content and substance,
the methods of retention and distribution, and the recipients of the information. ... Whether the existence of any
overbroad aspects of the intelligence-gathering system ...
has, or might have an intimidating effect on appellants
or others similarly situated."

In sum, just what the hell was the army into in its spying
on civilian political activity? Did all those dossiers really
have any relationship to the army's responsibility for
handling such massive civilian disorders as might arise?
Or was the army just collecting whatever it could find
about potential troublemakers, even though they had done
nothing unlawful?

After all, said the Court of Appeals in rather scary
language, "To permit the military to exercise a totally

unrestricted investigative function in regard to civilians, divorced from the normal restrictions of legal process and courts, *and necessarily coupling sensitive information with military power,* could create a dangerous situation in the Republic. (Emphasis added.)

But, we have been told, the army no longer spies on civilians, so why stir up a dead issue? Yet, as Senator Ervin noted in May, 1972, "It's going to be impossible" to destroy all the information the army has gathered. "Our investigations show," Ervin continued, "that while the army was engaged in spying on civilians, that it interchanged information that it collected with the FBI and with local law enforcement agencies throughout the United States, and there is no way we can run that down and get it out of their files."

Therefore, the issues raised in *Laird* v. *Tatum* are hardly dead. The Court of Appeals decision mandating that light be shed on army spying could have been a stunning breakthrough toward letting the citizenry see some of the inner workings of the total national political surveillance system into which the army secret police connect.

Most unfortunately, the Supreme Court thought otherwise. The government having appealed the Court of Appeals decision, the highest court dismissed *Laird* v. *Tatum* in June, 1972, The vote was 5–4, and in the majority were all four of Richard Nixon's appointees, including the redoubtable William Rehnquist. The latter participated in the decision even though he had been directly involved in the issues at the core of this suit against political surveillance while he was in the Justice Department. Rehnquist, moreover, had made it clear, when he was in the Justice Department and testified before Senator Ervin's Subcommittee on Constitutional Rights, that he opposed *any* limitation on government surveillance of *any* citizen.

The majority of the Court, in *Laird* v. *Tatum*, declared

that it isn't enough to claim that being spied on has a "chilling effect" on the exercising of your First Amendment rights. You have to be more specific and show palpable injury directly resulting from political surveillance —loss of a job or loss of income, for example.

In his vehement dissent, Justice William O. Douglas thundered:

This case is a cancer in our body politic. It is a measure of the disease which afflicts us. Army surveillance, like Army regimentation, is at war with the First Amendment. Those who already walk submissively will say there is no cause for alarm. But submissiveness is not our heritage. The First Amendment was designed to allow rebellion to remain as our heritage. The Constitution was designed to keep Government off the backs of the people. The Bill of Rights was added to keep the precincts of belief and expression, of the press, of political and social activities, free from surveillance. The Bill of Rights was designed to keep agents of Government and official eavesdroppers away from assemblies of people. The aim was to allow men to be free and independent and to assert their rights against Government. There can be no influence more paralyzing of that objective than Army surveillance. When an Intelligence Officer looks over every nonconformist's shoulder in the library or walks invisibly by his side in a picket line or infiltrates his club, the America once extolled as the voice of liberty heard around the world no longer is cast in the image which Jefferson and Madison designed, but more in the Russian image.

The Nixon four on the Court were not moved. Nor was one of John Kennedy's most egregious errors of appointive judgment—Justice Byron "Whizzer" White.

At first, the decision appeared to be a disastrous setback to those engaged in court action against the secret police. Whether the spying is being done by the military or the civilian branch of government, if you have to prove that you have been or will be injured as a consequence of your having been under political surveillance, the odds against you can be huge. Since, under present law, you have no right to find out what is in your dossier or to whom it is distributed, you may never know if a particular job application was rejected or a promotion denied because you were once photographed as a participant in an antiwar demonstration or any other activity that military or civilian secret agents consider "disloyal."

Nevertheless, several lower federal court decisions since *Laird* v. *Tatum* indicate that the door is far from closed to attempts, through the courts, to expose government ferrets gnawing at the Bill of Rights. The most significant development concerns a suit by a number of individuals, some of them peace activists, against the Security and Investigation Section (SIS) of the New York City police department. At least 365 police are assigned to this secret cadre, some of whose top officers received training from the CIA in September, 1972, in the handling of "large amounts of information." (In *The New York Times* of December 17, 1972, a spokesman for the CIA admitted that secret police agents from other cities around the country have also been given similar instruction by the CIA in Washington.)

The essence of the suit against New York City's very own secret police was well summarized by Federal District Judge Edward Weinfeld, who was asked by the police department to dismiss the action against it. The judge observed that the charges against SIS are that certain of its practices and some of its conduct infringe the plaintiffs' constitutional rights by subjecting them to, among other things, electronic surveillance and infiltration of organizations to which they belong. What it comes down to, the judge continued, is that these police practices "have a 'chilling effect' on plaintiffs and members of their class in the exercise of their constitutional rights of freedom of speech, assembly and association; that they violate their rights against unlawful search and seizure because the

SIS proceeds [sometimes] without obtaining warrants or judicial authorization; also that they violate their rights of privacy and to substantive and procedural due process."

Just as secret police all over the country do.

Judge Weinfeld, despite *Laird* v. *Tatum,* refused to dismiss the suit against SIS. He pointed out that he regards "the use of secret informers or undercover agents" as "a legitimate and proper practice of law enforcement and justified in the public interest," *but* "those so engaged may not overstep constitutional bounds. The Bill of Rights protects individuals against excesses and abuses in such activities."

As for *Laird* v. *Tatum,* Judge Weinfeld emphasized that that case had been decided by the Supreme Court on narrow grounds and that the majority, in its decision "specifically acknowledged prior Supreme Court authorities which 'fully recognize that Governmental action may be subject to constitutional challenge even though it has only an indirect effect on the exercise of First Amendment rights.'" Missing in the plaintiffs' argument in *Laird* v. *Tatum*—according to the Supreme Court majority—had been proof of *specific* present or future harm because they had been or still are under political surveillance.

The charges against the New York City secret police, however, are specific as well as general. For example, Judge Weinfeld cited the claim "that an anti-Vietnam organization of veterans disbanded due to the actions of a named informer working with SIS, who urged members of the veterans orgainzation to participate in unlawful conduct at demonstrations as part of. a plan fostered by SIS to create an atmosphere among its members of mistrust, suspicion and hostility so as to prevent their free and lawful association with one another and to chill their interest in the exercise of their right of free expression and association."

The case must proceed, Judge Weinfeld ordered.

In a similarly encouraging decision since *Laird* v. *Tatum*, a federal judge in Philadelphia has refused to dismiss a suit against the police department of that city for keeping files on all demonstrations and known demonstrators in Philadelphia. And on October 25, 1972, a federal judge in the state of Washington settled a suit by ten antiwar demonstrators against the police of the city of Longview who had taken pictures of antiwar marches in the fall of 1969. That court order requires destruction of all police photographs of the plaintiffs, who in turn have agreed to drop their claim for damages.

So, the court route to protect our Constitution—and ourselves—from the secret police remains open. Future suits will focus on specific harm—direct or indirect—resulting from police surveillance; not only evidence of disruption of lawful organizations by police infiltrators but also proof that secret police procedures and tactics have actually inhibited people from exercising their First Amendment and other rights.

Some of these cases will be lost; but there is reason to believe that others can be won. Even a losing case may produce a dissenting opinion that will later guide both lawyers fighting for the Constitution and judges in other jurisdictions. Such a potentially important dissenting opinion was that of Federal Judge Winter on August 1, 1972, in a suit that challenged Richmond, Virginia, police for photographing and keeping dossiers on individuals attending demonstrations.

Judge Winter declared (and this decision has been circulated to all ACLU lawyers around the country who are bringing actions against our secret police):

Laird v. *Tatum* was decided by the majority of the Supreme Court on the premise that none of the plaintiffs alleged or tendered any proof to show any harm to himself or any violation of his constitutional rights. The instant case is far different.... These witnesses were photographed by the police, without their

permission and arguably against their will, while they were
engaged in the peaceful exercise of their First Amendment right
to assemble ... and petition their Government for a redress of
their grievances. ... *There was evidence that others declined to
exercise their First Amendment rights* ... after they had once
had the experience of being photographed by the Richmond police. While in *Tatum* there was only knowledge of surveillance
or fear of the consequences of surveillance, here there was
actual exposure to the challenged police methods. In short, if
photographing on the part of the police constituted an impermis-
sible violation of constitutional rights, there was an abundance
of proof that actual harm and an actual violation of rights occurred. I can only conclude that *Tatum* is distinguishable and
hence not a precedent that is controlling." (Emphasis added.)

If this kind of "actual harm" can be clearly demon-
strated and if, furthermore, a convincing argument can be
made that the *purpose* of police surveillance tactics is to
chill the exercise of First Amendment rights—because in
a particular case the police can show no other reasonable
purpose for their spying—victories for the Constitution
are quite possible.

Consider, for instance, an important—and little-noted
—decision handed down by Federal District Judge Constance Baker Motley in New York in June, 1971. Local
police spies in New Rochelle, New York, for some years
had been eagerly collecting and distributing information
about the political activities of some of the more liberal
citizens of that city. One such "suspect" citizen was
I. Philip Sipser, a New York labor lawyer and campaign
manager for U.S. Senate candidate Paul O'Dwyer in 1968.
New Rochelle detectives had carefully filed information
that the potentially dangerous Mr. Sipser had actually
been seen participating in marches led by a local black
organizer employed in a community action program.
Moreover, suspect Sipser had picketed a construction
site as a member of a group asking that more black workers
be hired on that particular job. These activities placed

Mr. Sipser's name in a dossier that, for all Mr. Sipser knew, was now common knowledge to police departments throughout the country as well as to an unknown number of federal agencies.

Sipser and other spied-on residents of New Rochelle sued the police department—and won. Judge Motley ordered the police to stop spying on people "neither suspected of criminal activity nor engaged in criminal activity." She also instructed the police to deliver to the court the files and documents that had accumulated during political surveillance of those who had brought the suit. And lest there be any ambiguity in the decision, New Rochelle police were also ordered to stop "distributing, circulating, publicizing, or making known in any other way to any persons, group, or entity, public or private, the contents of any and all records heretofore obtained by any form of surveillance on such persons."

This kind of police surveillance, routine throughout the country, was declared by Judge Motley to be "without authority in law and violative of the rights guaranteed and protected by the Constitution of the United States."

In addition to continuing the battle in the courts, another sector of the campaign against the secret police is legislative. Among a number of bills now pending in Congress to stem the assault on privacy is New York Congressman Edward Koch's federal privacy act. The measure requires that each government agency maintaining records on any individual must:

—notify the person that such a record exists;
—disclose such information records only with the consent of the individual, and in that case, notify the person of the disclosure;
—maintain an accurate record of all persons to whom any information is divulged and the purposes for which the information was given to them;

—permit the individual on whom there is a record to inspect it, make copies of it, and supplement it;
—remove erroneous information of any kind, and notify all agencies and persons to whom the erroneous material has been previously transferred that it has been removed.

Although it's a useful start, there are weaknesses in the Koch bill—a basic flaw being its exclusion from these privacy safeguards of records "specifically required by Executive order to be kept secret in the interest of national security."

No government can safely be allowed simply to pronounce "national security" and thereby seal off whatever it wills. At the very least, in any court case under a privacy act, the burden of proof in each instance has to be on the *government* to justify any attempt to keep secret the records maintained on an individual or a group.

Another fundamental weakness in the Koch bill is its exclusion from privacy protection of "investigatory files compiled for law enforcement purposes, except to the extent that such records have been maintained for a longer period than reasonably necessary to commence prosecution."

As I have indicated, this clause would leave inviolate that swiftly growing mass of data being collected by federal agencies and individual states and cities for the FBI national data bank at the National Crime Information Center. And Koch's attempt to mitigate that clause in his bill by the term "reasonably necessary" is so broad and vague as to be useless.

But the intent behind the bill is commendable, as is Congressman Koch's recognition that "some types of surveillance and data collection should be forbidden absolutely." Again, at the very least, no government agency should have the right, for one example, to engage in the kinds of political surveillance of lawful activity that have been condemned by Federal Judge Constance Baker Motley.

Other kinds of legislation—city, state and federal—along with persistent court actions are necessary to safeguard privacy against the myriad secret police. But even so limited a federal privacy act as the Koch bill could become a quickening force in creating public pressure for stronger legislation and in awakening the courts to the seriousness of the issue.

A useful stimulus to eventual congressional action was the publication in July, 1973, of *Records, Computers and the Rights of Citizens,* a report by an advisory committee to the secretary of Health, Education, and Welfare. Among the committee's recommendations was the following legislation mandating that any organization operating an administrative personal data system shall:

1) Inform an individual asked to supply personal data for the system whether he is legally required, or may refuse, to supply the data requested, and also of any specific consequences for him, which are known to the organization, of providing or not providing such data;

2) Inform an individual, upon his request, whether he is the subject of data in the system, and if so, make such data fully available to the individual, upon a request, in a form comprehensible to him;

3) Assure that no use of individually identifiable data is not within the stated purposes of the system as reasonably understood by the individual, unless the informed consent of the individual has been explicitly obtained;

4) Inform an individual, upon his request, about the uses made of data about him, including the identity of all persons and organizations involved and their relationship with the system;

5. Assure that no data about an individual are made available from the system in response to a demand for [that] data made by means of compulsory legal process, unless the individual to whom the data pertain has been notified of the demand; and

6) Maintain procedures that (i) allow an individual who is the subject of data in the system to contest their accuracy, completeness, pertinence, and the necessity for retaining them; (ii) permit data to be corrected or amended when the individual to whom they pertain so requests; and (iii) assure, when there is disagreement with the individual about whether a correction or amendment should be made, that the individual's claim is noted and included in any subsequent disclosure or dissemination of the disputed data.

As for prospective court action safeguarding privacy, not all judges are somnolent as we slide toward postconstitutional America. Federal District Judge Gerhard Gesell, sitting in Washington, warned in 1971 that: "Systematic recordation and dissemination of information about individual citizens is a form of surveillance and control which may easily inhibit freedom to speak, move about and work in this land. If information available to Government is misused to publicize past incidents in the lives of its citizens the pressures for conformity will be irresistible. Initiative and individuality can be suffocated and a resulting dullness of mind and conduct will be the norm."

Judge Gesell's acute perception of the mounting dangers to the Bill of Rights is not yet representative of the majority of his brethren on the bench. Nor are a majority of legislators or the citizenry at large yet awake to what is happening to the Constitution.

But if the Koch bill, or one similar to it, could be passed, the provision that everyone on whom records are kept must be told about it might well startle at least some of the populace from sleep as their liberties are being computerized away. Under such a law, huge numbers of Americans would have to be informed that dossiers with their names on them are in some agency's files (and thereby, through computer interfacing, are likely to be in *many*

agencies' files). Accordingly, a tougher federal privacy
act might conceivably follow the passage of a relatively
mild bill if enough previously quiescent citizens were
stirred to anger on finding out that they too—not just
"extremists" and other freaks—are in the secret police
files.

Maybe. But we'll never find out unless and until there
is first enough sustained public concern to get an initial
federal privacy act passed—along with city and state
privacy bills. One vital element in any such privacy bill
should be the mandate that certain information already in
the files be erased. Among those records to be expunged
would be erroneous data and records of arrests that did
not lead to convictions.

It is also important to provide, by law, for the erasure of
a considerable amount of other material now in state and
federal files that has no business being there—from the
names of dissenters who have lawfully used their First
Amendment rights to information gathered by credit
bureaus about the private lives of citizens applying for
charge accounts.

Absolute erasure is impossible because some federal
agencies and police departments are likely to squirrel
away some information files for vague future use. But at
least the doctrine in law that certain information harmful
to an individual *should* be erased will place the secret
police on notice that their keeping illegal raw files can
subject them to a court suit if a citizen ever finds out
about it.

A strong rationale for erasure is provided by privacy
expert Alan Westin. "Look at the way the property system
has established rights in our capitalist system. You wipe
out records of bankruptcy, for example, and it is part of
the commercial system that after a certain period of time
we simply do not continue to record certain kinds of com-

mercial failures because we want to encourage people to come back into business. The same thing should be true of our personal records and our personal privacy."

Why, for example, should the following information in FBI files (as detailed in an October, 1971, *Freedom of Information Center Report* of the University of Missouri School of Journalism) not be erased, *by law*. It should never have been collected and filed in the first place. The report cites:

5,500 files on black Americans, including... Floyd McKissick, Mrs. Martin Luther King, Jr., entertainers, and "just plain folks." ... One file, on a prominent black female singer, notes that she "was suing her husband... for a divorce as a result of Mrs. —— catching her husband in bed with ——."

The FBI file on 25-year-old Michael Reuss, son of Rep. Henry Reuss (Democrat-Wisconsin), notes that he is the friend of a member—though not a member himself—of the Central Committee of the Bay Area Revolutionary Union and that once in 1969, was known to be opposed to the draft. The file also notes that Reuss was a Vista worker, and was arrested during a civil rights demonstration in 1965 in Mississippi.

In addition to provisions for erasure of material already in information files that ought not to be there, effective federal, state, and local privacy bills will also have to affirm each individual's right of access to any file kept on him. The best single recommendation in this area that I have seen is contained in Sarah Carey's *Law and Disorder III*, a remarkably informative book published in 1973 by the Lawyers' Committee for Civil Rights Under Law:

"Each individual should be granted the right of access, notice and challenge to all information pertaining to him. A person should receive notification when his file is opened, and upon each entry he should be informed of his right to access and challenge. *During a challenge, to protect the individual from incomplete and inaccurate information, an embargo should be placed on use of the information."* (Emphasis added.)

Law and Disorder III also proposes that regulatory laws (including right of access) "should be passed to control all information systems, 1) developed and maintained by agencies of the federal government, 2) operated by state or local agencies but supported wholly or partly by federal funds and 3) interfacing with federal systems or federally supported systems."

I do not believe this proposal goes nearly far enough. No state or local agency, whether supported by federal funds or not, has the constitutional right to invade any individual's privacy—at the very least without his knowing about it or being able to take action against it. Furthermore, since private agencies, such as credit bureaus, exchange information with government agencies, they too should be included in laws regulating *their* collection and distribution of information.

An even stronger supplementary safeguard has been proposed by attorney Richard Miller in *Trial* magazine, as reported in the University of Missouri's *Freedom of Information Bulletin*: "He would like to see state laws providing that public agencies, private firms and agents in the business of gathering and distributing personal data be liable to injured parties for passing out false information or knowingly disseminating true information for a defamatory purpose."

This liability, I would emphasize, should also extend to federal agencies and personnel in the data-collecting and data-distributing business. The liability, moreover, should consist of money damages for the injured party and sanctions against those agents, whether public or private, who are found to have caused the injury. When private citizens start collecting damages because they have been abused by secret police and other information gatherers, and when some of these secret agents are demoted or otherwise punished for mugging the Bill of Rights, the zeal to snoop may well be markedly diminished.

One starting point for legislation aimed at making dossier collectors and distributors responsible for the damage they do is recommended by the Lawyers' Committee for Civil Rights Under Law. It proposes that such legislation "should probably . . . waive sovereign immunity on behalf of the United States and the states and make them jointly liable with any individual who disseminates information to an unauthorized recipient, on a strict liability basis. The law should include minimum damage penalties, attorneys' fees, and a provision for treble damages." The committee suggests the same sanctions should apply to those who distribute erroneous information. I would also add as liable for punishment those who disseminate information they had no authority to collect, let alone distribute.

On federal, local, and state levels, there should also be independent commissions to make sure that new laws safeguarding privacy are being enforced. The Lawyers' Committee restricts its recommendation to a national independent commission that would conduct audits and spotchecks and would report to Congress. But independent state and local commissions also ought to be functioning in a similar way, and they should report to state and local legislative bodies.

These commissions, as the Lawyers' Committee recommends, "should include constitutional lawyers, representatives of citizens' groups and other civilians."

There is not the slightest doubt that the Bill of Rights badly needs this and other kinds of protection in a time of increasingly sophisticated technology, including computers, directed at subverting individual liberties.

Even children are no longer immune to the omnipresent eye of surveillance. An unintentionally chilling press release has been issued by Eastman Kodak Company. It concerns the school system of Polk County, Florida, which, Kodak observes, has an enrollment of 60,000 students and "operates more schools in more towns than any other system in the United States. It controls 58 elementary schools, 14 junior highs, 10 senior highs, and one vocational-technical school."

Here is an augury of what *may* be ahead for more Americans than only Polk County students:

SURVEILLANCE CAMERAS HELP ADMINISTRATORS MAINTAIN ORDER IN FLORIDA SCHOOLS

BARTOW, FLORIDA—Smiles and friendly greetings now far outnumber scowls and random left hooks among junior and senior high school students throughout Polk County, Florida.

That's because their actions are being recorded on film, and if anyone does anything to seriously disrupt school routine, the odds against establishing an alibi are far from even.

For the School Board of Polk County, plagued like 23,000 other systems in the United States with unrest, vandalism, and confusion, recently became the first in the nation to install a new automatic super 8 camera security system to monitor unfavorable situations, provide positive identification of troublemakers, and establish concrete evidence through which administrators can take remedial action.

Polk County's system employs recently marketed Kodak Analyst super 8 cameras encased in sound-absorbent boxes that are set to snap a picture every 30 seconds. A number of the cameras, costing less than $240 each, are already in operation in Polk County junior and senior high schools. More are to come. [At that price, what school can afford not to have such a system? —N. H.]

Located in corridors, outdoor campus areas, problem classrooms, and other areas, each Analyst super 8 camera will automatically take 7,200 pictures per hundred feet of Kodak MFX film, which is contained in standard-size drop-in cartridges. The films can be processed to make conventional photographic prints, or reversal processed to show on a projector.... In addition to the mounted cameras, junior and senior high school principals also are being supplied with Analyst cameras....

W. W. Read, superintendent of the Polk County School Board, emphasizes that this is by no means a snooping operation. Although the cameras operate constantly during school hours, the film is processed and viewed only when disruptions have occurred. [Scout's honor—N. H.]

"We're neither interested, nor do we have the time to 'spy' on our students when they are conducting themselves in manners normal [sic] for their age levels," he explains. "We process and look at the film only when incidents have occurred that require establishing responsibility for them."

Although the super 8 surveillance cameras have been in use only a short time, Read reports that their psychological impact already has reduced disruptive incidents, and they already have had a definite effect on the total tenor at the schools.

Liberation News Service asked some of the kids how *they* felt about the era of smiles, friendly greetings, and surveillance cameras that had come upon the Polk County school system. After all, those super 8 cameras are constantly working for the benefit of the students. Superintendent Read had said so, pointing out that "the students have been told the cameras are there and that it is possible for us to positively identify not only those responsible for trouble, but also those who are innocent of wrong-doing. Thus, both buck-passing and alibis are eliminated and the innocent are protected."

Said a subversive senior high school student, who probably reads Jefferson and Thoreau on the sly: "In any type of trouble, everybody the camera photographs is sent to the office. After all, they can't tell who caused the trouble because they don't have sound cameras. They don't know who said what to whom, and anyway, the instigation of trouble might just happen to fall during the 30 seconds the camera isn't photographing."

Said another student: "Nothing has changed but the amount of subterfuge and fear. It's like being in jail for six hours a day."

But school, after all, is supposed to be preparation for adult life. And the Polk County school system may already be shaping the subdued citizens of postconstitutional America.

Twelve Anguished Jurors

Paul Cowan

To a very great degree, the left underrates the intelligence of Middle America when it claims that there is a large, ready constituency for repression in this country. That became apparent to me when I interviewed seven of the twelve jurors who had been involved in the trial of the Harrisburg 7, a case I had covered for the *Village Voice*. The unusually long voir dire, which lasted about a month and involved 465 prospective witnesses, revealed a parade of rural, conservative Americans who seemed untouched by the war in Vietnam, who seemed willing to accept all their government's domestic decisions. When I interviewed some of the excused veniremen after the final panel was chosen, they told me they'd overheard several people who were still seated making anti-Catholic, antialien remarks. Newsmen covering the trial picked up those interviews; they reinforced the conviction of the defense lawyers and many journalists that xenophobia and reflexive patriotism would make the jury heed the testimony of the government informer Boyd Douglas and the panoply of FBI agents and Justice Department lawyers behind him, no matter how dubious their case.

Yet ten of the jurors voted to acquit Father Philip Berrigan, Sister Elizabeth McAlister, and their codefendants of conspiring to kidnap Henry Kissinger, to bomb federal heating systems, and to raid draft boards, though they did convict the priest and nun on some minor letter-smuggling counts. To me, that seemed the most extraordinary thing to come out of the case.

During the months after the trial, I conducted about twelve hours of tape-recorded interviews with seven of the jurors (those who agreed to talk with me), combining some questions about the case with others about the internal dynamics of the jury during the two harrowing months of sequestration and deliberation. The interviews left me feeling that my attitudes toward that group of Middle Americans (like those of most lawyers, defendants, and reporters connected with the case) were considerably more narrow and parochial than was *their* attitude toward the people we were once so sure they'd be unable to judge.

Throughout the voir dire, the defense had the unusual cooperation of a team of sociologists headquartered at Columbia and spearheaded by Jay Schulman, a friend of the defendants. This team had surveyed the eleven-county region from which the jury would be chosen. Since they didn't think it was likely that many people in the Middle District of Pennsylvania would feel active sympathy for the defendants on trial, they were seeking to find ways to identify veniremen who would at least remain open-minded until all the evidence was presented or who might even feel active antipathy toward elements of the government's case. Their hope, at the time, was to uncover two or three people—enough to hang the jury—who would hold out for acquittal. They didn't think the defense could expect anything better than that.

Their findings, like my posttrial interviews, challenged easy liberal assumptions about Middle Americans. For example, urban instincts said the best-educated jurors would be the most open-minded, but the sociologists' research suggested that people who acquired intellectual restlessness along with their diplomas hurried away from the Middle District of Pennsylvania, while the more conservative, tradition-bound types stayed home. In general, the sociologists thought, the defendants should reject college graduates.

And in the male-dominated region, where wives rarely participate in public life, they felt that women would be friendlier to the defense than men. That was particularly true because of the facts of the case. Schulman felt strongly that, given Boyd Douglas's credentials as a gigolo–con man who had used his relationships with Bucknell coeds Jane Hoover and Betsy Sandel to obtain information for the FBI, women, particularly young women, would take a quick, visceral dislike to him. So he thought that women in their twenties and thirties should be the jury's dominant numerical force.

Each night the lawyers and defendants met with Schulman to rate the veniremen on a scale of one (acceptable) to five (unacceptable). Those judgments became vital when the peremptory challenges began. (The defense had a great advantage there. Judge R. Dixon Herman had worked out a formula that allowed the defense to reject up to twenty-eight potential jurors, while the government could reject only seven.) The group's decisions once again bore out the importance of abandoning liberal biases when dealing with Middle Americans. One choice, which defied the survey's findings, turned out to be an inspired piece of guesswork. Harold Sheets was not only a college graduate, but a businessman as well—a sixty-one-year-old tax consultant from Harrisburg, with a degree from the Wharton School of Business, who had run his own office for thirty years. He told the judge he didn't want to be sequestered during tax season because it would mean the loss of a great deal of money. Paul O'Dwyer and Schulman wanted to strike him off the jury with a peremptory challenge, but Terry Lenzner, the defense team's toughest investigator, guessed that a lifetime of fighting tax cases in court would have left a residue of skepticism about the government. Sister McAlister also had a gut feeling that Sheets would make a responsive juror. His sympathy could be particularly important, the defendants reasoned, because the predominantly female jury would be likely to choose a calm older man as foreman. When J. Thomas Menaker, the local lawyer on the defense team, said his friends in town had reported that Sheets was reliable, there was a consensus that the accountant should remain on the panel.

But the three decisions that were the products of stereotyped liberal responses to obvious personality traits proved to be mistakes. Vera Thompson, the wife of a liquor store dealer from Carlisle, was automatically acceptable because she was black. The defense was told that Lawrence Evans, sixty-one, a retired supermarket owner from Dillsburg, had founded a business that supported the grape boycott. (Actually, Evans had been retired for several years, and a son who succeeded him honored the boycott.) In 1961, Evans had been a Democratic party ward captain and an ardent supporter of John Kennedy. During the voir dire he said he thought that priests and nuns should be even more involved in protests. Those opinions gave him such symbolic legitimacy that no one on the defense team even considered striking him from the jury. Mrs. Katheryne Schwartz, a fifty-eight-year-old grandmother from York, was a member of the Church of the Brethren and had four sons who had been conscientious objectors. That seemed to prove she'd support defendants whose actions had arisen from their pacifist beliefs.

The government didn't include any of the three in its peremptory challenges. They were the ones who voted to convict, though Vera Thompson eventually changed her mind.

Nine women and three men were finally impaneled. The seven I interviewed were Ann Burnett, twenty-four, a caseworker in the Dauphin County welfare department; Mrs. Jo-Anne (Tracy) Stanovich, a machinist's wife from Harrisburg; Robert (Fuzzy) Foresman, a firefighting instructor from Lewistown; June Jackson, forty-eight, an interior decorator's wife from York; Pat Shafer, thirty-five, from Etters, the wife of a construction engineer who'd helped build military bases in Thailand and Vietnam; Harold Sheets; and Mrs. Thompson. The other five were Pauline Portzline, fifty-one, the wife of a self-employed plumbing and heating contractor; Miss Frances Yachlich, thirty-eight, the only Catholic on the jury, a bookkeeper at a small heating company in Lebanon County; Nancy Leidy, a four-months-pregnant stenographer-typist for the state government; Mrs. Schwartz; and Lawrence Evans. (Evans actually did talk to me on the night of the verdict, when he granted angry interviews to most of the reporters covering the case. But he never let me interview him again.)

The deliberations that followed the defense's totally unexpected decision to rest its case without putting on a single witness took six and one-half days, a record for a federal case. Throughout that exhausting period it was clear that the lawyers and defendants who had chosen the jurors really didn't trust them. Most speculation focused on which one or two were holding out for acquittal. There was widespread fear that the few who were friendly to the defense would eventually be battered into submission by the overwhelmingly progovernment majority.

So when it turned out that nine of the jurors had favored acquittal from the first poll of the panel, the people close to the case evolved a set of myths to explain that unex-

pected behavior. All the myths highlighted the brilliance
or the decency of the radical defendants and their liberal
lawyers. None allowed for much sensitivity or intelligence
on the part of the jurors.

One myth was that the defense team, and particularly
Terry Lenzner, a brilliant investigator, had done such a
skillful job of delving into Douglas's past that the government was devastated by the facts they brought out on
cross-examination. But my interviews show that, though
Harold Sheets and Pat Shafer thought Douglas's testimony
might be plausible when the government was questioning him, most of the jurors didn't need a dramatic courtroom confrontation to size up the informer. They tried to
keep an open mind, but they disliked him from the start.

To understand their feelings, one has to imagine Douglas, with his carefully combed hair and his neat suits, his
pudgy, slack face and his droning voice, sitting in the witness chair day after day, answering every question with
the same carefully rehearsed stock response.

"I didn't like him from the first time he walked to the
witness stand, with his $200 Johnny Carson suit on,"
Tracy Stanovich told me. "And the more he talked, the
deeper in the hole he got. He always sounded like Goody-
two-shoes. But I think he did that to impress us. Soon I
began to ask myself, is this what the government's case is
all about? Who needs this thing?"

Tracy is a lively, red-haired machinist's wife from Harrisburg. Her physical appearance and apparent background caused many of the outsiders who saw her during
the voir dire to classify her as a potential ally for the prosecution. But she'd been a childhood acquaintance of Tom
Menaker's, and he was certain she'd be open to the defense's arguments. (Throughout the trial Tom's judgments
of the jurors were more accurate than were the other
lawyers'.) She's a Lutheran, married to the son of Serbian
immigrants, and she has twined her husband's religion

and customs to her own. When she was younger she studied ceramics in art school. Recently, she's begun to use those talents as a dental technician, molding caps for teeth, a job she enjoys enormously. And she turned out to be the jury's jokester, a free spirit who said anything that came into her mind and teased the more depressed panelists until she freed them from self-pity.

When I asked her what she thought Douglas's motives were, she referred to a letter he'd written his FBI handler, Delmar Mayfield; in it, he asked for $50,000 for his work as an informer. (Ironically, it was not the defense investigators who uncovered that crucial fact. It had been contained in a letter that was among some material the government handed over to the defense in the course of the trial.) "It seemed like he had a plan," she said. "He thought, 'Well, I have it all wrapped up in my head, and I'm going to walk out of here a rich man.' I think he lied about everything."

June Jackson is an older, more settled, more affluent woman than Tracy Stanovich. I interviewed her in her spacious York home, and our talk lasted three hours. Sometimes memories of the trial made her laugh. More often they brought her close to tears. The experience seems to sit like a rock in her stomach. Of all the jurors I interviewed, she appears to be the one the trial affected most deeply.

In accord with her sacred duties as a juror, she tried to suspend her judgments about the case until the deliberations began. But, "There was just something about Douglas I didn't trust. His eyes. His whole manner. But I tried to separate my emotional feelings about him the way I was supposed to, and just listen to him."

But that became more difficult for her when agent Mayfield took the stand. "There was something about him I didn't trust either. I mean he should have been telling the truth. Or maybe I just want to think that because he was an FBI agent. But call it a woman's intuition, or a hunch. There was just something about him that nagged at me, something I didn't like."

The nonverbal messages that Mayfield and Douglas sent out influenced the jurors at least as much as their actual testimony. The jurors were not particularly influenced by the drumfire of revelations that Douglas had exploited one Bucknell coed after another, although during the trial many observers felt that the turning point came during cross-examination, when Douglas laughingly admitted that he had proposed to Betsy Sandel, urged her to go to a demonstration at the Lewisburg prison, and fingered her for the FBI, all on the same day. In his closing argument, Ramsey Clark called that scene a "window into the man's soul." But the jurors didn't feel the same genteel pity for fair damsels in distress. They felt the girls got what they deserved.

Ann Burnett used the saltiest language of any of the jurors I interviewed. (During the voir dire she had seemed so crabbed and mousey that the defense nearly challenged her.) In the first few weeks of sequestration, her brash, talkative brilliance and her unabashed descriptions of her love life created some tensions between her and the other jurors. ("When that broad was born she was vaccinated with a phonograph needle," Vera Thompson told me, chuckling.) But by the end of the trial, she was bound to them by deep ties of mutual respect. She described her feelings about Betsy and Jane as we sat on the floor of her sparsely furnished Harrisburg apartment, which could have been a pad on New York's Upper West Side or in Berkeley. Her words were surprisingly blunt, but her sentiments were ones that all the jurors I interviewed shared.

"I think Jane and Betsy should have been smarter. They shouldn't have copied those letters: They knew Boyd was in the penitentiary, right? Now, regardless of what bullshit he fed them about what he was in for, I don't think I would like to be an accessory with, and before, and after the fact of a crime. I don't care what kind of piece of ass he was. There's just too many dicks in the world to worry about one guy like that, unless he's really got something going for him upstairs, which Boyd Douglas obviously does not have."

The men I interviewed felt more sympathy for Douglas than did the women. Even those like Fuzzy Foresman, who disbelieved the informer, found qualities about him with which they could identify.

Foresman is a warm, outgoing man, an addict of practical jokes who loves to garden and hunt and fish. He gets great satisfaction from fighting fires and from teaching the trade to younger men who take week-long courses at the academy where he works. He feels that the people in his town are somewhat limited partly because, until recently, they've resisted the more modern methods of firefighting he's tried to show them. The fact that he's a Lutheran with a Catholic wife who is raising his children inside her faith may increase his sense of being different from most people in the community. Nevertheless, he shared a purely masculine moment of friendly laughter with Douglas when the informer admitted the lies he'd told Betsy Sandel. Why? "It was so much in character, and it struck a couple of comical points in my own life, when I'd done the same thing with women in my younger days. . . . I think Douglas was a hell of a guy. He's got a sense of humor. It was a little flakey at times, but I could go along with that. But I just . . . I wouldn't care to be in his company much because he doesn't have a solid moral background to do things the way I'd do them—not that I'm perfect or anything. But I wouldn't trust him any further than I can see him."

Indeed, to Foresman, Douglas was "a fortune-hunter and a liar." That was an early impression, and nothing in the cross-examination deepened it very much. It carried over into the jury room, though, when Foresman looked through the photostats of the Berrigan–McAlister correspondence and found something that brought out the Perry Mason in him. He decided that Douglas must have forged some passages in Philip Berrigan's letters that seemed to advocate violence. "The writing was different. I could see where an 'i' was different in those parts of the letters than in the others. So I concluded that whoever had written those words hadn't written the whole thing."

Not a single defense attorney ever claimed that the letters were fakes. And, in press interviews, though not in court, the defendants had agreed they were genuine. But Foresman had begun to say to himself, "Well, my God, this guy was in jail for forgery." So he asked Judge Herman for the original copies of the letters. But they were unavailable to the jury because the prosecution, in a surprisingly generous mood, had acceded to a defense request to excise romantic passages between the priest and the nun. So only the photostats, with those portions clipped out, could be introduced as evidence.

Foresman had no way of knowing about that transaction, and it deepened his suspicions of the government. "When we couldn't get the originals, I had to say to myself, well, this is their evidence. And it looks to me like Douglas is playing games. So, as far as I'm concerned, throw it out."

Thus, for Foresman, that deduction, his own, meant the government no longer had a shred of a case.

To most of the urban liberal defendants, lawyers, and reporters who were involved with the trial, Harrisburg seemed like a menacing foreign culture where there were few clues to correct behavior. In that setting, Ramsey Clark's prestige, his aura of authority, and his brave decision to embrace the defendants' belief in nonviolent resistance provided a talismanic sort of comfort. Besides, his easy, folksy southwestern manner seemed more likely to appeal to the jury than Leonard Boudin's impatient, flashy brilliance, which might arouse Middle America's ancient distrust of New York Jews.

When Clark delivered his eloquent opening and closing statements (with their awesomely sincere appeals to the jury's patriotism and its religious faith), most of the contingent of outsiders felt that he had muted the favorable impression that—we felt then—the presence of a government informer backed by FBI agents and Justice Department lawyers had left with the jurors. Some, like Harold Sheets and Tracy Stanovich, were impressed by his oratory. But most seemed to feel that his attempts at eloquence were insults to their intelligence. For example, June Jackson saw him as "a politician who was much too oratorical and ineffective. All his eloquence didn't hit me at all. No way. No sir."

Fuzzy Foresman was the former Attorney General's most outspoken critic. To him, Clark was "a little childish in the way he handled himself." Though he was impressed with part of Clark's closing speech, he was offended by a reference to Boyd Douglas as Judas. "He sort of left it hanging as to what the defendants were. And damn well they ain't Christ. . . . He was playing too much on our sentiments, on our emotions. And we had too much material to deal with for that sort of thing."

By contrast, the jurors felt both affection and respect for Boudin. He was theatrical, too, certainly more theatrical than Clark, but he redeemed himself with his playful, self-mocking good humor and his obvious command of the facts. Because of his heart condition—he has a pacemaker—the judge had given him permission to roam the courtroom at will, and he often walked over toward the jury or the spectators and delivered an ironic, hammed look of anguish when the prosecution—or another defense lawyer—made a point that seemed specious to him. His absent-mindedness became a legend. Once he lost a contact lens and had to get on his knees in front of his wife, Jean, while she found it and replaced it. Another time he poured water into a cup that wasn't there. After a brief recess during Delmar Mayfield's testimony, he approached the witness stand with a fierce vigor, prepared to ask a vital question—only to find that Mayfield was on the other side of the room.

Yet behind the antics there was a deep passion, and that's what June Jackson sensed. "At the beginning of the trial, I thought to myself, 'I wouldn't have you if you were the last man on earth.' But when he performed in court and I looked into his eyes, I thought 'that's the man for me if I ever need help.' He was all lawyer. He seemed to know everything."

To Foresman, Boudin was a marvel. "I teach [fire instruction] but I'm not very good at it. I enjoy people who can think on their feet like Boudin. God, he has a fabulous mind. And he and I . . . I don't know whether I'm saying this right or whether it's correct or not, but I think he and I had a kind of rapport. We had a lot of eye contact, and we had a lot of fun together."

None of the lawyers on the defense team received as much praise from the jurors as did William Lynch, the prosecuting attorney. Lynch was no great favorite of the media. His quick temper in the courtroom and his relative surliness when reporters tried to interview him in the corridors made him the object of a great deal of verbal abuse. Thus, when Daniel Berrigan came to court one day, noticed the upward flap of Lynch's arms whenever he rose to object, and characterized the prosecutor as a "ruptured seagull," the disdainful phrase became a popular epithet with most journalists. But Ann Burnett was the only juror I interviewed who shared that view. Fuzzy Foresman considered him "extremely good." Vera Thompson and Pat Shafer both praised him. Harold Sheets thought he was "a good lawyer, though he'd get a little radical [angry] at things."

June Jackson described her admiration for Lynch in the context of her perplexity about the entire trial. I had asked her why she thought the government had brought such a frail case to court. "I don't know," she said. "That's the $64 question. It was my first personal experience with the government. And you know"—here she began to laugh, but a little uncomfortably—"they blew it. I can't believe it. I absolutely can't." Her voice quickened, her breathing became audible. "Intelligent men. And I think that Lynch is . . . oh, I'm crazy about Lynch. He wasn't flamboyant like Boudin, or young like Menaker or Lenzner. Oh, there was something about him. I really felt sorry for him."

That last statement startled me, so I asked her why. There was a slight catch in her voice when she said "I don't know how they could have let this idiotic thing come to trial when even we, little laymen who knew absolutely nothing, saw what a farce it was. I guess that's the reason Lynch deserves an awful lot of credit. Because he did so much with"—another slightly tense giggle—"with nothing."

Before the trial began, many of the defendants believed that they could use the courtroom as a forum to convert the jurors, and part of the public, to their belief in non-violent resistance. Even though the charges were murky and confusing, they hoped that their resourcefulness and the presence of the media would allow them to stage a re-run of *The Trial of the Catonsville Nine*. When it turned out that the encounter in court was to be a battle more of legal wits than of political principles, they grew intensely interested in their nonverbal relationships with the jurors. As they sat in court day after day, they imagined that intense emotional encounters lay behind each brief eye contact. They were confident that their bearing in the courtroom—their ability to laugh and convey sorrow and retain visible bonds of community—would constitute silent proof of their righteousness and innocence.

It did for some jurors. For example, Harold Sheets said, "When I looked at those fellows I just kind of wondered how they could do what they were accused of doing." And Ann Burnett was impressed with their "vitality." But for others their most effective defense was not their high spirits (which many criticized as a sign that they didn't take the proceedings seriously enough) or even their sanctity, but their apparent ineptitude.

For example, on the first day of the jury's deliberations, Fuzzy Foresman outraged Lawrence Evans—who was convinced they were all guilty—by saying, with a laugh, "If I was ever going to kidnap anybody I wouldn't have those jokers do it." Vera Thompson, the black woman from Carlisle, had a stepson who had been a marine in Vietnam and had come home filled with technical details about explosives like primer cords, which the priests and nuns were allegedly planning to use to blow up the Washington heating system. "I had sat around listening to him and his friends talk enough to know that those people had had no dealings with explosives whatever. Why, I knew more about it than they did." One reason she changed her vote from guilty to innocent was her recognition that even if they had wanted to carry out their scheme they never could have done it. "To me, that was just a dream they had. It would take an act of Congress actually to carry it out."

Perhaps because none of the defendants ever took the stand, their hopes and plans and actions—which did emerge in the extensive McAlister–Berrigan correspondence—confused more of the jurors than they converted. For example, Tracy Stanovich respected Father Berrigan's intelligence and wanted very much to meet him, "but I kept thinking how can a man of his education get involved in stuff like Draft Board raids? I guess he truly believed in it, but I kept thinking that with all the knowledge he's learned, he should be teaching other people instead of doing those things." Vera Thompson said plaintively, "If I could meet him, I'd just want to ask him why he did all that."

And the defendants' physical appearance, far from conveying holy fervor, kindled vagrant thoughts in the jurors' minds whose contents the defendants could never have imagined. For example, Tracy Stanovich "couldn't believe Father Berrigan's ankles and his calves. They were so thick. I've never seen anything like that. But Fuzzy told me that it was because he came from a poor Catholic family which exercised by kicking a soccer ball around a lot." Ann Burnett found Father Joseph Wenderoth "quite virile, the sort of man who could go out and build a house."

Some of their impressions could have contributed to a guilty verdict if the government's case hadn't depended on a witness they found as shady as Douglas. For example, Vera Thompson had no use for Eqbal Ahmad, the Pakistani scholar who was the only non-Catholic in the group. She had the idea that he'd gotten involved with the Catholic left as an agent of his government whose conscious purpose was "to bring America down to Pakistan's level." Fuzzy Foresman's view of Philip Berrigan was almost as dour. "I'm almost sure the defense would have done themselves some harm if they had put Philip on the witness stand. He struck me as an individual who was chomping at the bit, someone who was just a little bit on the arrogant side. If he had started ranting and raving about his political insinuations, I don't think that would have helped him any. The fact is, it would have irritated me."

That last comment of Foresman's suggests a strong feeling that all the jurors I interviewed, except perhaps Ann Burnett, seemed to share. For them, it was not the cross-examination of Boyd Douglas, not Ramsey Clark's eloquence, not the defendants' courtroom presence, but the shocking decision to rest the case without putting on a single witness that probably saved the defendants from a conviction. Their evident incompetence wouldn't have been enough to spare them if the government could have proved that they were trying to carry out a mature plan.

June Jackson recalls that when Clark first announced the decision to rest she was "in shock, in complete shock. We had ourselves all revved up for another couple of months in court. Plus, we all wanted to hear the defendants speak. We wanted to know what they had to say for themselves." In retrospect, what did she think of the decision to rest? "It was the best thing they ever did," she said. "Maybe had they taken the stand we would not have found them not guilty. They may just have dug their own graves, so to speak."

"That was probably what the prosecution was hoping for," I said.

"Not probably. Absolutely. We could see that. How stupid did the government think we were?"

Then I asked her whether, in her gut, she felt that the defendants might have been guilty.

"Of course. Of course. Of course. I think they might have had a plan, yes. And they might have tried to carry it through. Now they didn't. They were caught before they did. But I think they were capable of doing it. They wanted to. They were against the war and this was their way of doing something about it. But in the evidence we had we didn't have anything where they said, 'Yes, tomorrow we're going to go off and kidnap Henry Kissinger.' That's where the fine line was. Where does an idea become a fact? I'll be doggoned if I'd want anybody to convict me on the evidence we had to go on."

Yet nothing the jurors saw in the courtroom left as bitter an aftertaste as the interpersonal conflicts that emerged during the six weeks of sequestration and, particularly, during the six days of deliberation. Nothing was as frustrating as their inability to arrive at a unanimous verdict.

Most of the tensions revolved around Lawrence Evans, the grocer from Dillsburg, who had made such a good impression during the voir dire. Evans was convinced that all the defendants were guilty. He told most reporters that on the night the verdict was announced. Then, he was the only juror who mentioned the tensions that made sequestration such an ordeal. But later I called him and visited his house so that he could tape his own, amplified version of the schisms he'd once alluded to and other jurors had since described. He consistently refused to talk to me. So I've had to rely on other jurors' accounts of schisms that Evans first revealed to the press.

Sequestration itself was a terribly arduous process. The reason for it was Judge Herman's fear that the jurors would be unable to arrive at a just decision if, every night, they were exposed to press accounts of the trial, to reporters' persistent questions, to friends' opinions, and to the disruptive demonstrations that were scheduled for Easter week. The defense lawyers argued strenuously that sequestration would be an undue hardship for the jurors.

The people I interviewed hated sequestration but they felt in retrospect that their verdicts might have been different if they'd maintained contact with the outside world. Harold Sheets said, "I think it was necessary as far as I'm concerned, and I think I'm a fairly strong person." The demonstrations would have been a problem: "I'm sure there would have been peace people trying to get next to us if we had been alone outside the federal building. I think that would have gotten me angry enough that I wouldn't have been quite as rational about analyzing the facts." And his work would have been a problem, too. "We run an accounting business. After the trial my wife told me about comments from good clients of ours, people who I know very well. I guess 90 percent of them thought they were guilty. Just guilty. I'm not too sure if I'd heard that, I'd have felt the same way about the case."

To keep the jurors unbiased, the court created a sterile, strictly policed refuge for them in Harrisburg's Penn-Harris Motor Inn. Since they weren't allowed to discuss the trial even with each other, marshals were present all the time, auditing their conversations. Their mail was strictly censored. They had to eat every meal together and travel to and from court in a sealed-in bus. The only visitors they could receive were members of their immediate families, who could only come on weekends. Those meetings took place within the marshals' sight, which meant, of course, that the jurors were deprived of conjugal visits. Ann Burnett says that many of them got very horny.

Their media diets were carefully supervised. All political and international news had to be clipped from the newspapers before they could receive them. They weren't allowed to watch news shows or talk shows like Dick Cavett or Johnny Carson, where they might hear topical discussions or jokes, or dramas like "Gunsmoke," "Ironside," or "Bonanza," where they might see a courtroom scene or a scene of violence that might have a marginal effect on their perceptions of the case. Ann Burnett tried to bring a collection of great love stories to the motel with her, but a marshal seized it because he noticed there was a short extract from the opera *Carmen* in the book that contained a courtroom scene.

June Jackson was acutely aware of the moods she shared with other jurors during those weeks. "At first everybody stayed together, all the time. Every time we went to our own rooms we cried. We missed our families. And we were scared to death. We didn't know what tomorrow would be like, what would happen to us."

The thing that troubled her most was that, throughout the trial, "we'd always have to have our party manners on. I got awfully tired of getting up every morning and smiling at everyone, and putting on my makeup and combing my hair so I'd look nice in the courtroom. But it wasn't just that. You felt like you had to be on your good behavior all the time, to be nice to everybody. There were days when I got up and felt miserable, for no apparent reason. But I had to act happy-go-lucky.

"There was no one you could talk to about that feeling. It was all very private. And it was worse because we weren't allowed to discuss the trial either. And we couldn't turn off our brains as soon as we left the courtroom. But all of a sudden I was a party girl again—watching television, washing my hair. There were nights when I just wanted to be alone. I used to sit at my window and watch the cars go by. What else could I do? I couldn't read. I couldn't keep my mind on that.

"I remember one night when I was sitting in Tracy Stanovich's room, using her hair dryer. She was putting her clothes away. And all of a sudden I thought to myself, here I am. I've never met this girl in my life, and now I'm using her hair dryer, and she is putting her clothes away. And I said, what am I doing here? Who is this person? I shouldn't be here at all. I should be at home getting dinner. You know that TV show, 'Twilight Zone.' That's what the whole thing felt like. Very, very strange."

Most of the twelve jurors and six alternates eventually found ways of accommodating themselves to the situation and to each other. "When you're living in one little wing of one hotel, you have to get along," June Jackson says. Ann Burnett learned to listen as well as talk, and she fascinated Tracy Stanovich with explicit tales of her past exploits. June Jackson and Pat Shafer did a great deal of knitting and crocheting for their families. Some nights Vera Thompson, Fuzzy Foresman and Harold Sheets would play pinochle till midnight. Other times Fuzzy would join Tracy and some of the alternates in a card game called "pit." Pauline Portzline, who missed her husband terribly, would shut herself in her room and cry almost every night. Larry Evans, a sports fan, spent his evenings reading *Sport* or *Sports Illustrated,* or practicing putting on a makeshift green he'd constructed in his room. Each morning he'd get up at five, do fifty push-ups, and work out on an exerbike. An alternate, a fisherman, spent much of his spare time tying flies. On weekends the marshals would shepherd the whole group to special events like an ice show at the Hershey Arena or to picnic spots where they'd play touch football.

Larry Evans was the only persistent source of conflict for the jurors. At first they had liked him. Tracy Stanovich recalls that "he seemed like a very happy-go-lucky guy. He'd buy people drinks at night. He seemed very nice." But soon they tired of his jokes and anecdotes, which he repeated meal after meal, day after day; they became irritated by his unshakable assumption that he knew every answer, by his unwillingness to listen to anyone else. So, by the third or fourth week of sequestration, most of them had begun to avoid his company.

By that time, many of them had been shocked by his furious competitiveness and his occasional bursts of cruelty. Tracy Stanovich recalls the night the jury went bowling for the first time and Evans lost. "He just went wild. He was really mad about the whole thing. When we asked him why, he said, 'Well, I always win. I always win. I'm tops. Now I've got to win, too.'"

He was particularly harsh with the two youngest women on the jury, Nancy Leidy and Ann Burnett (and he singled them out for criticism in his posttrial interviews). Ann has a quick wit and a sharp tongue, but one night Evans teased her so much at the dinner table that she ran to her room crying. He was always accusing Leidy, the daughter of a prosperous family and four months pregnant when the deliberations began, of being spoiled, whiney, and narrow-minded.

Tracy Stanovich recalls that he was also cruel to Richard McGinn, an alternate who had recovered from a childhood case of polio with a body that was permanently bent and twisted. One weekend night all the jurors were dining together at a restaurant. Evans bought a bottle of champagne to share with Richard and another alternate. Someone else came by and took the last swig of liquor. When Evans saw that the bottle was empty, he accused McGinn of stealing his drink. He threatened to hit the cripple, and banged the empty bottle on the table. Often he taunted Richard with such remarks as "I'm going to send you out with Ann."

During sequestration, no one saw Evans's volcanic behavior as a portent of his conduct during deliberations. June Jackson, for one, didn't notice it at all. "I knew that he was a little peculiar, but aren't we all, to a certain extent." In conversations with Sheets, Foresman, and Tracy Stanovich, Evans did make a great point of his past experience on juries—he claimed to have served on five—and of the fact that he'd always been chosen foreman. But no one saw those boasts and his periodic hearty free-spending moods as attempts to campaign for foreman of the Harrisburg jury.

Then the defense made its surprising decision to rest without putting on a case, the lawyers made their summary speeches, and Judge Herman issued a long, self-contradictory charge as to how the jury was supposed to evaluate the conspiracy indictment. (The charge was so confusing that the jury had to ask the judge to reread it three times. He never gave them a copy of it. Most of them told me they never did get it straight.) After that, at last, the jurors were free to discuss the experience that had bound them together for six difficult weeks.

Their first task was to select a foreman. Their vote was split, six votes for Fuzzy Foresman, six for Harold Sheets. They flipped a coin, and Sheets, the more prudent and judicious of the two, won. In retrospect, Foresman feels that "the good Lord above had a hand in choosing the foreman."

That vote seems to have helped trigger a wild rage in Larry Evans. Within ninety minutes of the beginning of deliberations, after the foreman had been chosen but before a shred of evidence had been evaluated, he was off on a long speech that all the jurors I interviewed described as a tirade. Maybe he was angry because he'd been shut out in the vote for foreman; maybe, as Harold Sheets suspects, he wanted a quick guilty verdict so that he could get home by dinnertime and watch his son-in-law play in an important hockey game that night. Anyway, he had already made up his mind that the defendants were guilty (most of the other jurors pride themselves on the fact that they were still suspending judgment at that point, waiting to see the evidence and hear each other's views). He thought they should be jailed immediately. "Larry just blew up," June Jackson recalls. "I couldn't believe it." He yelled and screamed and banged on the table. He invoked God's will and his children's future. His veins stood out and his face got beet red. "I was really frightened," Ann Burnett says. "I kept thinking, this man is going to have a stroke."

Ann knew at once that Evans's fervor would make any rational discussion impossible. "And I started getting very upset. At first I just stood there. I was numb. I felt like I was sinking into my chair. It was the feeling you get when you know that all is lost. I was ready to sit there and talk for weeks on end if necessary. But what was the point of that, seeing how Larry felt? I started to cry. I was so upset I was shaking, and I had to get up and go to the ladies' room because when I get very, very upset I have something like an asthma attack. I just can't breathe." All of the jurors were shaken by Evans's outburst and Ann's flight. Shortly afterward, the day's deliberations ended.

June Jackson's room at the Penn-Harris Motor Inn was next to Evans's. At about midnight that night she was awakened by some loud talking that seemed to be coming from his room. "I thought someone else was in there. I walked over to the wall to listen. And I realized he was talking to himself about another jury he had been on. Some of the other jurors had apparently talked him into acquitting a defendant he thought was guilty. Then, a few days after the trial was over, that defendant died of a heart attack. And Larry was saying that God was punishing the defendant even though the other jurors had talked him out of doing it. And, he said, they are not going to do that to me this time. He said, if we stay here for six months I will not change my mind. He said, they are guilty. I knew it the minute I walked into that courtroom.

"And then he started to sing 'Rock of Ages.' That's when I realized he had been talking to God. And then I kept hearing doors opening and banging shut. I stood there absolutely petrified. I was close to in shock myself."

If she had left her room that night, the marshals would have intercepted her before she could talk with Foresman or Sheets, the only people she trusted enough to help her decide what to do about Evans. She didn't want to get in trouble that way, and by then she had a sort of clannish loyalty that made her want to protect Evans, too. But the next day, still terribly shaken, she did talk to Foresman and Sheets. They considered writing a note to the judge about Evans's behavior. Sheets says that "we didn't because of my stubbornness in thinking that I could bring him out of that state. I kept thinking of the job we had to do, the decision we had to make. I didn't want to disrupt it." Instead, the men tried to calm June Jackson down and to prevent a recurrence of the situation by getting one of the marshals to let June change her room. (She never even did that.)

Sheets, the rationalist, the calm psychologist, was convinced that a hung jury would be an emotional disaster for everyone concerned. So he kept trying to devise ways to reach Evans. One day, for example, he asked all the other jurors to remain silent while he and Larry had a face-to-face debate about their opinions of the case. Sheets spoke for twenty minutes, describing the contradictions and gaps in Douglas's and Mayfield's testimony that had convinced him the government had failed to prove a conspiracy. Evans just spoke for a minute or two, insisting that he had read the testimony, too, and that he was serving God's will by holding out for a conviction.

By then, Evans only had one ally on the panel, Mrs. Schwartz. (A speech and a diagram by Pat Shafer had convinced Vera Thompson to change her vote.) She was not an instinctive pacifist, as the fact that she had four conscientious-objector sons had led the defense to believe. Instead, she had a fundamentalist's belief in the Church of Brethren creed, and she agreed with Evans that the defendants' intent was tantamount to a crime. "She'd never been exposed to this sort of thing in her life," Sheets says. At sixty-eight, "she was a lady who'd spent her whole life in a kitchen. Her husband made all the decisions for the family. I don't think she made any decisions except, probably, what to feed the kids. She raised a big family, and I'm sure she did a good job at it. But she was thoroughly confused at the trial."

Few of the jurors agreed with Sheets that Evans, or Mrs. Schwartz, could be converted. For them, the six days of deliberations became a blurred, grueling, timeless period of irrational arguments, of trips into the courtroom where they'd try to make sense of the judge's impenetrable charge, of nights at the motel, which seemed more and more like a cage. "I was sick the whole time," recalls Tracy Stanovich. "I had a terrific headache. Couldn't eat anything. Couldn't sleep."

And Evans became more unbearable every day. Once, according to Tracy Stanovich, he threw some pieces of paper towards Pat Shafer. Throughout the sequestration and deliberation, Mrs. Shafer had been one of the strongest, most diligent members of the jury. Since she has three school-aged children, she could have been excused automatically, but she decided to serve because she wanted to do her duty as a citizen. Though she provided a comforting presence for some of the younger women, she set exacting standards of performance. In her terms, Frances Yachlich, with whom she constantly consulted during deliberations, was a "good juror"; few other women on the panel rated that gentle form of high praise. But there was a moment when Evans's stubbornness shattered Pat's calm: she began to cry, and Sheets had to comfort her.

Evidently, Evans was accustomed to controlling his small world—his family and his business. Under the strain of sequestration and deliberations, he apparently developed a broad range of tactics for irritating the other jurors, whose independence of his will must have been one deep source of his frustration. Sometimes, in the midst of a discussion, he would begin to laugh disruptively, uproariously, and walk out to the men's room until he could control himself; at other moments he was sanctimonious. When Tracy Stanovich tried to explain why she favored acquittal, he said he felt sorry for her, that he would pray for her soul. He kept telling Mrs. Schwartz that "God is making us do this work, Katheryne."

He treated Nancy Leidy worse than any of the other jurors. Tracy Stanovich remembers one morning when Nancy, who eventually had a miscarriage, was riding to court in a station wagon instead of a bus because she felt sick. Evans was there, too. "He hassled her the whole way over. Finally, a marshal had to tell him, 'Larry, get off her back.'"

When they got to court, Nancy couldn't bring herself to ride on the same elevator with Evans. Fuzzy Foresman noticed that and heard her sobbing. "So I walked over to her and I saw that she was extremely emotional, emotional to the point where she couldn't catch her breath. And I just took hold of her and rubbed her shoulders a little bit and just talked to her gently. I said, 'This guy isn't going to hurt you or anybody.' I just kept talking to her, and calmed her down real well. She behaved pretty good after that."

But Foresman found himself getting progressively angrier at Evans. He provoked the man time and again with his mocking, irreverent wit. But at a deeper level his clashes with the Lutheran grocer, who kept asserting that his opinions about priests and nuns were tied to God's will, may have represented a sort of reenactment of fights Foresman had had several decades earlier when he married a Catholic woman from the coal town of Shamokin, where he and his friends used to journey for carefree evenings of dancing the polka and enjoying the beautiful women.

"Before we got married, very close personal friends told me that the Catholic church would do all sorts of nasty things to me. For example, we were married in a church. A mixed marriage in a church. The first one the priest had performed. My Lutheran friends had said it was impossible. Not only did it happen, but I invited them, and they were there." Nevertheless, afterwards his friends kept warning him about the Catholics' prejudices. "It was bullshit. I've had more problems with the damned Protestants than I had with the Catholics in regard to religion."

So, when Evans began to say that he knew the priests

and nuns were guilty as soon as he entered the courtroom, one of Foresman's thoughts was: "'Larry, I've heard all this before. I've been down this road before.' And it irritated me because the jury room was no place for that."

Foresman says that he kept trying to restrain himself, to submerge anger in wit. But on the sixth day his wrath erupted. Evans had been telling him how he'd pray for him, how his insistence on the defendants' innocence was endangering his grandchildren. "I got tired of his bullshit, you know. I just had to get up on my feet and get to the front of him. So I just jumped up and yelled, 'You're never going to convince me with that method, Mister. You're way out in left field. Who the hell do you think you are, telling me how to think?' I blasted that right into his face. But I never intended to hit him."

Tracy Stanovich, who hates conflict, recalls that she cringed at the scene. Vera Thompson, who was furious at Evans, says, "I was hoping that Fuzzy would knock him on his ass." Here is how June Jackson saw it.

"We women were already just broken. We realized that we couldn't get through to Larry, no way, no how. Then, he really took off on Fuzzy, telling him how he should think about the case. It was another tirade. His face was beet red. He was screaming at Fuzzy. No human being, no matter how strong, could take that forever.

"So Fuzzy walked over, Larry got up, and we could see there was going to be a problem. They were actually ready for a fistfight. And how we protect our own! We didn't want one marshal in there to see what was going on. So someone stood over by the door to keep them out, and Hal Sheets went over to break them up. As soon as Fuzzy realized what he was doing he went back to his seat.

"Oh, we all cried for Fuzzy. We felt so sorry for him because we knew what kind of person he was and we saw that he was crushed. And he apologized to us. He was ashamed of himself, and he said that he just couldn't believe another human being would act the way Larry did. But somebody did. And that scared me, too. I guess it's something I still don't understand. I hated to see somebody break another person."

That episode persuaded even Sheets that there was no chance for a unanimous verdict. Indeed, in retrospect Sheets blames his unyielding desire to forge a consensus for the terrible last days of deliberation. "I'm usually able to handle people, but I just couldn't handle this one. I couldn't get through to him. That's the thing about the trial that still frustrates me."

A few minutes after Foresman and Evans had squared off, Sheets notified the judge that the jury had concluded its work. And, within half an hour, those twelve men and women trooped into court to announce their verdict.

After the verdict was announced, the jurors returned to their motel to gather their belongings. It was a sentimental moment, the end of the most harrowing experience any of them had undergone. Most of them joked or cried as they prepared to leave with their kids or spouses or parents. But Evans not only shunned the whole scene, he kept the door to his motel room locked until all the other jurors had parted. At one point Sheets knocked on Evans's door until he finally answered. But he couldn't extract even a trace of warmth from his angry, hurt antagonist.

The jurors don't see each other much any more. June Jackson and Pat Shafer occasionally lunch together. Tracy Stanovich and Frances Yachlich joined them for dinner one evening. Harold Sheets and Fuzzy Foresman have phoned or visited some of the other jurors. Some have exchanged Christmas cards. But there are no reunions, no lingering sense of camaraderie. Nevertheless, the seven jurors I interviewed have more in common than they may have realized. The trial had affected them quite deeply, shaken their faith in American justice in ways that many of them couldn't quite communicate to their families or friends.

Indeed, Pat Shafer says that if she and her husband had to vote, "it would be a hung jury." Barney Jackson respects June's judgment, but it's hard for him to cope with the deep emotions the trial unleashed in her. Without quite meaning to, he makes her feel hysterical and overwrought whenever she tries to talk about her new uncertainties.

Most of the jurors saw the trial as a waste of money. Some of them absorbed an unexpected new fear from it: Tracy Stanovich and Fuzzy Foresman, the most impulsive, outspoken people in the group, both wondered aloud whether fantasies they set down in letters could—like Philip Berrigan's and Elizabeth McAlister's—be used to bring them to trial for an unprovable conspiracy. All of the jurors I interviewed had fresh doubts about a Justice Department that had been forced into hasty, punitive action because J. Edgar Hoover had once made an ill-advised statement about a plot that involved the Berrigan brothers. And all of them wondered about a jury system that allows men like Larry Evans to make crucial decisions about justice. But they don't know what to do about those feelings. They are scattered through Pennsylvania, isolated people whose frustration and rage still sit in their guts like rocks.

They don't want to feel that way. They wish they had been able to retain the faith in the government they had when the trial began. Ann Burnett found a metaphor most of the other jurors responded to when she said, "The trial was like a pregnancy where you never gave birth." Partly, that was because they never reached a unanimous verdict. But it was partly because the government's case was so inconclusive. There was a time during every inter-

view I had when a juror who voted for acquittal said he
would have supported conviction if only the government
had been able to furnish one or two credible witnesses
to corroborate Douglas's testimony. Even Ann Burnett
sounded sad when she said that. It was as if they had voted
to acquit against their will, because the government they'd
been trained to love had violated the sense of justice they
revered even more.

Most of them made comments that vindicated the defense's strategy of fighting for an extended voir dire and
using careful sociological measurements to select the jury.
They asserted that most citizens of the Middle District of
Pennsylvania were more like Larry Evans than themselves. Harold Sheets's clients, Tracy Stanovich's friends,
many of June Jackson's and Pat Shafer's relatives had
strongly disagreed with the verdict they rendered. Fuzzy
Foresman thinks that most people in his home town of
Lewiston would have voted as Evans did. "They refuse
to get involved in anything outside their own little ickey-
wickey bailiwicks," he said.

Yet, paradoxically, they are offended by the contempt
that the government, the defense, and the press displayed
toward them. That became particularly clear in my interview with Pat Shafer. Early in the trial an excused juror
had told me that he'd overheard anti-Catholic remarks
she had made during the voir dire. I wrote a *Village Voice*
article about that (though I suppressed her name), and the
defense attorneys and other reporters picked up the story.
Maybe that was the reason her conversation with me was
so much more guarded than that of the other jurors. But
it became animated when she criticized the press. She
showed me a sheaf of clippings that attacked the jury, and
in the hurt voice of a good citizen who has been wronged,
she said that no other aspect of the trial had caused her
such pain.

June Jackson felt the same anger, except in her case it

was directed at the government and its attitude toward America. Still, I felt a haunting regret about the fact that she could have been talking about the lawyers or the defendants or the sociologists or the press or me.

After the verdict she'd become aware that the Justice Department had located the trial in the Middle District of Pennsylvania because they thought the place would yield a sympathetic jury. "How stupid did those people in Washington think we were? Did they think that by just picking a certain part of the United States they could get a guilty verdict? Don't they know that people are people whether they come from northern Florida or southern California? I mean we all have minds and feelings. I don't care where we're from. Don't they have enough faith in human nature to know that?"